Educators ON THE Frontline

Advocacy Strategies for Your Classroom, Your School, and Your Profession

Jill Lewis
New Jersey City University
Jersey City, New Jersey, USA

Kathleen Stumpf Jongsma
Zayed University
Abu Dhabi, United Arab Emirates

Allen Berger
Miami University
Oxford, Ohio, USA

INTERNATIONAL
Reading Association
800 BARKSDALE ROAD, PO BOX 8139
NEWARK, DE 19714-8139, USA
www.reading.org

The International Reading Association attempts, through its publications, to provide a forum for a wide spectrum of opinions on reading. This policy permits divergent viewpoints without implying the endorsement of the Association.

Editorial Director   Matthew W. Baker
Managing Editor   Shannon T. Fortner
Permissions Editor   Janet S. Parrack
Acquisitions and Communications Coordinator   Corinne M. Mooney
Associate Editor   Charlene M. Nichols
Administrative Assistant   Michele Jester
Assistant Permissions Editor   Tyanna L. Collins
Production Department Manager   Iona Muscella
Supervisor, Electronic Publishing   Anette Schütz
Senior Electronic Publishing Specialist   R. Lynn Harrison
Proofreader   Elizabeth C. Hunt

Project Editor   Matthew W. Baker

Cover Design   Linda Steere

Web addresses in this book were correct as of the publication date but may have become inactive or otherwise modified since that time. If you notice a deactivated or changed Web address, please e-mail books@reading.org with the words "Website Update" in the subject line. In your message, specify the Web link, the book title, and the page number on which the link appears.

Library of Congress Cataloging–in–Publication Data
Lewis, Jill, Ed. D.
  Educators on the frontline : advocacy strategies for your classroom, your school, and your profession / Jill Lewis, Kathleen Stumpf Jongsma, Allen Berger.
       p. cm.
  Includes bibliographical references and index.
  ISBN 0-87207-554-0
  1. Education and state--United States.   2. Politics and education--United States.
3. Educational change--United States. I. Jongsma, Kathleen Stumpf. II. Berger, Allen. III. Title.
  LC89.L43   2004
  379.73--dc22

                                                                    2004019205

We dedicate this book to all education advocates who daily put themselves on the frontline, fighting for whatever they believe is best— often under difficult circumstances and at great personal cost.

—JILL LEWIS, KATHY JONGSMA, AND ALLEN BERGER

CONTENTS

PREFACE

*Our lives begin and end the day we become silent
about things that matter.*

—Martin Luther King, Jr.

At a 2002 Governor's Education Summit, educators and policymakers were discussing new education initiatives that the state should pursue. Everyone on the panel of educators and legislators agreed that any new plan or action must support excellent standards and result in high achievement for all students.

As part of her comments, Barbara LaSaracina, the New Jersey state teacher of the year and a panel member, stated, "Teachers get so little respect; they have so little power. Teachers think that the only route to recognition and reward is to leave the classroom and go into administration." Many other audience and panel members seemed to concur with her statement.

One purpose of this book is to suggest that there are rewarding paths in education that do not require leaving the classroom and through which educators can and do make important contributions to their classrooms, their schools, and their profession. We illustrate how educators working independently and collaboratively, and often through their professional organizations, have advocated for change. We share stories in which educators' actions make a significant impact on their students, their schools, and their teaching practices. We also discuss initiatives that have produced long-lasting changes that continue to affect successive generations of educators and students.

We three authors—Jill, Kathy, and Allen—are professional educators with many years of experience in education. At various points in our careers, we were all classroom teachers, and some of us were district supervisors, administrators, or education consultants. Allen also was a professional journalist. Currently, we all are university professors, teaching a variety of courses in literacy and in educational policy. We present regularly at education conferences and write articles for education journals. We author texts and materials used in school and university classrooms. We care deeply about students, educators, schools, and our own individual beliefs about learning and teaching. Consequently, we spend much time and energy advocating for education concerns.

Throughout this book, we use examples from our own personal experiences and concerns, as well as from the experiences of other teachers, administrators, professors, parents, and community leaders. The strategies we describe are those that any education advocate can use, regardless of issue or viewpoint. Other professionals writing an advocacy book would focus on the careers and issues that they know best. Although their issues might look quite different from ours, we would probably approach advocacy for our ideas in similar ways.

We write primarily for classroom teachers. However, we envision that other school- and university-based personnel—such as school administrators, central office staff, school librarians, school board members, and professors—can benefit from knowing how to successfully communicate their views to others and how to take actions that result in positive changes.

Organization of This Book

The chapters in this book show you how to be an effective education advocate, and they provide examples to inspire your efforts. We also point out missteps that you will want to avoid.

In chapter 1, we explain advocacy in its broadest sense and discuss why advocacy is important to your work. We ask you to assess your current advocacy skills and set goals for developing additional ones.

Chapter 2 explains the types of education concerns that bring people to advocacy. We introduce ways for advocates to work individually as well as how to develop advocacy coalitions.

Chapter 3 provides guidelines for developing a deeper understanding of your concerns and anticipating and analyzing education issues, including monitoring and evaluating current and pending legislation for both intended and unintended consequences.

Chapter 4 introduces the planning process for successful education advocacy initiatives. We discuss how to identify less obvious resources within your reach that can help your cause.

Chapter 5 offers a host of strategies for getting your message disseminated in printed formats such as newsletters and newspapers. We give step-by-step suggestions for implementing each strategy successfully.

Chapter 6 provides ideas for successful public service announcements, radio spots and interviews, websites, and e-mail messages. We also explain how to hold successful meetings with board members and legislators and how to give testimony at hearings. Finally, this chapter offers strategies for developing relationships with policymakers.

Chapter 7 offers a detailed story of advocates using many of the ideas from earlier chapters to change opinions and legislation. Jill Lewis describes her frustrations and mistakes, as well as her successes, and how she modified her strategies along the way. There also are examples of the materials advocates used to reach different audiences.

Chapter 8 provides benchmarks for evaluating the success of your advocacy initiatives. We explain how to recognize and celebrate your advocacy successes and how to rethink your strategies if they are not working effectively.

In chapter 9 we ask you to reconsider your advocacy skills after working with this text. Then, we encourage you to set new goals for continuing the development of your education advocacy skills and for increasing your advocacy efforts.

The appendixes contain examples of materials referenced in the chapters and used in various advocacy campaigns. These materials punctuate and add additional dimensions to the stories we tell. Included in Appendix A is "A Declaration of Professional Conscience for Teachers" by Kenneth Goodman, a well-known advocate on behalf of teachers and students; published letters to the editors of leading newspapers; a transcript of testimony presented at a hearing of a state assembly committee; a resolution adopted by a professional educational organization; and selected published articles containing information complementing the chapters in this book. We selected these items with care and with an eye toward their usefulness and practicality. In Appendix B you will find a list of websites that are useful to education advocates. These are in addition to the many websites to which we refer you throughout this book.

We know that finding funding is an advocate's ongoing concern, so in Appendix C we include a list of resources for information on funding and for learning more about grant writing. Fundraising is not, however, our focus in this book. Instead we offer an in-depth look at the role of education advocates and a wide array of advocacy strategies that they use for getting their messages heard.

A Word About Vignettes

Throughout the book, we share our personal experiences and the experiences of others who have chosen to engage in advocacy activities. These vignettes illustrate the use of widely differing advocacy strategies. Most of the vignettes tell an advocacy story in the words of the person who lived it. Some of the advocates accomplished their desired goals, and other advocates present works in progress where the outcomes are not yet known. Still other advocates describe efforts that were not totally successful. As you read these vignettes, we suggest that you think about each advocate's approach. After each vignette, we offer questions to guide your own reflection on the advocacy experience. These questions may serve as motivators for journal writing or for discussion in professional study groups or university classes. Consider how each advocate became involved in advocacy, what strategies the advocate used, and whether or not these strategies were effective. Put yourself in the advocate's shoes. Think of what you might have done in his or her place. Determine if there are lessons from the vignette that may help you as you consider your advocacy issue and plan how you will address your education concerns.

Education advocacy is rewarding, frustrating, time-consuming, exhilarating, and challenging. Those who do it are part of a responsive, expanding community that does important work. Won't you join us?

CHAPTER 1

A Close Look at Education Advocates: What They Do and Why They Do It

I f you are reading this book, you probably hold strong beliefs about education. These beliefs might be about what students should learn, how they should be taught and tested, what decisions ought to be left to teachers and school administrators rather than to politicians, how schooling should be funded, and how monies should be allocated to individual schools. You probably share your beliefs with colleagues, neighbors, friends, and family members. Occasionally, you also might share your opinions with members of civic and professional organizations to which you belong.

Many of us talk about our education concerns and our wishes for needed education reform with those whom we know well and with whom we interact on a regular basis. Only a few of us go a step further and present our opinions to those who make districtwide education decisions or to those who write or enforce the state and national laws that determine education policy. We call ourselves *education advocates*.

Definitions can help us understand the many behaviors involved under the broad umbrella term *advocacy*: "From the Latin ad vocare: to speak for, to plead the cause of another, to make others' case" (Mental Health Association in Alaska, 2002).

The Association for Supervision and Curriculum Development (ASCD; 2002) adds another dimension to the definition of *advocacy* when it suggests that advocacy involves building respectful relationships as the foundation for change.

Definitions of the related term *advocate* also indicate the range of individual actions involved: "1. One that argues for a cause. 2. One that pleads on another's behalf." (*The American Heritage Dictionary*, 1994, p. 13).

Thus, one who engages in advocacy, an advocate, is performing several functions: supporting, assisting and aiding, speaking and pleading on behalf of others, and defending and arguing for people or causes (Wrights Law, 2002).

Advocates do not sit passively or idly on the sidelines. Advocates get involved. Advocates engage in a variety of activities to bring issues or problems to the attention of others. By drawing attention to their causes, advocates begin to remedy identified problems.

What Does Advocacy Look Like?

If you are new to advocacy, perhaps you are concerned that you do not have the appropriate background or skills to participate. The following vignette may reassure you that you can engage in this work at the local level and that you do have the skills to make a difference. The vignette's author, Toni Tsatoke, became involved in advocacy as an undergraduate student. She saw a need while she was student teaching and, with the support of her supervising teacher and the school principal, began her advocacy for the students in her school.

Filling Boxes—and Lives

Toni Tsatoke
Student Teacher, Haskell Indian Nations University School of Education,
Lawrence, Kansas, USA

During my senior year, the teacher education program that I graduated from required a one-year student teaching commitment. The first semester involved observation and some instructional assistance to the supervising teacher. The second semester was a gradual process of assuming lead teacher responsibilities and then phasing back out. I was paired with a master teacher who welcomed my input and ideas. Our extended time together allowed us to build a working relationship and allowed me to better acquaint myself with the needs of our kindergarten students.

I reflected on the many times it cost money for children to participate in school activities (e.g., extracurricular clubs, book fairs, holiday gift-buying programs, class pictures, sports team sales, and school T-shirt sales). I also acknowledged the benefits of book-buying opportunities for students. As for weekly book orders, the children eagerly anticipated the arrival of "the box." Something had to be done for those who repeatedly had nothing in the box.

I realized that schools must be creative fundraisers in order to function. Although I was mindful of not overstepping my boundaries, I was compelled to speak with my supervising teacher about my concern for these students. In turn, she conveyed these concerns to the principal and asked and received permission for me to try to locate outside resources to supplement the materials available in our class.

Through a friend I contacted the local community center. I discovered that many community-based social centers receive donations from a variety of sources, and those donations include children's books, toys, and clothing. The local community center donated books that could be kept in our classroom and used in a reward system that was truly inclusive and didn't require any money from our students.

My advocacy didn't require a title or a bunch of letters behind my name. My experience was truly rewarding because I realized that anyone can be an education advocate. The end result gave all of our students something to look forward to as well as meeting our literacy objective to increase our students' access to age-appropriate books.

FOR YOUR CONSIDERATION

• What personal qualities does Tsatoke bring to her advocacy efforts?

• What personal qualities do you have for successful advocacy work?

• If you were going to meet with Tsatoke, what questions would you ask her about her advocacy work?

Why Do Educators Need to Advocate?

Perhaps we educators advocate in support of our convictions. These times are troubling for many of us. Long-standing beliefs and practices about instruction and assessment are receiving intense public scrutiny. Often the outcomes of these investigations are less than complimentary of existing policies and practices, or even of individuals working in the education field. Mandates from state and national governments—such as those connected with curricula for early childhood, literacy, or math—require practices that we may not easily accept. Letters to the editor in *Education Week* and in a host of educational newsletters and journals suggest that current education policies go against much long-standing research and practice and are contrary to the beliefs of many professional educators about how students learn or how they should be assessed. Although some of the new mandates do correct inequities or ineffective practices of the past, others—such as the No Child Left Behind Act's (NCLB) Adequate Yearly Progress (AYP) requirement and student retention policies—appear more problematic. Letters to the editor or op-eds (opinion-editorials) in our local and national newspapers suggest that the following are frequent areas of concern:

class size

student–teacher ratios

aging school buildings

overcrowded schools

outdated materials and equipment

programming for English-language
    learners (ELLs)

vouchers

charter schools and school choice

the achievement gap between
    minorities and other students

funding for arts education

school leadership

textbook selection

gifted and talented education

teacher quality and teacher
    certification

gender equity

parents' rights

school violence

As Kenneth Goodman reminds us in "A Declaration of Professional Conscience for Teachers" (see Appendix A, p. 234), it is our responsibility as educators to pledge ourselves to do what is best for our students. Therefore, every educator must advocate for policies and actions that facilitate best practices in instruction and assessment. Policymakers and members of the community at large need to hear our voices when we have concerns about schools and how schools are or are not working for the students they are intended to serve.

The annual *Phi Delta Kappa/Gallup Poll of the Public's Attitudes Toward the Public Schools* often serves as a barometer of public opinion. The latest poll (Rose & Gallup, 2003) suggests that the public has high regard for the schools in their communities, wants needed improvements to come through those schools, and is not interested in seeking alternatives to their existing public schools. However, the poll also reports that few people understand the implications of recent legislation such as NCLB, and when they are informed of NCLB's requirements, hold points of view differing from many of the mandates. For example, 83% of poll responders believe that decisions regarding what is taught in the public schools should be made at the state level or by the local school board, rather than by federal intervention. Although NCLB bases judgment of educational effectiveness on statewide tests administered annually to students in grades 3–8, 66% of the poll responders believe a single statewide test cannot provide an adequate judgment of whether schools need improvement. Eighty percent of poll responders were concerned that limiting testing to English and math would mean less emphasis in the school curriculum on art, music, history, and other subjects. Poll results suggest that educators will need to help parents understand many of the education policies and mandates that affect their children. Educators also may need to help parents advocate for what they believe is in the best interest of their children's education.

Other education and policy organizations have stated that there is less positive support for public schools and educators than the Phi Delta Kappa/Gallup poll would suggest. The authors of the Public Education Network's *A Community Action Guide to Teacher Quality* (2003), state, "Surveys suggest that 70 percent of registered voters—approximately 91 million people—believe our public education system needs to be completely replaced or changed in a significant way" (p. 1). In addition, ASCD (2002) indicates that public support for education is surprisingly fragile. In response to this knowledge, the association's website states that "the time for advocacy on behalf of students is now. And the voice needed is yours.... Just as teaching and learning require commitment, energy, and perseverance, so too does advocacy" (n.p.).

Further, ASCD (2002) suggests,

> When we do not create effective channels of communication with legislators, the media, and community members, others define the policy agenda—and make decisions without the critical information we can furnish. The consequences of such ill-informed efforts, even when well intentioned, can be devastating to children and learning. The stakes are simply too high for educators not to engage in advocacy efforts. (n.p.)

As professional educators, all of us need to work tirelessly to provide the best education programs possible for our communities. We—you and the three of us—are the individuals who know the students and their strengths and needs. Therefore, we are the individuals who can best advocate on their behalf. Collectively, we are able to provide local, state, and national policymakers with reliable and current information for making wise fiscal and programming decisions for schools and the students those schools serve.

The Complex Roles of Education Advocates

The work of education advocates is multifaceted. They participate in public deliberation about policies that have an impact on their students, their teaching, and their schools. They understand that through well-informed public discussion and an open exchange of ideas, they can influence choices and policy decisions that may have short- or long-term consequences, both intended and unintended, for students, teachers, and schools. They work at the local, state, and even federal levels, depending on the issue and which policymakers will be making decisions.

Advocates are willing to take responsibility for problems. They recognize that by participating energetically in education-related decision-making processes, they can make a difference in how problems are resolved. They believe that if they do not engage in these deliberations, they share some of the blame for harmful policies.

Education advocates present specific solutions for resolving particular problems. What they propose may be at odds with the views of others. In the process of discussion, public debate, or both, they frequently agree to compromise on their individual or their organization's positions and work toward building consensus. Advocates usually feel that compromising or getting some concessions is preferable to not advocating and getting only what others decide to give them.

Advocacy groups do effect educational change. John Willinsky (2002), director of the Public Knowledge Project at the University of British Columbia in Vancouver, British Columbia, Canada, specifically commented on the effectiveness of educational advocacy by stating,

> Whether it represents industry alliances, social issues, environmental concerns, or consumer groups, the interest group has increasingly come to represent the forceful public voice of advocacy with significant political clout. Interest groups have been particularly active around educational issues, getting behind state referendums on bilingual education and affirmative action, for example, as well as the teaching of evolution. (p. 613)

And Willinsky spoke positively about the role advocacy plays in effecting public policy, noting,

> Now it may be tempting to think of interest groups as a distortion of the course of democratic processes, to see them as the opinionated and vested ganging up against the individual expression of equal citizens, but interest groups also represent a freedom of association around deeply felt values, issues, and interests, if only in response to a politics of issue-less candidate consumerism. (p. 613)

Education advocates play a key role in school improvement. Often, their school improvement efforts involve recruiting others to their causes. When parents or other community members are included in advocacy activities, they usually become more involved in their local schools, volunteering their time and working harder to make their schools successful for their own children, as well as for the children of others. As noted by the U.S. Department of Education in a 1998 report, "When families and communities are involved in education, students learn more and schools improve" (p. 32). In addition, when their voices of concern are added to the advocacy efforts of others, the impact of the advocacy message increases, and policymakers often take notice.

The author of the previous vignette was a student teacher. Classroom teachers and educational support personnel—such as librarians, counselors, and school psychologists—also advocate for students and programs in their own schools and school districts. The next vignette illustrates how the advocacy actions of school psychologist Avivah Dahbany made a significant difference in the educational planning for a specific student.

On Behalf of Lively Youngsters

Avivah Dahbany
School Psychologist, Franklin Township Public Schools, New Jersey, USA

As a school psychologist, I often learn from school staff of students who are having academic, social, or behavioral problems. On one occasion, a teacher asked me for assistance in helping her deal with a student who was having academic and behavioral problems. The teacher and principal wanted this student referred for an assessment to determine his eligibility for special education and related services.

When I went to the teacher's classroom to observe the situation, this first-grade child was jumping off his desk and chair. He skipped and ran around the classroom. The teacher then assigned students to different learning centers, and this child started working on the computer appropriately. I went over to him to ask him what he was doing, and he easily described his activity. Then I asked him about his classroom behavior. He admitted it was "bad." When I asked why it was "bad," he said his behavior was "dangerous." I thought that someone had said this to him, so I asked him what "dangerous" meant. He said it meant he could hurt himself or hurt others. Based on these responses I knew that this child was not a special needs student.

I arranged to meet with the parents, homeroom teacher, principal, and other subject area teachers to discuss the child's behavior and his apparent cognitive strengths. Because his behavior was usually so inappropriate, many attending the meeting were unaware of his cognitive strengths. We jointly developed a behavioral plan with expectations and consequences. The parents would get a daily progress report from the teachers and provide behavioral consequences for their son at home. The teachers would provide the child with more challenging academic tasks to stimulate his intellect.

Today this student remains in the regular classroom and is making good academic progress. Generally, his behavior is appropriate. When he behaves inappropriately, he knows the consequences and readily adheres to them in school and at home. This success story is an example of what can happen when parents, teachers, and other school staff work together for the best interests of a child.

FOR YOUR CONSIDERATION

- What strategies did this school psychologist use to bring people with different viewpoints to consensus on what was best for the child?
- Some people say that labeling special needs children is a political act. Do you agree with this premise?

Through such advocacy in the education arena, educators build the capacity to provide students with a quality education. They also inform the public and enlist support from many different constituent groups in responding to and then solving education problems. By reaching out to others and including them in educational decision-making, educators build commitment for schools and for school programming. A public that is committed to its schools will more likely make the financial sacrifices necessary to attract and retain quality teachers, provide a safe learning environment that is conducive to learning, and purchase up-to-date learning materials for all children (Dilley, 1995).

The Public Education Network (2003) offers us the following challenge:

> Think about that: 91 million Americans want a dramatic overhaul of public education. Now think about this: what if those 91 million people *did something* about it? What if 91 million people took action on an issue they said was important to them? An engaged, empowered public is not an ideal—it is a necessity for good, sustainable decisions about our education system, our economy, our environment, our security, our future. (p. 1)

Your hard work as an education advocate helps to build that engaged, empowered public. Through your advocacy efforts, you educate others about your concerns. When you inform others and work with them to find solutions to problems, you are building important coalitions that can make a difference for schools.

Are You Engaged in Education Advocacy?

Have you ever advocated for someone or something in your school, for your students, or for something in your profession that you really cared about? Perhaps it was for a student whose educational programming was not meeting his or her needs, for a school sports or academic team that needed more funding or better equipment, or for professional development that was more targeted to your needs. What were some things you tried to do to get your ideas heard and to accomplish your goals?

The education advocacy self-assessment that begins on the next page provides an opportunity for you to determine your current level of advocacy involvement and set goals for future advocacy efforts. Take a few minutes to rate yourself by taking the self-assessment. (You may choose to photocopy it first because you will be asked at the end of this book to retake it.) As you complete the self-assessment, consider any type of educational advocacy you may have done. If you are new to education advocacy, do not be intimidated. Whether you are just getting started or are a seasoned advocacy veteran, the rest of this book will help you with suggestions for and examples of participating in advocacy.

Education Advocacy
Self–Assessment

Your Current Education Advocacy Activities

On a scale of 1–4, rate how often you have engaged in each of the following advocacy activities. Circle your response.

1 = Not at All   2 = On Rare Occasions   3 = Sometimes   4 = Very Often

1. Met with a teacher to discuss a school issue that concerns you

   1   2   3   4

2. Met with a group of teachers to discuss a school issue that concerns you

   1   2   3   4

3. Met with a parent or a group of parents to discuss a school issue that concerns you

   1   2   3   4

4. Met with a school administrator to discuss a school issue that concerns you

   1   2   3   4

5. Discussed an education concern with the local board of education or with a school board member from the school district where you live

   1   2   3   4

6. Discussed an education concern with the local board of education or with a school board member from the school district where you teach

   1   2   3   4

7. Organized for advocacy with other groups that you believed shared your concerns

   1   2   3   4

8. Sent a letter or an e-mail message to one of your state or Congressional legislators to discuss proposed education legislation

   1   2   3   4

(continued)

9. Invited a policymaker to your school to observe your programs and students in action

| 1 | 2 | 3 | 4 |

10. Written a letter to the editor of your local newspaper supporting or opposing the viewpoint expressed in an article on an education issue

| 1 | 2 | 3 | 4 |

11. Written a letter to the editor of your local newspaper about a concern, a program, or a practice in your local schools

| 1 | 2 | 3 | 4 |

12. Encouraged a group of parents to protest an action taken by their board of education

| 1 | 2 | 3 | 4 |

13. Encouraged a group of teachers to protest an action taken by their board of education

| 1 | 2 | 3 | 4 |

14. Telephoned one of your state or Congressional legislators to discuss proposed education legislation

| 1 | 2 | 3 | 4 |

15. Met with a state legislator who represents you to discuss an education issue

| 1 | 2 | 3 | 4 |

16. Met with a state legislator who does not represent you to discuss an education issue

| 1 | 2 | 3 | 4 |

17. Testified in support of or in opposition to an education bill before a state legislative committee (e.g., your state assembly's education committee)

| 1 | 2 | 3 | 4 |

18. Testified in support of or in opposition to an education policy before a state board of education or a board of regents

| 1 | 2 | 3 | 4 |

(continued)

19. Testified in support of or in opposition to a bill before your state assembly or Senate

        1   2   3   4

20. Discussed education issues in an interview with someone from your local newspaper, radio station, or television station

        1   2   3   4

Your Potential Education Advocacy Activities

On a scale of 1–4, rate how comfortable you would be doing each of the following advocacy activities. Circle your response.

1 = Not Comfortable at All   2 = Somewhat Comfortable   3 = Comfortable
4 = Very Comfortable

1. Meet with a teacher to discuss a school issue that concerns you

        1   2   3   4

2. Meet with a group of teachers to discuss a school issue that concerns you

        1   2   3   4

3. Meet with a parent or a group of parents to discuss a school issue that concerns you

        1   2   3   4

4. Meet with a school administrator to discuss a school issue that concerns you

        1   2   3   4

5. Discuss an education concern with the local board of education or with a school board member from the school district where you live

        1   2   3   4

6. Discuss an education concern with the local board of education or with a school board member from the school district where you teach

        1   2   3   4

(continued)

7. Organize for advocacy with other groups that you believe share your concerns

1	2	3	4

8. Send a letter or an e-mail message to one of your state or Congressional legislators to discuss proposed education legislation

1	2	3	4

9. Invite a policymaker to your school to observe your programs and students in action

1	2	3	4

10. Write a letter to the editor of your local newspaper supporting or opposing the viewpoint expressed in an article on an education issue

1	2	3	4

11. Write a letter to the editor of your local newspaper about a concern, a program, or a practice in your local schools

1	2	3	4

12. Encourage a group of parents to protest an action taken by their board of education

1	2	3	4

13. Encourage a group of teachers to protest an action taken by their board of education

1	2	3	4

14. Telephone one of your state or Congressional legislators to discuss proposed education legislation

1	2	3	4

15. Meet with a state legislator who represents you to discuss an education issue

1	2	3	4

16. Meet with a state legislator who does not represent you to discuss an education issue

1	2	3	4

(continued)

17. Testify in support of or in opposition to an education bill before a state legislative committee (e.g., your state assembly's education committee)

1	2	3	4

18. Testify in support of or in opposition to an education policy before a state board of education or a board of regents

1	2	3	4

19. Testify in support of or in opposition to a bill before your state assembly or Senate

1	2	3	4

20. Discuss education issues in an interview with someone from your local newspaper, radio station, or television station

1	2	3	4

After you have completed the self-assessment, total your scores for both sections. If you scored 70 or above on your current activities, you are definitely an experienced education advocate; a similar score on potential activities suggests that you are ready to take some of the actions we have suggested in this book. If you scored between 60 and 69 in either part of the survey, you are probably comfortable with the idea of being an education advocate and are excited about developing some tools for this role. If your score was below 60, consider whether there is a particular aspect of advocacy work that you find uncomfortable. Perhaps the idea of speaking in front of a group, giving testimony, makes you nervous. Maybe you are concerned you won't find the right words for a letter to or a meeting with a legislator. Remember, you do not need to work alone. Try some small steps. It's fine to write out what you want to say, even in a small planning meeting. And talk to others who might serve as role models for you.

1. What conclusions can you reach about your activities as an education advocate?

2. What goals would you like to set for yourself as an education advocate?

Why You?

Given all that has been said about the hard work, the amount of time you will invest, and how frequently you will need to compromise in order to get anything accomplished, why would and should you get involved in education advocacy activities? Isn't educational advocacy something that is better left for the big guys, the ones who already have the money and power? Don't professional education organizations or education coalitions hire professional lobbyists to communicate with officials, committees, or boards about their concerns? How can educators individually, or even as a small or large group, make a difference when lobbyists and organized and heavily financed lobbying campaigns have the attention of policymakers? Why would anyone want to listen to you or be at all concerned about what you know or believe?

The answer is simple: You have knowledge and experience that you need to share. You have information that no one else can give. It is easy for the naysayer or the skeptic to sit back and say that the opinions of individuals do not count and that no one will pay attention to an individual's interests or concerns. However, the three of us have filled the pages of this book with examples to the contrary.

Pause for a minute and reflect on several recent examples in which individuals' input into potential U.S. education policy mattered. For example, you could ask your representatives to Congress how many constituent phone calls, e-mail messages, letters, and personal visits they received over the years as the Individuals with Disabilities Education Act (IDEA) of 1997 was proposed and passed, as amendments were considered to the original act, and as procedures began for reauthorization of it in 2003–2004. According to Richard Long, Director of Government Relations for the International Reading Association, droves of educators and parents wrote to legislators about their concerns, especially about the overidentification and labeling of students as having learning disabilities (personal communication, February 19, 2003). They asked for more opportunities for early intervention before testing began for referral to special services. They wrote about the need to protect the rights of individual students. They protested about unfunded mandates. Over the years, legislators listened to many of these concerns. Some were incorporated into the original IDEA legislation and into its subsequent amendments. Success of recent advocacy actions related to the 2004 reauthorization of the act are uncertain, however, as decisions had not been made as this book went to press.

You also could check with your representatives about the number of constituents who contacted them in response to proposed cuts in funding for Title I. Such proposed reductions have always triggered tremendous constituent concerns, and legislators have listened (Richard Long, personal communication, February 19, 2003). Funding cuts might have been greater if educators had not acted to prevent them.

Finally, you could find out from your representatives how many constituents they heard from recently in response to the George W. Bush administration's proposed changes to the Vocational Education Act, which was originally signed into law on October 31, 1998. The first formal hearings on the act were held during April 2004, so the outcomes were uncertain when this book went to press, but members of Congress were deluged with constituents' comments describing how the proposed changes might affect their schools and the programs they implement for their students.

At the state level, your state legislature and board of education also make critical decisions that affect your students, your school, and your profession. They may decide which specific textbooks school districts may use for social studies, science, or reading classes. They can require particular content for teacher certification or professional development programs. It is in their purview to determine which programs will receive state funding and which will be cut, what legal student–teacher ratios are, and what criteria will satisfy the provisions of No Child Left Behind for Highly Qualified Teacher requirements.

As you have seen, advocacy efforts are important at both the national and state levels. U.S. federal and state legislators' education aides will tell you that what individual legislators hear from their constituents influences how the legislators make their decisions in committee work and how they vote on bills before the House of Representatives or Senate. Your professional organizations know the impact of constituents' messages. That is why they frequently send out alerts to you and other members, asking you to phone or fax your legislators to let them know how specific legislation will affect your lives and the lives of your students.

Although advocacy is essential at the state and national levels, activism is necessary at the local level as well. Your conversations with local officials, business leaders, and school board members can make a difference. Your local policymakers and community leaders do want to know what you think and believe. A handwritten letter, a phone call, or an in-office conversation may have a significant impact on their thinking. Remember that you often can be most successful in advocating for issues in your own community.

Perhaps the following letter, written by Karen Atwood Cook (2004) of Boothbay, Maine, USA, to her state's Commissioner of Education, explains best why advocacy is part of your professional responsibility.

Dear Commissioner Gendron,

I have never written a letter like this. As I write, I realize that I may not be sending it and that you may not be the one actually reading it, but the process of writing it and pondering its content is serving an important purpose for me right now.

I am a teacher. I began my teaching career in 1978, although teaching has been part of my life for its entirety. My father was Ralph M. Atwood, a teacher, coach, principal, and superintendent in the Messalonskee School District. I had the good fortune to have Duke Albanese—former education commissioner—as a high school teacher, and when he became my dad's assistant we became good friends. My brother is a former teacher, coach, and assistant principal who now works at a small liberal arts college. I have a long list of relatives and friends who are or have been teachers.

My dad used to say "teaching is a way of life." You couldn't find a stronger advocate for the profession than he. He has been gone now for 6 years, but his memory and love for education live on in the school that bears his name in Oakland, as well as in the many people he influenced, including my brother and myself, who chose teaching as a career path.

I had many talks with my Dad about education. When Duke was commissioner, Dad and I chatted about the way things were going, how Duke would discuss things with him, and he joked about being glad that he was retired. When I think about what he would have to say about what is going on in education today, I am sure he would reply with one of his usual quotes, "The more things change, the more they remain the same." Then, when he had the time to listen to me whine about the selected topic of the week, he would remind me to "Go into my classroom and make a difference."

Commissioner Gendron, I am finding that it is becoming more and more impossible to "Go into my classroom and make a difference." I have a pit in my stomach right now because I need to get my DRA's done by next Friday since they are due to the principal. The reading lab is not up and running yet because the "data" has not been completed. My special needs children and children reading below level need to be helped. It is next to impossible to administer DRA's without some type of assistance with the rest of the class. I have new math (investigations) and new phonics (Fountas and Pinnell) programs to implement (both excellent by the way). I need to get prepared for my meeting with our consultant on Tuesday as she visits to help us become users of "best practices." Ironic, though, for the past 20+ years I have been proud of my reputation as a teacher who people come back and see and refer to as someone who was an outstanding teacher for their child. I now need to know these "best practices"?! I need to attend a meeting to review MEA scores tomorrow at lunch, since my team ran out of time at yesterday's staff meeting. I have to make sure that I am prepared for the math assessment in two weeks even though I am not sure why we are giving it, except that the state is telling us that we need to have one done. I will make substitute plans because I will have to miss a day in my classroom to score the assessment. Since we have no common planning time, I will try to locate my colleagues in the hall and on the way to lunch and specials to discuss some of the other things that we have due in preparation for our visit with our K–2 literacy consultant. I need to refer a student to special education and am going to try to bypass the SAT, since that would be another meeting for which I would have to have a sub. State says I have to have SAT, though! Even though his parents want him tested and he is struggling...got to jump through those hoops to have a committee of 8 people tell me what I already know which is that this child needs help.

The previous paragraph is only a beginning and I am absolutely certain you hear this often. It is not intended to be whining, but rather to provide an entry to my final point:

I will not encourage either of my own bright, talented children, ages 16 and 12, to enter the field of public education. I will not encourage them, yet I will not DIScourage them if that is the path they choose. I have, however, chosen to be honest about what being a teacher means today, and more importantly, what is does not mean. Not to worry, they had it all figured out anyway!!! My daughter told me, "Mom, the songs you teach your kids are the things they will remember, and if they are made to feel happy and safe in school, they will do well. It won't be because of a rubric." I am certain that my father would be in agreement with me on this, considering the recent circumstances of the field. This absolutely breaks my heart. The long line of teachers in the Atwood family will become broken; it has been a proud line. None of my nieces and nephews are considering public education, either. What I am doing lately is not teaching. It is meeting, assessing, scoring, meeting, reviewing, analyzing, meeting, coming home so tired and emotionally drained that I am close to tears almost every day. It is not teaching, it is trying as hard as I can to find time during the day to share myself as a person, share a song, share a memory, share something with my children that does not have to be assessed. Meet the standard? Yes, I have a standard to meet! That standard is a way of life for myself and my family that is reasonable and important. Right now, as I prepare to head off to school tomorrow and meet those eager second graders, I am going to try really hard to stay focused on what is important, even though I will need to get those assessments done and get ready for those meetings and review those results and wait as my principal paces the floor in anticipation of the publication of "The List."

A way of life? Yes, teaching always will be for me. I will always love it with all of my heart and soul. However, I am considering leaving it, at least in the public arena, because it simply is becoming something other than what it is supposed to be. The way of life that it is becoming is one that will destroy morale and make people physically and emotionally ill. Someone needs to take a good look at what is REALLY happening and do something about it before it's too late. Students not meeting standards? How about teaching jobs with no one to fill them? Perhaps the people who do fill the positions will be people who really enjoy how things in education are going. Perhaps there are people who really think these Learning Results are going to actually work! Perhaps these are people that pore over assessment rubrics on the web at night, not look for the latest children's books that are out there, or checking on which show on PBS they might tape for their class. My bet is that those are not going to be people whom their former students are going to see years later and give them a warm and sincere hug and say, "I loved having you as a teacher."

Thank you for listening.

Sincerely,

Karen Atwood Cook

Boothbay, Maine, USA

As it turned out, the author of this letter did send it to the Commissioner, with very positive results. Within 24 hours, Commissioner Gendron wrote a personal reply to her, and shortly after, the Commissioner began surveying Maine's teachers about the stressors in education today. The Commissioner indicated that she will be making recommendations for some relief from these stressors. Your advocacy can make a difference!

Even if you have not given much thought to advocacy activities in the past, the time is right to consider what stances you can and will take now and in the future. We as educators need to decide what issues matter to us and what we are willing to do to get our important ideas heard by the people who make the important decisions for us, for our community, for our state, and for our nation. As Alan Farstrup, Executive Director of the International Reading Association, writes in an introduction to the *IRA Advocacy Manual* (2002),

> Your advocacy is critical because there is a vital need to deliver our message. The education of our children has become a top priority of our nation's policymakers and the public. In this time of overwhelming reform of public education, policymakers are making more and more decisions that will directly affect your classroom. The need for advocacy is greater than ever due to the barrage of federal laws and regulations placing tough mandates on local school districts. In addition, at a time where states are facing a budget crisis, our leaders in Congress and in state legislatures must understand that education is too important an investment to be sacrificed. It is imperative for educators, administrators, and parents to make their voices heard. (n.p.)

You may still need to convince yourself that your ideas do matter, that without input from you, your community leaders, legislators, and fellow citizens have limited information for making decisions. You need to keep reminding yourselves that the more your community leaders and policymakers know, the better able they are to make informed choices and decisions. Sharing your ideas with others and hearing their comments and concerns broadens your own understandings of issues. At the same time, you help to broaden the understandings of others.

At times your advocacy concerns will be intensely personal, linked tightly to issues that affect your own students and teaching. You also might wrestle with issues that not only affect you but also are significant concerns for others. Issues of concern to you are worth advocating for. Others can tell your story, but because you live it, no one can tell it nearly as well as you can. Share the implications of a particular policy or piece of legislation for your teaching. Describe how a proposed practice will have a positive or negative impact on your students. Let legislators and policymakers know how your school will be affected by actions they are proposing. Tell your story with vigor and passion, and tell it well. Like Toni Tsatoke, Avivah Dahbany, and Karen Atwood Cook, you may find that what you say and what you write makes a difference for your students, your school, and your profession.

The Consequences of Inaction

Ultimately, the decisions of your leaders and policymakers may not be those you or your colleagues favored. However, if you have not given information, asked questions, or provided feedback, you have missed valuable opportunities to have any input into a practice or a policy. Providing information or testimony before decisions are made is a valuable proactive activity. Complaining after an issue is resolved is much less fruitful. Reasoned arguments, well presented, do make a difference and do influence the thinking and responses of others in a manner that you will find both supportive and pleasing. No matter what the issue, your opinions, experiences, and knowledge do matter, and your ideas need to be heard by those who can make the difference in an outcome or event.

As Farstrup states,

> Education has become a top priority of our nation. However, this does not mean the education community can back down and assume our job is over. It is now more important than ever for the education community to stick together and be vocal about the importance of public education. (IRA, 2002, n.p.)

You need to engage in advocacy for education because schools need support. Competition for monies is keen, and schools are not the only institutions needing more attention and funding. In many communities, especially those with large numbers of senior citizens, education has lost much of its traditional support base, the parents of the students. When community residents no longer have children in the schools, many lack familiarity with either the physical structures or the needs and concerns of campuses. Often the image of school that many residents hold is an image of schools past, rather than those of today.

As an educator, you know what schools need. You recognize the strengths of the institution. You also are well aware of the problems. If you do not communicate your concerns to others, the necessary messages may not reach the appropriate ears and eyes.

Positive Results From Action

Have we encouraged you to begin or to continue your advocacy practices? We hope so because we believe that there are many positive outcomes of advocacy participation. We believe that advocacy matters. Perhaps the following vignette will help us illustrate that the advocacy activities of individuals do make a difference. This educator used different strategies to successfully accomplish her advocacy goals. As you read Priscilla Shannon Gutiérrez's story, consider the ways her activities were similar to Tsatoke's and Dahbany's, described in the two previous vignettes, and how they differed. Also, think about how some of her issues are reflected in Cook's letter.

Upholding the Law as It Relates to Parental Rights

Priscilla Shannon Gutiérrez
Director, Rocky Mountain Deaf School, Lakewood, Colorado, USA

Several years ago when high-stakes testing was just starting to gain momentum, I was working for a large urban school district in California. Under state law, parents of non–English-speaking students have the right to waive out of testing if they feel their child is not fluent enough to succeed on the test.

Most parents were not aware of this right, and so I developed a letter in Spanish to inform them and sent it home. In spite of their right, not very many opted out that year. It seemed they were eager to have their child learn English and they viewed the test as a measure to gauge their child's progress in English.

The following year, as state testing time rolled around, the district informed all teachers that they were not to advise parents of the right to waive their children out of testing. The district's position was that everyone had to take the test, regardless of his or her fluency levels in English. We were told that there would be consequences if any teacher violated the district mandate.

Naturally, I was incensed that the district intended to supersede the rights of a particular language group, who by and large were already subjected to marginalization (e.g., no materials in Spanish, no communication to home in Spanish). And so, in spite of the threat of potential consequence or sanction to me as a professional, I made the decision to write a letter in Spanish informing parents of the right to waive out. And, fortunately for me, my site administrator backed me up.

The district wisely decided not to pursue any type of consequence or sanction, realizing that to do so would expose their flagrant violation of state law and parental rights.

My story illustrates the power of just one teacher and the difference teachers can make in protecting both parental and student rights if they stand up to district mandates that violate said rights.

FOR YOUR CONSIDERATION

• How did moral and legal considerations influence Gutiérrez's fight for parental rights?

• How would you assess the pros and cons of what she did?

• How do the advocacy strategies used by Gutiérrez compare and contrast to those used by Tsatoke and Dahbany?

If you are successful in expressing your ideas to others, as the four education advocates telling their stories in this chapter were, we think several important things may happen. You may build and broaden a constituency around the issues of concern to you. You may get your message out to more people who can then help you and support you as you work for change. You will increase visibility for yourself, your cause, perhaps your organization, and certainly for the ideas you wish to put forth.

We believe you will find that engaging in education advocacy rejuvenates you and sends you back to your job or your community with increased vigor and dedication. Frequently, you may become more resolved to your cause as you seek new ways to communicate your important message to others. Through advocacy, you often will build relationships as your work for a common cause strengthens the bonds between you and others with similar concerns. As you plan your strategies together, you may find collegiality and friendship.

Negative Results From Action

Of course, engaging in advocacy activities may have its downside. It would be unfair if we did not present and learn from some of the less-than-positive stories. Taking stances that others find unpopular or antithetical may lead to difficult personal situations. You may lose some friends over differences of opinion on ideas or strategies for change. You may find yourself in arguments as you passionately espouse your opinions.

In some situations you may find that your views, your stances, and your activism may place you in even more uncomfortable positions. Some teachers who have advocated for specific beliefs and practices have found themselves vilified by parents, colleagues, or administrators. In the worst-case scenarios, teachers were transferred to other positions or faced administrative hearings for their involvement in advocacy activities. Some lost their jobs.

These are, of course, extreme scenarios, which might have been prevented by greater care and diplomacy in expressing ideas. However, advocates frequently are passionate people who care a great deal about the ideas and positions they espouse. Expressing those views to others may necessarily involve some risk. You need to decide your personal comfort level with advocacy positions and know the limits that you must set in putting forth your positions. Then, you must implement logical plans to lead to positive results.

Conclusion

In May 2003, Cathy Roller, Director of Research and Policy for IRA, spoke to education leaders at a meeting of the National Conference of Research in Language and Literacy at the IRA Annual Convention in Orlando, Florida, USA. In response to discussion about the many policies that recent U.S. government initiatives were mandating, she suggested educators had three alternatives: (1) We could vent, (2) we could circumvent, or (3) we could invent. In the chapters that follow, we present suggestions to help you with the last approach, advocating your ideas in a positive light.

We believe that your advocacy work is important and that you can make a difference in policies and practices at the local, state, and national levels. We want to help you affirm the importance of advocacy activities for your personal and professional growth, and we believe that planned and organized advocacy activities will help you present your education-related beliefs and practices to a variety of audiences.

CHAPTER 2

Deciding to Advocate

A s we begin this chapter, we are mindful of the statement of Richard Long, IRA's Director of Government Relations, at the Governmental Relations Symposium, a meeting of educators from across the United States. During opening remarks, Long reminded those attending, "You have power. You use it or you give it away." Although the content of the symposium focused on advocacy strategies at the state and national levels, Long's statement applies across the board. Whatever the concern and whatever the level—local, state, or national—we as educators can choose to participate and to advocate for our causes or we can give our power away. If we are proactive and advocate for our positions before all decisions are reached, we may be able to accomplish many of our advocacy goals.

As an education advocate, you must make choices about your work so that you efficiently and effectively use the limited time you have. How do you decide which of your concerns about education merit your time and efforts? Once you decide to get involved, how and where do you begin? Should you work with others? If so, how do you form coalitions of like-minded individuals who are willing to work together? These are but a few of the questions addressed in this chapter.

Concerns That Motivate Educators to Advocate

Concerns at the Personal Level

Advocacy efforts often grow from personal concerns. You read something or you witness or experience something that so greatly affects you that you can no longer sit back and remain detached. You decide to get involved. All educators have stories to tell of situations in which we made that choice. Misty Sailors's vignette suggests that caring deeply about an issue may be the most important requirement for taking an advocate's stance. As you read Sailors's story, consider how her convictions about what is right for students and teachers drove her to principled advocacy actions.

Politics, Romance, and Teaching: Confessions of a Reading Teacher Educator in Texas

Misty Sailors

Assistant Professor, University of Texas at San Antonio, San Antonio, Texas, USA

Some years back I was introduced to the book *Love Lessons*, a Harlequin romance novel focused on a young elementary school teacher using controversial teaching methods with her inner-city Hispanic students. Ricardo, an investigative reporter, is on a quest to expose her and save her students from her radical methods. As romance novels go, Ricardo becomes more interested in the instructor than in the instruction. I later discovered that Sandra Lee, the author, was actually a graduate student in education writing novels to support her studies. I smiled to think about the extremes some people go to and the compromises they make in order to achieve lifelong goals. I had no idea at the time how much I would have in common both with the author of the novel and with her main character.

I left classroom teaching to enter full-time doctoral study in the fall of 1999. The precipitous drop in salary had me scurrying for outside income because I was also the mother of three young children. I tutored. I collected data for research projects. I conducted teacher workshops. When the opportunity to lead inservice sessions for the Texas First Grade Reading Academies presented itself in the summer of 2001, I jumped all over it. One week's pay equaled my monthly university salary.

Governor George W. Bush's Texas Reading Initiative and the "retraining" of all primary-grade teachers in the state were in full swing that summer. The initiative focused on beginning reading instruction and the critical role that phonemic awareness played in reader success. The Texas Center for Reading and Language Arts, the Regional Service Center, and the Texas Educational Agency designed the Academies' training materials. To insure standardization, scripts were written and the rules for "trainers" were clear: There were to be no script deviations, no answers to questions other than what the script said, and no discussions that might depart from the scripts. This made me uncomfortable, but the money was just too good. I had almost convinced myself I would be OK until my first workshop with 60 first-grade teachers began. They were smart, insightful, and very knowledgeable about the content of the workshop. As a result, they asked questions, offered descriptions of their classroom reading and writing instruction, and critiqued the "formulaic" curriculum being presented to them. I listened to what they were saying and changed my approach from a deliverer of a script to a teacher who was reflective and responsive to her learners— the kind of teacher I had always been.

I encouraged teachers to share their own expertise and raise their own questions. Although the teachers responded positively, my fellow trainers did not. Some frowned; others asked me to stop "subverting the curriculum." During the third workshop, representatives from the Regional Service Center reminded me to "follow the state curriculum" so that "all teachers in Texas heard the same thing." Furious, I taught the rest of the sessions holding the script prominently in my hands but continuing to teach the way I believed was right.

For unknown reasons they allowed me to complete the last set of Academies. The following summer, I applied for the same position but discovered that I was not considered a "team player" and, therefore, would not be invited back. Imagine my surprise in the summer of 2003 when a new director called to invite me to present. I can only assume she was unaware of my history of noncompliance. I was just finishing my degree and was still incredibly broke, but this time I said no. I said that I simply could not follow a script and meet teachers' needs.

I completed my doctoral program and now serve as a university faculty member. My beliefs and my teaching are now protected through the traditions of "academic freedom." I have no doubt that my beliefs and principles will continue to face challenges. We can never escape the responsibility to act in ethical ways regarding our profession. Teaching is a moral act. Whether we choose to creatively comply, strategically adapt, actively subvert, passively resist, or directly confront policy mandates or other forms of intrusion into our professional lives, there will always be difficult choices to make. This is no romance novel we are living. Our passion for children and their learning cannot be redirected as easily as a plot twist. Yes, the risks and the costs for taking a principled stand are real, but our actions are part of a political and professional struggle that will affect future generations of educators. We must dig deep to discover who we are as educators and seek to live by those beliefs.

FOR YOUR CONSIDERATION

- Ernest Hemingway said that courage is grace under pressure. In what ways did Sailors demonstrate courage?

- "Teaching is a moral act," Sailors says. Yet critics say that public schools are value neutral. What examples can you give of how ethics and values affect education?

- How might journaling or discussing ideas with a teacher study group help individual teachers "dig deep to discover who [they] are as educators and seek to live by those beliefs?"

For many professional educators, advocacy efforts begin in their individual classrooms or at the school or district level. Perhaps without realizing it, we were behaving as education advocates when we questioned building or school district policies, spoke out in defense of a specific educational practice, or worked for the implementation of a particular instructional strategy or curriculum. We also were advocating when we spoke up for a student, lobbied for a student's classroom placement or curriculum, or protested when we thought disciplinary procedures were inappropriate. When we supported a parent and spoke up in support of the parent's concern, we were advocating as well. In each of these cases, we decided that something needed to be done, and we personally stepped in to see what could be changed.

There are numerous other examples where educators similar to you or to the three of us took their personal concerns about policies and practices in their schools or districts, decided that change was necessary, and turned their concerns into advocacy actions. As you read some of these stories, think of what advocacy strategies were used and why they were or were not successful. We three encourage you to use these ideas to plan your own advocacy activities; reading about what others have tried may give you ideas for your own initiatives.

Concerns at the School or District Level

Many individuals and organizations focus advocacy energy on larger legislative and policy issues. However, local daily events may lead to advocacy as you reflect on what is happening in your school and to your profession. Often, your advocacy efforts at the local level will be your most productive endeavors. You may more readily see your influence, and you often will get results more quickly.

As an educator, you probably advocate often on behalf of specific students. You arrange meetings with teachers, administrators, and support personnel to raise issues related to curriculum and assessment. You work for changes when students are inappropriately placed or denied access to programs that might better meet their needs. You plead for additional financial or curriculum support on behalf of the students you serve. In the following vignette, Carol Karpinski shares a story in which Melissa, a colleague, would not accept other teachers' assessments of her situation and searched for solutions to better help her students learn. As you read about Melissa, think back to times you have heard negative statements about students, administrators, or specific district poli-cies. How did you or others around you respond to what was said? Were there any positives that developed from these original negative thoughts? Are there any insights from Melissa's story that you might consider when you work with others who share different points of view than you?

Mutual Respect

Carol Karpinski
Programmer, New York City Public Schools, New York, New York, USA

When Melissa entered the faculty room on the first day of school, a colleague fired, "You and I share the class from hell—Homeroom 718." Another teacher piped in, "Yeah, I had some of those kids last year, and you'll be looking for a straight jacket by December." Melissa brushed off their remarks and left the faculty room, apprehensive and angry, but thoughtful. She was determined to do more than keep the lid on. She believed it was unfair that these teachers had spoken so negatively about these students whom she had just met. She was determined not to prejudge Homeroom 718, but rather to give them every opportunity to prove these teachers wrong.

Yet, as a veteran teacher, Melissa knew that high expectations for students were not enough. She restructured her American literature plans to maximize student input, opened a dialogue with students about life experiences, and gently led them to explore the required reading. She developed an effective technique that began with a detailed exploration of an author's life. Students saw the writer as a person with problems and experiences as real as their own. This became the core of her approach.

Conscious of her white middle class perspective, Melissa avoided value clashes by not "preaching" to her students. She knew her approach was working when Lamont, regarded by peers as a student leader, raised his hand during a book discus-sion and said, "I want to go to West Point like that guy." Lamont's comment indi-cated that he made a connection with the character in the book they were reading, linking his personal experiences to actions and events from the text. Through these open discussions with her students, Melissa created a classroom environment in which student opinions were valued. As she respected her students, they grew to respect their teacher and to respect learning.

FOR YOUR CONSIDERATION

• The three of us believe that working to change programs and curricula that are not working successfully for students is an important form of advocacy work. Do you agree?

• How could Melissa have involved others in her building in her advocacy efforts?

• What issues in your own building or district need your advocacy attention?

Another teacher, Machelle Dahl, also saw inequities at the local level and advocated for their correction. As you read Settlage and Dahl's vignette, consider how their actions were similar to and different from those Karpinski shares in Melissa's story.

Who Belongs at the Science Fair?

John Settlage
Associate Professor, University of Connecticut, Storrs, Connecticut, USA

Machelle Dahl
Fourth-grade teacher, Escalante Elementary School, Salt Lake City, Utah, USA

Science is the subject that is notoriously difficult for children of color and students whose first language is other than English. Time and again this "fact" is shown through test scores, course enrollment patterns, and career choices. When a new school was opened on Salt Lake City's west side, there was little reason to expect any break in this time-honored pattern. After all, the demographics of this neighborhood would not suggest the presence of budding scientists.

Not only is English not spoken in many of the students' homes but also many families were recent immigrants from areas such as Bosnia and Somalia. The cultural transitions are difficult for them, as are the economic challenges. Nevertheless, the staff of Escalante Elementary School (*Escalante* translates into *explorer*) made a commitment to provide quality science instruction to all the students.

Machelle's principal won a grant to sponsor an after-school science club. The goal was to have each of the students prepare an original science project for the April school district science fair. Rather than leaving attendance to chance, Machelle was persistent in her efforts to attract all types of students into the program. And she was tenacious at keeping them there. All of her hard work prevailed.

The school district science coordinator was one of the judges and was very complimentary about the students' projects. In fact, there were enough projects of sufficient quality that the decision about which to send to the district-level competition was a difficult one.

When the winners were announced at the district-level science fair, one fourth of them were from Escalante. The students who were responsible for them were not your typical "science types": Three were girls, and all were English-as-second-language students from southeast Asia and Mexico. While there may have been some grumbling from parents and schools on the other side of town, it was hard to dispute the fact that "those kids" had done so well in science. Machelle explains that advocacy is about doing what needs to be done and not believing that the supposed barriers, such as race and class, cannot be toppled.

FOR YOUR CONSIDERATION

- What local education problem did this advocate need to confront?
- What steps did she take on behalf of her students?
- In what ways were her advocacy strategies similar to those Melissa used?
- What "time-honored pattern" exists at your school that you would like to see changed?

Many school advocacy concerns center on curriculum issues. School personnel may find themselves passionately defending a book, a particular instructional strategy, or even a particular program. One of the authors of this book remembers the extensive hours she and others spent in districtwide meetings, defending specific books from censorship challenges brought by individual parents or other members of the community. Even with a well-established school district policy for reconsideration of books, hours of preparation often were necessary to prevent each title from being removed from the classroom, the building library, or all libraries throughout the school district.

The advocacy team presented testimony on each book's appropriateness to the curriculum. They orchestrated support for keeping, rather than banning, each book. And they sought informed opinion from professional reviews in library and education journals. These advocates called school district citizens who believed in open access to books and urged them to speak on a book's behalf. Students were invited to present statements on why they felt a book should remain in the curriculum or in library circulation.

Often, the advocacy of the opposing side was equally rich as the challengers organized individuals to present their ideas on why the book should be removed. Sometimes at the end of the hearings, when the superintendent would finally make the decision on the book's placement, the advocacy team would be disappointed. Contrary to advocates' personal wishes, the text might be removed from the library or left on the shelves but with specifications for carefully controlled access.

Evaluating the outcome of these efforts, it would be easy to be discouraged. However, without this advocacy, the likelihood of keeping the book on the shelf or in the curriculum would have been minimal. With testimony, the school district had a chance of keeping the book for ongoing use in the curriculum. Concerns for freedom of information merited the time and efforts the advocacy team dedicated on behalf of each text.

Advocating for strongly held educational beliefs at the school or district level may come at considerable personal cost. ReLeah Lent's passion for her high school students, her role as their publication advisor, and her concern for First Amendment freedoms show strongly in the following vignette. Taking her stance and her ensuing positions put her at considerable personal and economic risk. For details on this case, as well as on book censorship in the same school district, read the account in Pipkin and Lent's book *At the Schoolhouse Gate: Lessons in Intellectual Freedom* (2002). For their work, Pipkin and Lent received the John Phillip Immroth Memorial Award and the NCTE/SLATE (Support for Learning and Teaching of English) Intellectual Freedom Award.

Freedom of Publication

ReLeah Lent
Area Two Coordinator, Florida Literacy and Reading Excellence (FlaRE) Center,
University of Central Florida, Orlando, Florida, USA

Emma Goldman, a major figure in the history of American radicalism and feminism who was an influential and well-known anarchist in her time, once said, "The free expression of the hopes and aspirations of a people is the greatest and only safety in a sane society." Few would disagree with her words as they apply to adults; many, unfortunately, would question the sanity of allowing students to enjoy free expression in their publications, especially their school newspapers.

The principal of Mosley High School, where I sponsored an award-winning student newspaper for many years, censored an advertisement for a meeting by a gay support group. I was subsequently removed as newspaper sponsor because he felt the students who worked on the newspaper were engaging in too much investigative journalism and spending too much time writing "negative" articles that did not portray the school in a positive light. In response to his position, I filed a federal lawsuit on behalf of my students' rights for free expression.

We eventually settled out of court, fearing the creation of "bad law" that would do more harm than good. The result? According to the Student Press Law Center in Arlington, Virginia, USA, which was supportive of the case from the beginning,

> For the student press community, nationwide...the case is a victory. The clear message to other school administrators: if you're going to fire a good adviser for publishing a solid newspaper instead of a public relations puff piece, you're going to pay the price—both in terms of substantial money and shame. Sadly, though, the highest price will now be borne by Mosley's students. (Pipkin & Lent, 2002, p. 199)

FOR YOUR CONSIDERATION

- What do you think Lent meant when she said she and her students feared the creation of "bad law"?
- Lent quotes the Student Press Law Center's response to the judgment. How do you interpret this response?
- What other actions might have been taken by Lent as the sponsor of the student publication? What might have been the outcomes of these actions?

Another example of school-based curriculum advocacy is well described in *You Can Make a Difference: A Teacher's Guide to Political Action* (Keresty, O'Leary, & Wortley, 1998). This book chronicles the actions of three teachers and reading specialists in the Metropolitan School District of Madison, Wisconsin, USA, who mobilized their energies and actions when their school district's Reading Recovery program was threatened with elimination. Losing the program would mean that

20 teachers in the school district would lose their jobs and almost 200 children would not receive the reading instruction their teachers felt they needed.

You Can Make a Difference describes how these three educators organized their colleagues, garnered parents' support, worked with the media, and lobbied their school board and their legislators. Their well-organized campaign worked, and funding for the program was restored. Particularly insightful in their text are the authors' comments about what to do after you win or lose. They state, "If you lose, resolve to come back again. If you win, celebrate, and then resolve to come back again" (p. 26). They recognize that a singular success or failure is just one piece of an ongoing concern: Those who are interested in advocacy need to remain vigilant for the next problem they may need to face.

Advocacy concerns also may center on broader school or district policies. A particularly well-orchestrated campaign by parents and a few teachers in one elementary school serves as an excellent example of advocacy in action. A group of parents wanted the school to implement a uniform school dress code. They felt that students' wearing of uniforms would be more economical for most families and that this dress code would contribute positively to school discipline and school unity. Working together, several parents and teachers brought their wishes for a dress code to the building administrator, who, following school district policy, suggested procedures that needed to be followed, including a vote of all parents who had children attending that school. This small group of parents and teachers then organized a campaign to inform other parents of the benefits of uniforms. They reviewed the research literature. They collected estimates of the costs involved. They brought samples of possible uniforms to the school. They distributed fliers, wrote pieces for the parent newsletter, and made presentations at meetings that were organized at different times of the day so that most parents could attend. They also made phone calls and home visits to inform parents whom the other methods of communication had not reached. They achieved their desired outcome when parents cast their votes in favor of the uniforms.

What can we learn from this story? Parents and teachers, believing that their cause was important, organized to present their ideas to others. Where an individual parent or two might not have been successful, the parents and teachers working together accomplished their goal. Although they were successful, what may be more important was their feeling of ownership of their idea and their recognition of the important role they played in that school community. The parents were empowered by their advocacy efforts, and many became even more active in school affairs as a result. In addition, the teachers discovered new allies they might tap when they needed parent support for future advocacy initiatives at the school. As they worked together on the one concern, they formed relationships that would be helpful when working to support or oppose other school-related projects and policies.

Concerns at the Community Level

Let's look at some education advocacy examples that involve educators working beyond their school and in their larger community. In these cases, both individual and group advocacy activities were necessary to reach the desired goals.

One example is still playing out in the community of one of this book's authors. With the help of the local newspaper's education reporters and their strategically placed articles, the community learned of the deplorable state of many of the school district's middle school and high school libraries, especially the libraries at schools that were minority-student dominant. To illustrate the desperate need for new and current information, the newspaper articles featured text examples from the books that were currently on the shelves in these school libraries. Some science texts gave information that was clearly incorrect in light of current research and knowledge. For example, some discussed the possibility that the United States would someday engage in space exploration and land a man on the moon. Some books on careers had outdated information and inappropriate stereotypes and sexist language.

When the newspaper articles appeared, community members were outraged. Letters to the newspaper's editor were strong in their condemnation of school district policies that would allow such materials to be available to students. Many letters spoke to the issue of equity, commenting that the books that appeared most dated in their information often were found in the neediest schools. With the public incensed, school district policies were quickly changed. The superintendent issued a call to all schools for the removal of books with aged copyright dates. Although budgets were tight, somehow monies were found to begin the process of replacing obsolete texts and bringing collections in line with current recommendations for library and media materials. None of these changes would have been possible if the initial problem hadn't been "leaked" to the reporters by parents and teachers who knew the dreadful state of the library collections in the schools. The parents' and teachers' advocacy began the chain of events leading to new library appropriations.

In the same school district, students, parents, teachers, and interested community members rallied on another issue, working together to defeat a possible proposal to change the schools' starting times. As a solution to ongoing budget deficits, the school district had considered a later start to the school day for middle school and high school students. By starting classes for these schools at a much later hour, the bus runs could be adjusted so additional equipment and drivers would not be needed. Apparently, how this change would affect extracurricular activities, athletics, and students' work schedules had not received much consideration by school district administrators and school board members until articles in the local newspaper called attention to the proposal. Then, students, parents, teachers, and community members began to organize themselves to advocate on this issue. Letters to the editor both supported the idea and illustrated its folly. Many students, parents, teachers, and community members presented testimony to the school district's board of education about the difficulties such a time deferral would create for students who needed to work after school hours. Others from these groups spoke to the problem of those families that would have children on many different academic schedules. Although some proponents testified to the value of starting school later—given research on adolescents' sleep cycles—most of the students, parents, teachers, and community members spoke in opposition to the plan. The proposal lost steam, thanks to the many concerns expressed by these groups. Proponents were successful in defusing the plan because they were able to show the impact of the school time change on the community as a whole. By the number of and diversity of the comments from individual citizens and from business representatives across the community, school district representatives knew that the public as a whole was concerned. This was clearly an issue that moved beyond individual school borders to become a concern of the larger metropolitan community.

Concerns at the State Level

Many advocacy efforts emerge as responses to state-level education policies. Two areas that seem to be ongoing concerns in many U.S. states are textbook adoptions and high-stakes testing.

TEXTBOOK ADOPTIONS. In some states—such as California, Florida, and Texas—state-level decisions direct book selection for all school districts across the state. School districts are encouraged to select from a state-approved list because only books selected from this list will be funded by the state; school districts pay for texts not on the list.

As you can imagine, it is very important for textbook publishers to get on the state-approved lists. They spend millions of dollars developing materials that meet the state education standards and the requirements of the textbook proclamations in these very large states. Consequently, publishers rarely make major changes in their books when they try to sell them in other geographic areas. Thus, what is prepared for a few key states influences what is available for school districts in other parts of the United States.

Because of the widespread impact of textbook selection decisions, textbook adoptions always trigger responses from both individuals and organized advocacy groups. States that have state-approved textbook selection systems usually have elaborate procedures for material review. Advocates are familiar with the process and do what they can to be a voice in the decision-making process.

Often, textbook adoption procedures start with submitted materials facing a first round of stringent reviews by a committee of educators from across the state. If materials meet this first review, which is a very extensive process, they may be placed on a list of texts for possible consideration by the state's department of education. From that point on, the textbook adoption procedures accelerate. Materials are disseminated for community viewing. Hearings are scheduled, and individuals sign up to testify for or against particular materials. Citizen action groups and special interest groups may disseminate information in newsletters or e-mail messages to their constituents. They urge their followers to sign up to testify, often suggesting specific issues the followers may want to consider in their written or spoken testimony. Group members may arrange individual meetings with personnel in the school districts to inform the personnel of the group's concerns about the texts and to ask for school district acceptance or rejection of the materials in light of the concerns the groups present.

Note how many advocacy activities may be at play here. People who want to testify study the materials carefully and do research on various aspects of the texts. They may organize meetings to create opportunities for viewing the texts and asking questions about them. They may prepare fliers describing the advantages and disadvantages of particular texts. They may organize individuals to testify in support of or in opposition to the texts and orchestrate media events to call attention to their concerns. They may present their ideas to the public through letters to the editor and appearances on local radio programs.

Because there may be a series of meetings, often in different places across the state, individuals who wish to advocate in support of or opposition to specific texts accomplish more by connecting with others who share their concerns. Working together, they can arrive at a common message that they then disseminate to a wider audience.

Textbook adoption periods often galvanize individuals who do not engage in advocacy on a regular basis. Many people feel strongly about the materials that will be used to educate children, and these people get involved in this educational concern but not in others. In Texas, where one of this book's authors taught for many years, busloads of supporters for a specific position would turn out for a textbook adoption hearing. Recently, at a hearing on high school biology texts, more than 160 individuals signed up to testify before the state board of education. Advocates knew how to marshal their supporters quickly and effectively so the members of the state board of education heard the advocates' views on the texts.

HIGH–STAKES TESTING. The other issue that seems to mobilize education advocates is high-stakes testing, an issue on which few individuals are neutral. Advocates use a variety of approaches to voice their opinions, including letters to the editor, e-mail messages, letters, phone calls, and office visits to their legislators. In Florida, teachers have converged on their legislators in Tallahassee, the state capital. Many teachers have shared their stories about the impact of the state test and the implications of present testing practices for their school and their students. Other teachers visited their legislators at their offices in their home districts or invited legislators to visit their schools or speak to meetings of their parent–teacher associations. (See chapter 6 for details on how to use legislator visits effectively.)

Often, these visits have helped to place human faces on the test results that were synthesized in state reports or summarized in area newspapers or on radio and television programming. When a teacher was able to share classroom stories about the impact of high-stakes testing in the classroom, including stories about the amount of time spent in test preparation rather than teaching, the limitation of the daily curriculum to those subjects that would be tested, or the impact of testing on specific students who had not performed successfully and might be retained rather than promoted, some legislators became more concerned. When teachers of parents shared stories about young students too upset to go to school, or coming home ill on testing day, a few legislators agreed to voice these concerns in appropriate committees and to work for change in state testing practices. Other legislators used their concern about the information from parents, teachers, and administrators to try to secure more funding for early intervention programs that might prevent students from failing and facing the possibility of being retained in a grade. However, budget obstacles usually interfered with securing the desired funding allocations. Results of all these visits with legislators were not always as successful as advocates wished; however, some legislators became more sympathetic to the educators' and parents' concerns, and advocates could, therefore, consider their strategies successful.

Martha T. Dever's success story illustrates that individual advocacy acts can also affect state assessment policies. As you read her vignette, consider the strategies she used and her diligence in pursuing her assessment concern.

From High Stakes to Low Stakes

Martha T. Dever
Professor, Utah State University, Logan, Utah, USA

One Saturday morning I opened the newspaper to learn that our state legislature had mandated the use of a standardized kindergarten readiness assessment. Knowing that standardized testing can be emotionally and educationally harmful to young children and that it often leads to inappropriate curricula and program placements, or to the application of disability labels for children at a very young age, I was alarmed!

I investigated and learned that *all* kindergarten children would be tested. I talked with the legislator who wrote the bill, and he explained as his reasoning that many children in juvenile court have poor reading skills. He thought testing to inform development of preschool programs was a solution; my colleagues and I, however, knew the pitfalls of testing children so young.

I got in touch with my local legislators and found one willing to listen to my concerns. After a while, she embraced my concerns about high-stakes testing in the primary grades. She invited me to share my concerns with the legislative education subcommittee and to help rewrite the bill. I also suggested an alternative way to obtain data to inform the development of preschool programs.

For nearly five years my colleagues and I advocated our position. We pled with personnel from the state school board and the state office of education to advocate against testing. We talked with legislators. I had all but given up that any change would come when my legislator called to say that she felt the timing was right (with the approaching legislative session) to introduce the rewritten bill. Three months later, the legislature voted to make the assessment optional, rather than mandatory. Now, the test no longer carries high stakes and teachers are empowered to use it or not use it as they think is best for the children.

FOR YOUR CONSIDERATION

• What made this advocate's strategies successful?

• If Dever had been trying to change the law today, what strategy changes might she have to make in light of the recent federal legislation on assessment and adequate yearly progress?

These stories showing advocates' responses to concerns about statewide issues demonstrate that advocacy efforts beyond the school and community levels require persistence over time. Results may be slow in coming because policy changes are not easily implemented. Often, advocacy performed at the state level requires the coordination and networking of many concerned individuals before the concern receives legislators' or state board or education members' attention. Although it is possible that with a great deal of diligence an individual may bring about change, more is usually accomplished when advocates band together. As you will see in later sections of this chapter, working effectively with others requires good advance planning and constant monitoring of all individual activities.

Concerns at the National Level

Often education advocates' initiatives target national issues and policies in the United States. Ultimately, most policies at the national level trickle down and influence what happens in the states or in local communities. Recent federal legislation for such programs as Title I, NCLB, the IDEA, vocational education, and teacher education has spurred educational advocates to action.

To have an impact on policies at the national level, you must communicate with Congressional representatives by meeting them when they are at home in their districts, inviting them to your school when they are in town, and sending them e-mail messages and faxes about your concerns. You can respond to their mailers and the information that they have posted on their websites. You also can call to let them know, usually through their office aides, your views on pending legislation. Through these mechanisms, you begin forming relationships with your legislators and their staffs that may serve you now or in the future. Seasoned advocates know that legislators are interested in their constituents' opinions. In chapters 5 and 6, we suggest some specific strategies for communicating effectively with your legislators.

Deciding to Advocate Alone or With Others

One of the first decisions you will need to make as an education advocate is whether you will work alone or with others. How you make that decision may be decided by the nature of your issue; the diversity of the audiences you want to reach; and your own time, talents, and financial resources.

Advocating Alone

As this chapter's vignettes and stories illustrate, there are many times that advocates work alone. Often, this is when the issue is intensely personal. Occasionally, advocates work alone because of time constraints or because they are unable to contact others to meet and plan a coordinated effort. Sometimes, though, advocates work by themselves because they feel that they lack the skills or the information to participate in a wider advocacy campaign.

Advocating alone is not a negative activity. Each advocacy act requires an intense personal commitment. You will need to exercise your personal power in the ways that are the most comfortable and appropriate for you. A decision to work by yourself means that you single-handedly take responsibility for the outcome of your actions, credit for your success, and criticism from those who disagree with you. It is a choice that you will make deliberately as you become increasingly skilled as an education advocate.

Advocating With Others

Generally, we believe that you will accomplish more if you seek out and work with like-minded individuals or members of groups and organizations sharing similar concerns. Forming partnerships or coalitions usually strengthens your approach.

Before making the decision to work solo or with others, ask yourself, Is my issue one that cuts across different fields or groups? Are there other organizations or groups that might be interested in working with me? Is a unified approach more likely to win support for my idea? Will the time and effort it takes to negotiate positions and resources be useful to me in the end? If so, consider whom you might approach. What groups or organizations share similar concerns? Who have you met who might be interested in working with you? Whom can you contact to help you make connections to people who can assist you?

When you work with others, you have a wider range of expertise and experience on which to build. You have more manpower so that responsibilities and tasks can be delegated. You also may have more funds to work with when you pool financial resources. If you put a coalition together, there are some benchmarks you can use to evaluate the success of your efforts or to guide your redirection and regrouping if you are not achieving your goals. (See chapter 8 for suggestions on how to judge the success of your coalition or redirect your joint efforts if they are not effective.)

Throughout the project, you will be working with others to achieve the group's desired outcomes of influencing opinion or changing current practice or legislation. Members of your group should feel a connectedness with one another, and mutual respect and trust should be evident as the group considers alternative suggestions for advocacy. Remember that your group members will have diverse experiences and expertise, varying levels of formal education and experience in the education system, and multiple personal goals. However, they are working with you on the same initiative, and that initiative needs to stay as your focus. As the group spends time together, you usually will find that communication improves and individuals pause to consider the various perspectives of the other group members. From time to time, especially if one group member is reluctant to speak up or if the ideas of others are ignored, it may fall to you to ask the group to listen to everyone's ideas. You want all coalition members to participate in the development of the advocacy plan.

When your group first meets, you begin what we sometimes call the *project development phase*. During this period, you want to accomplish several goals. First, you need to establish that each member values the project. If, for instance, your advocacy project is to obtain funding for playground equipment at all elementary schools in your school district, you need to be certain that each group member, or the organization he or she represents, values this goal. Some group members may have come to your first meeting without a clear understanding of its purpose or their role at your meeting.

During the project development phase, encourage extensive conversation about the issue before you develop your advocacy plan. The conversation will guide the direction of your plan and provide room for multiple perspectives.

After this time of initial conversation, you will need to develop a clear course of action. Strategies for developing your advocacy plan are discussed in chapter 4. For now, consider that there are some actions that group members may not be willing or able to undertake. They may see a conflict of interest or have a personal objection. They may be unwilling to invest the necessary funds. In such cases, consider alternative contributions these group members can make to the plan so they may remain involved.

Because you will have brought together a diverse group of individuals and organizations in the project development phase, you will want to identify each member's assets. Some members might be excellent public speakers or artists. Others might provide contacts, meeting space, or financial resources. Recognize the strengths that each member brings to the coalition.

Depending on the urgency of your issue, your group might not meet more than once a month, or it may meet even less frequently. With the group, make plans for sharing information. You will want to keep one another informed of any developments related to your issue as well as any other concerns that might present themselves and on which you might collaborate. Because your partners come from diverse arenas, they may learn about emerging issues earlier than you; for instance, your partners from the business community may find out that their local chamber of commerce is undertaking a study of education levels of county employees in order to identify how businesses must respond to the current education levels and what they need to ask of area schools.

There also are some challenges to collaborating with diverse groups. First, collaboration can be extraordinarily time-consuming, much more so than if you work alone. Depending on the size and diversity of your group, communication by e-mail and faxes may or may not be possible, but each member must be kept informed in order to stay committed to the effort. Second, group members must be clear about their roles in the group and that the work is a team effort. If after your first few meetings individual coalition members start to work on separate—but related—projects, you may find yourselves at cross-purposes. You will need to decide how to address this problem and re-focus the group.

Third, if you have been working on your own advocacy concerns, you may find it challenging to share responsibility and relinquish control. You will need to take deliberate steps to involve others. You also may have expectations of the group that are unreasonable. Your passion for this issue or for this work may be far greater than the enthusiasm of other group members. You might be willing to spend countless hours on the concern; they may not be. It will be critical to periodically assess your expectations.

Fourth, you also will need to verify that group members are willing to sacrifice self-interest for the group's interest and that they are willing to work toward consensus on issues. Consensus requires skill at recognizing the different agendas that group members may bring to your meetings. For example, some members may agree to be part of your coalition because they see the coalition as an opportunity to network and encourage interest in their own projects.

On occasion, individuals agree to join coalitions but do not have the time to participate in face-to-face meetings. In these cases, you will have a fifth challenge. You will need to decide whether it is still worthwhile to include these individuals as part of your membership and whether there are alternative ways for them to participate. For instance, if a member of the state legislature agrees to join and is willing to be listed as a part of your coalition, the legislator's addition may be inherently valuable for initiatives your group may subsequently undertake. Keep the legislator informed, invite his or her participation and advice, and double-check that the legislator is willing to be included on any materials you distribute that include coalition members' names.

A final challenge in working with a coalition is shifting the decision making to a group, rather than you having sole responsibility. There are some instances where individual decision making may be appropriate, but you will need to assess the effect of individual versus group decision making in each instance.

The benefits of working with a coalition are numerous, including ongoing communication with diverse stakeholders who bring multiple perspectives for your consideration. The wide membership lends legitimacy to your effort and provides it with greater visibility. If you represent a particular organization, its name and activities will become more familiar to others. Working together on one activity may lead to other joint initiatives and numerous possibilities for networking.

Jill Lewis's vignette below speaks to many of these benefits, but especially to the long-range networking that grew from the initial advocacy issue. As a result of working together, the organizations described in the vignette now collaborate on many education issues.

Keep Your Ear to the Ground

Jill Lewis
Professor of Literacy Education, New Jersey City University,
Jersey City, New Jersey, USA

While I was attending an out-of-state professional meeting, a colleague told me that a national association had just endorsed a position statement claiming that speech pathologists were able to teach reading and provide professional development in reading to teachers. Because I felt that speech professionals lacked the academic and experiential preparation for teaching students to read, I was concerned.

Coincidentally, when I returned home, a member of that organization's state affiliate contacted me. He wanted to meet to discuss literacy and what role speech pathologists could play in children's literacy achievement. At our meeting, I learned that he was unaware of the details of the position statement. He was a speech pathologist and felt unprepared to teach the entire scope of literacy, but he believed he could make some contributions, especially in the areas of phonological and phonemic awareness.

Working together, along with an advocate from a third professional field, we drafted a 13-point New Jersey Literacy Initiative Mission Statement that articulated our beliefs about the training of literacy professionals and the qualifications of individuals who work with struggling readers. We defined the respective roles of reading specialists and speech pathologists. We provided research-based support for each of our 13 points. (See Appendix A, page 237, for a copy of the mission statement.)

A number of the state's professional and business associations endorsed our mission statement. Then it was sent to the governor and to all members of the state legislature. We also met with legislators to discuss it, and we understand that the statement has been used by educators as they developed school and district curricula, and by policymakers as they developed literacy policies in the state.

As a result of working together, we produced a statement that can guide initiatives at the state level. We also have established a professional relationship among ourselves and with our state professional organizations. We continue to keep one another informed about shared educational concerns and visions.

FOR YOUR CONSIDERATION

- What might have been some turning points in this vignette, where the outcome might have been different had the individuals acted differently?

- The author of this vignette feels the outcome was positive. Do you see any negative consequences in the result? What are they, if any?

- In what ways might your education interests be positively affected by working with other professional organizations? What organizations would you contact?

Your combined effort also means there is shared accountability. If your advocacy work is not successful, together you and your partners can determine possible reasons for this lack of success and revise your plan accordingly. Most important, if you work with a coalition, you are more likely to achieve better results. Avivah Dahbany's vignette affirms the benefits that working with others can bring.

Lemons to Lemonade: Mobilizing a Coalition of Professional Organizations

Avivah Dahbany
School Psychologist, Franklin Township Public Schools, New Jersey, USA

What does a school district do when it eliminates its special services department that had a staff of 25 people, including school psychologists, learning consultants, school social workers, and secretaries? To save money, the school district replaced these department members with consultants from a county educational service.

In response to this action, members of several professional organizations met to develop a plan of action. This plan included contacting the state education association and the state department of education, and meeting with legislators. This working relationship later expanded to cover other issues beyond the issue involving special services personnel.

Among the information the coalition shared were findings about parents' displeasure with the services their children were receiving. During the years the county educational association provided this school district with services, the parents complained that their children were not receiving the services they required. In addition, the school district found that it was spending more money using the county educational service than it had spent with its original staff. After a few years of experiencing these difficulties and many complaints from parents and district educators about the quality of service, the school district reconsidered its position and decided to end its agreement with the county educational service. Although costs may have been less, the quality of service was not the same, and many of the original personnel were hired back to provide the necessary support for students and parents.

Representatives from these state professional associations continue to collaborate as a coalition of educators. They meet a number of times a year to discuss issues of mutual interest. They developed a position paper to explain their roles and functions. The coalition exhibits at a number of statewide conferences each year, educating others about their roles and functions and advocating for the use of special services personnel hired by the local school district. Coalition members also have made presentations about other issues affecting special education. Although this group started with one issue, it has developed into a professional collaboration benefiting everyone concerned.

FOR YOUR CONSIDERATION

- What benefits do you see in expanding the original coalition to an even larger group of professional associations? What are possible risks of expanding beyond the original groups?

- To what extent do you think this coalition should be credited with the change in district policy?

- What does the author use to gauge her advocacy success? What else might she consider?

Sometimes our interactions with others help us think through concerns that need our attention. One group in the area of St. Louis, Missouri, USA, meets regularly to discuss education issues and how group members will address certain education-related needs. Perhaps participating in such a group will help you refine your ideas and strategies. As you read the vignette, consider how the members of this group support one another in teaching and advocacy efforts.

Literacy for Social Justice Action Research Group

Mary Ann Kramer

Literacy Coordinator, Adult Education and Literacy, St. Louis Public Schools, St. Louis, Missouri, USA

The Literacy for Social Justice Action Research Group, founded by Rebecca Rogers of Washington University and myself, is made up of adult education instructors, elementary school teachers, and university faculty and students who are committed to the relation between literacy and social justice in classrooms, schools, and communities. Members of this collaboration between Washington University and the St. Louis Public Schools have met twice a month since the fall of 2001 to discuss educational readings, videos, CD-ROMs, presentations by guest speakers, and educational policy, and to explore how theory and practice work toward democratic aims in our classrooms. As teachers we are immersed in our students' learning on a daily basis and have questions and issues that arise in the context of our classrooms, schools, and the communities in which we work. The group serves as a forum where teachers pose questions and think of multiple possibilities for strategic action in their classrooms. This includes collecting resources (e.g., children's and adult literature, lesson plans, websites, and interactional strategies) that teachers can use in their classrooms. Teachers in the group conduct an action research project in their classrooms on the relation between literacy and social justice. They collect data on their interventions (e.g., examples of student work, transcripts of classroom interaction, and a videotaped lesson) and, with the group's assistance, analyze the data, looking for patterns and themes that can aid in further strengthening the teaching and learning in the classroom.

As a group we conceptualize our work as literacy advocates operating at the societal, institutional, and classroom levels. Participants experience a sense of connectedness with other teachers from different schools. We have participated in IRA's African American Read-In Chain and national conferences. We believe the unique combination of adult educators and elementary-grade teachers in this group allows us to conceptualize and act toward more socially just communities.

FOR YOUR CONSIDERATION

- If you were going to participate in Kramer's group, how would you introduce yourself and your connection to social justice?
- What action research project might you begin in your classroom or your school if you were participating in a group similar to this?
- How might Kramer's group members use their experiences to initiate advocacy activities outside their individual classrooms and schools?
- How might you organize a group such as this?

On almost any issue, finding like-minded individuals strengthens our efforts. When we work with others, we benefit from the group's collective thinking and the members' multiplicity of experiences. We also strengthen our advocacy appeal when we can show that our advocacy concern affects many others. By banding together, we broaden the circles of concern. We may also feel more secure in our position when we know we have the support of many.

Kaplan (2000) noted, "Given the multiplicity of interests, networks, and inconsistencies that tend to separate rather than unite education's representative groups, it is no simple task to rally the troops and their generals" (p. 213). But just because something is difficult, it should not deter us from what, in the long run, will be beneficial and rewarding. When you read news about what is happening in U.S. schools, recall the many groups that are expressing concern: parents, members of business and industry groups, politicians, individual educators, professional education associations, and senior citizens. All of these groups can be part of the coalition of advocates that you put together at the school, community, state, or national level. If you truly wish to strengthen your voice, you will seek to collaborate with these diverse groups to achieve mutually desired goals.

Successful collaboration involves joint planning, joint implementation, and joint evaluation. There are numerous examples of successful and large-scale education collaborations that can serve as models. For instance, the Committee for Education Funding in Washington, DC—a group that is more than 30 years old—has more than 100 members who represent diverse stakeholders. This group focuses on U.S. federal policy, especially on funding issues. Its members pledge not to undercut any other members' quests for appropriated dollars. The members also believe that when they work together on issues, individual priorities are not as important as the fair financial treatment of all members.

The Alliance for Excellent Education, also based in Washington, DC, is another national coalition in the United States that brings like-minded members from other organizations together. Members of the Alliance write position papers and work with legislators to draft bills that are mutually beneficial to all Alliance members and that aid Alliance goals of helping at-risk middle school and high school students achieve high standards and graduate prepared for college and success in life.

At the state level, one state's reading association has formed an advisory board for its Legislation Committee. The board comprises members from the state legislature, the state board of education, the state's Department of Education, businesses, the media, and the Parent–Teacher Association. Together, the board members draft position papers and mission statements, and plan conferences. Their combined efforts certainly give strength to their endeavors, spread word of their activities and positions, and lend legitimacy to their work. The chorus of their voices has a wider range than the education community singing solo.

Think of what coalitions you can put together for your advocacy issue. Consider individuals and organizations in your community. Who shares similar interests or concerns? Who might benefit if your advocacy efforts were successful? Who might be harmed if particular policies or practices were put into effect? Seek out these individuals, and invite them to advocate with you. In chapter 4, we will offer further suggestions for bringing people together in a common cause.

Conclusion

This chapter has focused on how you make decisions as to where you direct your advocacy efforts and whether you work alone or collaborate with others.

These two types of advocacy activities—independent and collaborative—are not mutually exclusive. When we are involved in working with others, we are still engaging in individual advocacy acts. We cannot and should not avoid telling our personal stories. Our stories make our issues real to the people we need to inform and influence. As Kathleen Kennedy Manzo, associate editor of *Education Week*, stated at the Government Relations Symposium in February 2003, "People in Washington, in your statehouse, and at your local level need to hear from you. You have important information to share."

In chapter 3, we will focus on how you acquire information for becoming a more informed education advocate because, whether you are advocating at the local, state, or federal level, you need to have well-researched information to support your issues of concern.

Becoming an Informed Education Advocate

When we approach others to discuss concerns we have about education, our listeners assess several things simultaneously: the legitimacy of our concerns, the logic of our arguments, the solutions we offer, and, perhaps, what we are asking of our listeners. Being an informed education advocate will make a difference in the kind of impression you leave.

Consider the following two fictional scenarios. How do they differ? In which situation are the advocates more likely to be successful?

Scenario 1

Scene: The office of state assemblywoman Pritchard, who is visited by two representatives of a state professional association—Elena Cassidy and Darren Johnston.

Ms. Cassidy:	Good afternoon, Assemblywoman Pritchard. My name is Elena Cassidy, and I'm here on behalf of the Kentucky Gifted Children's Association (KGCA). Thank you for seeing us. It's very generous of you to give us some time.
Mr. Johnston:	Yes. Thank you for seeing us. My name is Darren Johnston. I'm the president of KGCA. Here are some materials about our organization. We've heard a lot of good things about your voting record on education.
Assemblywoman Pritchard:	Well, thank you, and I'm pleased to meet both of you. What can I do for you?
Mr. Johnston:	Well, I'm sure you know that our state has many gifted children in our public schools in grades K–12. We are concerned

	that funding for gifted education programs is being cut this year, and we hope you can address this situation.
Ms. Cassidy:	Yes. We have many schools that are losing their gifted programs, and parents are complaining that their children's educational needs aren't being met.
Assemblywoman Pritchard:	Well, how can I help?
Ms. Cassidy:	KGCA believes that more state legislators need to become involved in supporting funding for gifted programs for children in grades K–12. Otherwise, the programs will be cut for sure. Teachers believe that the children need these programs in order to reach their full potential.
Mr. Johnson:	Yes. Budget decisions are being made right now, and without support for gifted education from legislators, we cannot guarantee parents that their children's needs will be met.
Assemblywoman Pritchard:	I see. I do chair the Assembly's Budget Committee. I can certainly tell them about your organization's concern, and those of the parents.
Mr. Johnson:	We would appreciate that a great deal. We think the voters would be very happy to know that you have taken our issue to heart.
Assemblywoman Pritchard:	Yes. I will mention your visit to the committee. Of course, I can't promise anything. As you know, these are difficult times for the state budget.
Ms. Cassidy:	KGCA appreciates whatever you can do. Thank you again for seeing us.
Mr. Johnston:	Yes. Thank you.
Assemblywoman Pritchard:	You're welcome. Good luck with your work.

Scenario 2

Scene: The office of state assemblywoman Pritchard, who is visited by two representatives of a state professional association—Farrah Ambugway and Ralph Canniday.

Ms. Ambugway: Good afternoon, Assemblywoman Pritchard. My name is Farrah Ambugway. I'm a parent of a child who has been identified by her school as gifted, and I'm here on behalf of the Kentucky Gifted Children's Association (KGCA). Thank you for seeing us.

Mr. Canniday: Yes. Thank you for seeing us. My name is Ralph Canniday. I teach fourth grade in Prescott Township. I'm also the president of KGCA, an organization of more than 2,000 parents, teachers, and administrators statewide. Here is some literature about KGCA.

Assemblywoman
Pritchard: Well, thank you, and I'm pleased to meet you. What can I do for you?

Mr. Canniday: Well, as you may already know, more than 20,000 of Kentucky's public school children in grades K–12 are identified on the basis of statewide tests and teacher identification as gifted. These children require additional classroom and out-of-classroom support to have their unique learning needs met. The proposed state budget for this next year cuts all of this support, including cutting jobs of teachers who provide additional enrichment support outside the regular classroom.

Ms. Ambugway: Yes. These programs are critical to the children's continuing academic and social progress. I have some information about this issue in this folder of material on gifted children's needs that we brought for you. One thing you will find is the results of a study available through the government-sponsored Educational Resources Information Center (ERIC) Clearinghouse on Disabilities and Gifted Education that describes some of the ways gifted children's needs can be addressed in regular classrooms. KGCA believes that gifted children should experience education that would allow them to fully develop their abilities, for their own benefit and for the benefit of society as a whole, and that this can be done with relatively inexpensive adjustments within regular classrooms. We've also included some letters from parents who are complaining to KGCA that their children's educational needs aren't currently being met and how the proposed budget cuts will provide even fewer services. We hope you can address this problem in funding.

Assemblywoman
Pritchard: Really? I didn't know how valuable these programs for gifted children are. Thank you for the material.

Mr. Canniday: Yes. Budget decisions are being made right now, and without support for gifted education from legislators, we cannot assure parents that their children's needs will be met. We also cannot assure the children that our state will help them to meet their potential and become all they are capable of being. Seven percent of our children have scored "advanced" on the statewide reading test, and 5% have scored "advanced" on the statewide math test. We cannot afford to deny these gifted children the special attention they need.

Assemblywoman
Pritchard: I see. I do chair the Assembly's Budget Committee. I can certainly tell them about your organization's concern, and those of the parents. Do you think you could send me some additional copies of these materials so I can share them with committee members?

Mr. Canniday: Of course. We will get them to you tomorrow, and we would certainly appreciate your sharing them. Or, if you'd prefer, we can also send them directly to the committee members and let them know you've asked us to distribute these materials.

Assemblywoman
Pritchard: That would be fine. Thanks.

Ms. Ambugway:	Well, thank you. We think the voters will be very happy to know that you have taken our issue to heart.
Assemblywoman Pritchard:	Yes. Of course, I can't promise anything. As you know, these are difficult times for the state budget. But I will discuss the issue with the committee.

FOR YOUR CONSIDERATION

• What differences did you notice in these two scenarios?

• What kind of impression might each set of speakers make on the assemblywoman?

• Which advocacy effort is likely to produce the greatest result? Why?

You no doubt noticed that the visitors in the second fictional scenario had done their homework. They offered evidence to Assemblywoman Pritchard that she can use to make a case to her committee when it reviews budget cuts. They also brought materials to share with her that directly addressed the issues. They were better prepared to present research-based arguments for their viewpoints. In this chapter, you will learn about the wide variety of resources available to education advocates to help them stay informed about issues, new policies under consideration, and the wide range of perspectives that different groups have on these issues and policies.

The Importance of Education Advocates Doing Their Homework

Where possible, you should provide research evidence to substantiate your opinions. School district officials and policymakers are always looking for research- or evidence-based information, especially related to school reform proposals under consideration at the state or federal level. When you include hard data with your arguments, you demonstrate that your concerns have a factual basis. You also help policymakers see that there are different perspectives on an issue when you present data from different sources. As a result, your evidence may become the basis for policy revision or for new policy and action. V. Darleen Opfer's story is a case in point.

Interpreting Data on the Segregation of Charter Schools

V. Darleen Opfer

Director and Associate Professor, The Ohio Collaborative: Research and Policy
for Schools, Children, and Families, The Ohio State University, Columbus, Ohio, USA

Policymakers absorb a great deal of research through informal routes. They read widely, go to meetings, listen to people, and discuss with colleagues—all without necessarily having a particular decision in mind. When they engage in the stream of activities that aggregate into policymaking, they draw from the knowledge they have gathered from these varied sources and apply it to their work. Because of this diffuse information-gathering process, influencing policy can be a slow and frustrating experience.

During the 2002–2003 academic year, I evaluated the charter schools of a southern U.S. state. In the process of doing this evaluation, it became evident that some charter schools in the state were being used as segregation academies—a way for white parents to remove their children from predominantly African American schools and school systems.

In a preliminary evaluation report, I presented findings from interviews and focus groups that supported this conclusion. Representatives from the state department of education took exception to my findings and asked that the section be removed prior to the final report. Ethically, I just couldn't do that, so in the final report I expanded the section to show that the problem of segregation in charter schools existed not just in the two schools in which I had conducted interviews and focus groups but in many charter schools in the state. I compared the racial composition of charter schools with their closest public school neighbors and with their districts. When compared to their neighboring public schools, half the charter schools differed from their respective districts' racial composition, with at least 30% fewer African Americans at the charter school than at the public schools. For example, one district system was 78% African American and 22% white, excluding the charter school; the charter school was 98% white and 2% African American. Again, state department of education representatives took exception and refused to allow the report to go before the state board of education for approval.

During this time, *The New York Times* covered a report released by the Civil Rights Project at Harvard University that showed similar segregation patterns across charter schools nationwide. Also, a session was conducted at an American Educational Research Association (AERA) conference on just this topic. I forwarded copies of the conference papers to the state department of education. In a conversation with a governor's aide, I mentioned the charter school problem, the Civil Rights Project report, and the AERA papers.

Shortly thereafter, the major newspaper in the state ran a favorable story about the governor's history on race relations while in the legislature. The article concluded by questioning whether he would maintain this record as governor. A week later, a representative from the state department of education called me to say they wanted to draft legislation to fix the segregation problem in the state's charter schools. This legislation was to be introduced in January 2004 (more than a year after I first raised the issue) when the legislature convenes. Unfortunately, this did not occur. The governor's office and the secretary of education decided against submitting a bill at the last minute and against making the issue public. Instead, as a warning to the rest, they did not renew the charter for the charter school that was the most egregious case.

Did my report influence policy? Perhaps. I had hoped for legislation to address the issue, but perhaps the warning will serve a similar purpose. The influence process is diffuse, and no one person or group of people can control it.

FOR YOUR CONSIDERATION

- What evidence is provided in this vignette that research helped Opfer present her case to state department of education personnel?
- What role did ethics play in this advocacy story?
- What can you learn from the experiences of this writer that you might use in your interactions with policymakers?

Researching Issues and Locating Information Resources for Education Advocacy

Finding evidence to support your positions takes considerable time and energy. Whether you work in conjunction with others or individually, there are nearly endless resources available to assist you with obtaining information and substantiating your viewpoints. Looking for material that is just right for you can be a bit overwhelming. To limit your search, consider your issue, your audience, and what and how much data you feel is needed.

What follows are descriptions of various categories of information sources, each of which offers something a little different. The figures contain thorough lists of online sources for you to investigate. Select those websites that will be most helpful for your advocacy issue. Their appropriateness will vary with the nature of your concern and your point of view.

When you review the information at any website, remember that the organization is advocating its specific viewpoints. An organization usually offers only those ideas that substantiate its positions. You will need to visit other websites in order to take a comprehensive look at the multiple perspectives on any single issue.

U.S. Department of Education

The U.S. Department of Education wants to present its programs in as positive a manner as possible. We can expect that its website will include information that presents its vision for education. If, for example, the U.S. Department of Education is pro-voucher, then we would expect that press releases, data, or research reports obtained at its website will explain the positive aspects of vouchers.

From the U.S. Department of Education's homepage (www.ed.gov), you can link to almost anything about education initiatives at the national level, including information on pending federal legislation, new regulations and policies, and grants and education resources for various content areas and topics such as accountability. Examples of the kind of information the different offices of the U.S. Department of Education provide and that education advocates will find valuable are described here. Additional information can be found in the websites listed in Figure 1.

NO CHILD LEFT BEHIND ACT. The U.S. Department of Education has a website devoted entirely to NCLB. Visitors to this website learn that it

> offers "one-stop-shopping" for links to legislation, Federal Register Notices, Policy Guidance, and Grant Applications for the No Child Left Behind Act of 2001. Links to Legislation, Regulations, and Policy Guidance for programs still being implemented under the Improving America's Schools Act are also on this site. (n.p.)

As this legislation continues to evolve, you can expect additions and changes to the information on the website, so it is the first place you will want to look to learn the current federal perspective on NCLB.

INSTITUTE OF EDUCATION SCIENCES. The Institute of Education Sciences, established on November 5, 2002, by the Education Sciences Reform Act of 2002, advances rigorous education research that will lead to evidence-based education practices. The Institute comprises three research centers: (1) the National Center for Education Research, (2) the National Center for Education Statistics, and (3) the National

Center for Education Evaluation and Regional Assistance. Each center provides important data to support your advocacy work. For instance, the website of the National Center for Education Statistics presents a great variety of statistical information about education in the United States, including information about libraries, vocational programs, service learning, community service, distance learning, and uses of technology for education. Its annual *Digest of Education Statistics* provides extensive state-by-state and national data on elementary and secondary education, including enrollment, programs for disabled students, teacher qualifications, private schools, dropout rates, drug use, and school violence.

OFFICE OF EDUCATIONAL RESEARCH AND IMPROVEMENT. Until December 2002, the Office of Educational Research and Improvement (OERI) was the primary source for education research reports funded by the U.S. Department of Education. Although the OERI is no longer in existence because it was replaced by the Institute of Education Sciences, its archived files can be found at www.ed.gov/offices/OERI/index.html. Research reports from the 10 regional laboratories administered by the OERI can be found in these archived files. Topics are of a very wide range, including adult literacy, character education, parent and family involvement, preschool education, math education, and education management. Readers visiting this website are cautioned, however, that the information is out of date.

WHAT WORKS CLEARINGHOUSE. The website for the What Works Clearinghouse highlights classroom interventions that have been researched reliably, are replicable, and have led to positive student outcomes. You can learn how the research was conducted on these interventions. You also will find reviews of the test instruments used to assess the interventions' educational effectiveness. The Clearinghouse notes that all reviews are "scientifically rigorous."

Special Committees, Boards, Commissions, and Other Advisory Groups at the Federal Level

The U.S. federal government often appoints specific bodies to address particular issues and provide advice. Two such groups are the National Advisory Committee on Institutional Quality and Integrity and the National Institute for Literacy Advisory Board. Other commissions and boards are listed at www.ed.gov/about/bdscomm/list/index.html.

Groups such as these frequently influence education policy. In April 1983, the National Commission on Excellence in Education produced its report, *A Nation at Risk: The Imperative for Educational Reform.* Even now, this short document of less than 100 pages provokes considerable dialogue at the local, state, and national levels. In 1997 Congress invited the director of the National Institute of Child Health and Human Development (NICHD), in consultation with the U.S. Secretary of Education, to appoint a panel of experts to determine the effectiveness of various approaches to teaching reading. This group, the National Reading Panel, examined a large number of experimental reading research studies to draw their conclusions. Their subsequent report (NICHD, 2000) played a significant role in federal legislation—especially in the formulation of NCLB—that included some very specific regulations regarding reading instruction.

National Research and Development Centers

University researchers sometimes form consortia for conducting research. When their individual institutional resources and strengths are combined, they are more likely to be successful with grant applications and to be able to conduct large-scale studies. Their websites include abstracts of their research and, often, the complete text of their studies. Some of the centers publish books that are available for purchase. The name of each center gives a clear indication of the kind of research you will find at the center's website. The centers listed in Figure 2 receive or used to receive federal funding.

Regional Educational Laboratories and Think Tanks

REGIONAL EDUCATIONAL LABORATORIES. Unlike the national research centers, the regional educational laboratories research a wide variety of education issues. Usually the laboratories are not-for-profit organizations that provide assistance to educators; policymakers; and labor, business, and community leaders. Their work helps to bridge the gaps among research, theory, and practice in education; they also may offer evaluation and technical assistance services. Some laboratories include archives of research documents compiled from other sources, which can save you time searching for relevant material.

As the name suggests, regional educational laboratories tend to concentrate their work in specific regions of the United States. Many of the laboratories work on projects in their local communities, including conducting and/or

Figure 2. National Research and Development Centers

Center for Research on Education, Diversity & Excellence
www.crede.ucsc.edu

Center for Research on the Education of Students Placed At Risk
www.csos.jhu.edu/crespar

Center for the Improvement of Early Reading Achievement (archives)
www.ciera.org

Center for the Study of Teaching and Policy
http://depts.washington.edu/ctpmail

Consortium for Policy Research in Education
www.cpre.org

National Center for Early Development & Learning
www.fpg.unc.edu/~ncedl

National Center for Improving Student Learning and Achievement in Mathematics and Science
www.wcer.wisc.edu/NCISLA

National Center for Postsecondary Improvement
www.stanford.edu/group/ncpi

National Center for Research on Evaluation, Standards, and Student Testing
http://cresst96.cse.ucla.edu

National Center for the Study of Adult Learning and Literacy
http://gseweb.harvard.edu/~ncsall

National Center on Adult Literacy
www.literacyonline.org/ncal.html

National Research and Development Center on English Learning and Achievement
http://cela.albany.edu

National Research Center on the Gifted and Talented
www.gifted.uconn.edu/nrcgt.html

applying research in schools or working with local residents on projects such as those designed to strengthen family literacy programs. The laboratories may provide professional development for teachers and administrators, offering workshops during the year as well as summer institutes on best and promising education practices. Project funding for the laboratories derives from multiple sources, including private foundations, state governments, and federal grants.

Figure 3. Regional Educational Laboratories

North Central Regional Educational Laboratory
www.ncrel.org

Northeast and Islands Regional Educational Laboratory at Brown University
www.cal.org/brownlab

Northwest Regional Educational Laboratory
www.nwrel.org

Pacific Resources for Education and Learning
www.prel.org

SouthEastern Regional Vision for Education
www.serve.org

Southwest Educational Development Laboratory
www.sedl.org

By combining funding resources and involving local neighborhoods and schools in their research projects, the laboratories obtain a richness of resources for their communities. A list of some regional educational laboratories that are currently operating appears in Figure 3.

THINK TANKS. Think tanks also can provide data and researched arguments for your advocacy work. What makes these groups unique is that they often reflect a particular bias about education issues, including views on such topics as assessment, standards, and teacher quality. Figure 4 includes an annotated list of think tanks, drawn from a list posted on the No Excuses think tank's website. Each annotation offers some insight as to the kind of information you will find on the think tank's website. Additional think tank web addresses can be found on the websites of some of the individual think tanks, such as the Thomas B. Fordham Foundation. You also can conduct a search on the State Policy Network's website (www.spn.org/resources/spn-directory/default.asp) to find think tanks located in your state.

The vignette on page 67 is an example of an advocate using research to support her effort. As you read this story, think about the resources this advocate used and how research facilitated her advocacy.

Figure 4. Annotated List of Think Tanks

Brown Center on Educational Policy at the Brookings Institute
www.brookings.edu/gs/brown/brown_hp.htm
> This think tank has a special focus on efforts for improving academic achievement in elementary and secondary schools. It also includes a comprehensive list of links to education sites.

Center for Education Policy
www.ctredpol.org
> This is a nonprofit, nonpartisan research and education organization that is part of the Georgia Public Policy Foundation. It is dedicated to providing practical ideas on key public policy issues.

Center for Education Reform
www.edreform.com
> This advocacy group serves as a clearinghouse for information on innovative reforms in education. It provides links to education reform organizations and resources and promotes school choice and charter schools.

Center on Reinventing Public Education
www.crpe.org
> This center's research focuses on charter schools, school contracting, school choice, and school system decentralization.

Education Quality Institute
www.naschools.org/contentViewer.asp?highlightID=57&catID=88
> This institute evaluates research-proven education programs to assist consumers as they select programs that meet locally defined needs. It provides technical assistance to ensure that high quality programs are implemented successfully.

Eduventures
www.eduventures.com
> This site provides education, technology, industry analysis, market data, and insight to buyers, suppliers, and users of e-learning products and services.

Empower America
www.empoweramerica.org
> This think tank encourages public policy solutions that maximize free markets and individual responsibility. An area of focus is education reform. The Empower America site includes links to research and reform organizations, state departments of education, newspapers and publications, and unions and special interest groups.

The Heartland Institute
www.heartland.org
> The institute provides a source of public policy information on education, including a link to *School Reform News*, a 24-page monthly newspaper reporting on school reform efforts nationwide.

(continued)

Figure 4. (continued)

The Heritage Foundation
www.heritage.org
> This foundation is a research and educational institute whose mission is to formulate and promote conservative public policies based on the principles of free enterprise, limited government, individual freedom, traditional American values, and a strong national defense.

Nation's Report Card
http://nces.ed.gov/nationsreportcard/
> This site presents the only nationally representative and continuing assessment of what U.S. students know and can do in various subject areas.

No Excuses
www.noexcuses.org/resources/think_tanks.html
> This project mobilizes public pressure on behalf of better education for the poor by bringing together liberals, centrists, and conservatives who are committed to high academic achievement among children of all races, ethnic groups, and family incomes. It issues its own reports; reports from other sources; links to other states, including state report card information; and links to statewide policy centers.

Pacific Research Institute for Public Policy
www.pacificresearch.org
> This institute is a not-for-profit, nonpartisan research organization that focuses on K–12 education reform strategies, including charter schools, public and private scholarship programs, academic standards, and education finance reform.

Program on Education Policy and Governance at the John F. Kennedy School of Government
www.ksg.harvard.edu/pepg/index.htm
> A Harvard University think tank, this program examines strategies of educational reform and evaluates important educational experiments. The program has specialists in governance and public management. The website includes links to research papers on school choice.

RAND Corporation
www.rand.org
> This nonprofit describes itself as "conducting research and providing analysis to address challenges that face the United States and the world." Although originally it concentrated on policies affecting national security, it has recently produced several reports on education that have received considerable attention.

Thomas B. Fordham Foundation
www.edexcellence.net
> The foundation supports research, publications, and action projects of national significance in elementary and secondary education reform. It provides extensive links to education-related organizations, think tanks, federal and state government sites, and publications.

Spread the Word

Jill Lewis

Professor of Literacy Education, New Jersey City University,
Jersey City, New Jersey, USA

A few years ago I heard about a bill that a state legislator was hoping to get through the New Jersey Assembly. The bill would fund a program called Spread the Word. The purpose of Spread the Word was to collect gently used books from New Jersey children and distribute them to children in the state who had few books in their homes. The bill narrative explained that the proposed program modeled a successful program in another state. I examined the other state's program and found that crucial to its success was adequate funding to hire someone to collect and distribute the books. The bill proposed for New Jersey contained no provision for staff.

I met with the New Jersey legislator and offered the support of my organization, the New Jersey Reading Association (NJRA), if he made some changes to his bill. I shared NJRA's concerns that the program could not be successfully implemented without adequate personnel. After discussion, the legislator agreed and revised the legislation to incorporate our concerns.

Members of my organization later testified on behalf of the revised bill; it subsequently passed in the legislature. Later, the assemblyman was awarded NJRA's Legislator of the Year Award for his willingness and open-mindedness in working with the state reading association.

This story is a positive example of an advocacy initiative. Working closely with the legislator, the NJRA influenced a piece of legislation that would significantly benefit New Jersey children. Unfortunately, our story has a less-than-happy ending. A few months after the bill passed, a new governor was elected. One of the last acts of the outgoing governor was to slash a few items from the state's budget. You guessed it! He slashed the funding for the position of the Spread the Word coordinator, leaving the legislation in place, but without any leadership to implement the program.

In retrospect, did members of our organization waste their time and energies advocating for this particular program? Probably not. By our participation the NJRA accomplished two major objectives: (1) We advocated for a program we believed was important for New Jersey children, and (2) we developed a positive relationship with a legislator who might be willing to work with our organization in the future.

FOR YOUR CONSIDERATION

• Lewis spent time finding information about the Spread the Word program's implementation in another state. How did her research help with her advocacy effort?

• What are some next steps you would suggest to this advocate to continue accomplishing her goals for the Spread the Word program?

• Find some examples of advocacy for education in your local newspaper. How do the strategies used by different groups differ from one another? What do they have in common?

State Departments of Education

It is critically important for education advocates to be familiar with the organization, leadership, and decision-making processes at their state's department of education. One way to reach your state's website is by visiting http://wdcrobcolp01. ed.gov/Programs/EROD/org_list.cfm?category_ID=SEA. Here you will find a website link to each state; in many instances, an e-mail address for the state's department of education also is provided. The site also offers you an opportunity to search for information on U.S. federal policies as well as research and statistics, and lets you select whether you want information pertinent to students, teachers, parents, or administrators.

Another option for locating your state department of education's website is to visit a page of the Chief State School Officers website. If you go to www.ccsso.org/chief_state_school_officers/index.cfm, you will have access to every state's department of education.

Both of these sites are useful for linking to your state and to search for comparative information from other states.

In recent years, state departments of education have been required to make public much more information about their state's schools. State report cards can be found at individual states' department of education websites. The report cards provide data on statewide test results, enrollment and dropout rates, ethnicities and socioeconomic factors within school districts, teacher certification, and so on. On these websites you also can find considerable information about new policies enacted or under review, special projects, departments within the state's department of education and their missions, activities, and contact names.

Professional and Business Associations

PROFESSIONAL ASSOCIATIONS. To which professional associations do you belong? Many individuals working in education belong to several, feeling that each association serves a unique purpose. For instance, one of this book's authors belongs to eight different education associations. Four keep her abreast of the most current research in her field—literacy; one informs her about education research and policy analysis in the broadest sense; another is an honorary education society; another gives her the perspective of administrators and other school leaders on important education issues; and another is the local union that represents her on contractual issues.

Education associations often develop position statements that can be used to bolster support for advocacy on local or state issues. You can request that their headquarters staff provide materials and contact information and assist you with formulating your ideas. These organizations sometimes will offer to provide issue-related testimony on your behalf at specific state legislature or state board of education hearings. Many education associations also have an individual on staff whose sole responsibility is managing government relations for the organization and its members; that individual can be a terrific resource for helping you with disseminating your ideas to the media and legislators.

CHAMBERS OF COMMERCE. You might think of your state or local chamber of commerce as a group that promotes tourism in your area. That is just part of what these chambers do. Many work collaboratively on projects with state departments of education and local school districts. They often have education committees, and sometimes these committees conduct research. Chamber members may serve on chamber- or state-appointed committees, or committees of other professional associations, that develop education standards, review state curricula, or consider state assessments.

You should work to develop partnerships with the business community, and your state or local chamber of commerce can help you establish these connections. A directory for all state and local chambers of commerce can be found at the National Chamber of Commerce's website (www.2chambers.com).

NATIONAL GOVERNORS ASSOCIATION. Many governors have made education their top priority. The National Governors Association (NGA) is a professional association that provides governors with an opportunity to share ideas and innovations.

The NGA has been very involved in recommending policy on such issues as the development of state content standards, state assessments, implementation of NCLB, workforce readiness, funding of special education programs, and teacher quality.

One way the NGA has been able to assist its members is through its Center for Best Practices, which provides technical assistance to governors and their staffs on a range of issues, including education. Among other services, the Center staff surveys states, analyzes issues, tracks policies, and forms focus groups on specific issues. The information obtained from the Center is often used for NGA's newest initiative, its Clearinghouse on Educational Policy Issues. At the Clearinghouse homepage (www.nga.org/center/topics/1,1188,D_5444,00.html), the visitor learns that

> this clearinghouse contains a collection of policy primers on emerging and important education policy issues in the states. Our goal is to disseminate best practices and research-based policy recommendations to states on topics such as student disparities in academic achievement (the "achievement gap"), turning around low-performing schools, educator quality, and more. (n.d.)

In 2003, the Clearinghouse published its first primer, *Closing the Achievement Gap*, which is available at www.subnet.nga.org/educlear/achievement/index.html.

The three of us contacted the governors of each state in the United States to ask their views on teacher participation in the policymaking process. Specifically, we asked, What is the best way for teachers and other educators to share their ideas with policymakers? In some cases, they, in turn, forwarded our question to officials at their state departments of education. Some of the responses appear in Figure 5.

U.S. CONFERENCE OF MAYORS. The U.S. Conference of Mayors (USCM; 2003) describes itself as "the official nonpartisan organization of the nation's 1183 U.S. cities with populations of 30,000 or more. Each city is represented in the Conference by its chief elected official, the mayor" (n.p.). If you explore the USCM website, you will be able to identify the large number of issues, especially urban issues related to education, that the organization addresses through its conferences, reports, and Best Practices Database. Because the USCM formulates policies, you may find support for such education issues as after-school programs, school construction, and school safety. You can access this group's website at www.usmayors.org.

Figure 5. What Is the Best Way for Teachers and Other Educators to Share Their Ideas With Policymakers?

I believe the most effective way for teachers and educators to communicate with policy-makers is to establish a direct personal relationship with the elected state officials, senators and representatives, in their local district. Also, through your elected officials, ask for an opportunity to appear before the appropriate legislative committees to convey ideas.
—*Secretary of the Cabinet, Office of the Governor, Commonwealth of Kentucky, September 18, 2003*

With the challenges and opportunities that face us under No Child Left Behind, it is even more imperative that we facilitate means to allow educators input into important policy decisions. For this reason, I've asked our Department of Education to coordinate a Teacher Leadership Conference...to invite teachers to share their ideas, concerns, and views as well as inform them about major issues related to education.
—*M. Michael Rounds, Governor, State of South Dakota, July 7, 2003*

Pennsylvania has a vast array of educational associations and the Department of Education meets with these associations, singularly and collectively, upon multiple occasions during the year. We also have several well funded "education policy groups" with whom we actively cooperate and which, as does the Secretary, have frequent and direct contact with the Governor. Our State Board of Education includes key members of the educational committees of both chambers and so they have a direct hand in both information flow and decision-making. Teachers have an indirect input through these associations and groups, but also though our two teachers unions, which have frequent and direct impact on chosen issues. During the course of a year, we receive direct input from approximately 1,000 of our classroom teachers. Through study and focus groups, and during frequent visits to school districts, we receive input from many more. It would be an oversimplification to say the system is complete, but we do receive policy inputs from a wide variety of sources.
—*Frank Meehan, Director of the Bureau of Teacher Certification and Preparation, Pennsylvania Department of Education, Commonwealth of Pennsylvania, July 1, 2003*

As I strive for excellence in government, the input and interaction of opinion leaders...are vitally important to me.
—*Governor, State of Michigan, July 2, 2003*

I believe the best way for teachers and other educators to share their ideas with policymakers is to do precisely what you did, commit thoughts to writing and mail them. Most successful policymakers, and all successful politicians, read their mail carefully and try to be thoughtful in responding. I also always encourage educators to stay involved in their state's legislative session and to attend relevant committee meetings whenever possible.
—*Mark Warner, Governor, Commonwealth of Virginia, June 27, 2003*

I value your input on issues. The participation of you and your fellow citizens will help us in seeking solutions to this and similar issues that confront our state.
—*Governor, State of New Mexico, June 26, 2003*

(continued)

Figure 5. (continued)

Teachers can attend local school board meetings, voice their opinions to their local union representative or school administrators, communicate with their state legislators or become actively involved in committees at the local or state level that help shape education policy.
—*Commissioner of Education, State of Connecticut, July 9, 2003*

Policymakers should require consulting teachers and educational organizations before any legislation is passed. Likewise, teachers should be required to and invited to attend policy-making forums, conferences and Senate meetings in which decisions are made concerning the educational system.
—*Dalia Rodrigues Aponte, Advisor to the Governor, Office of the Governor, Puerto Rico, June 24, 2003*

Teachers have a number of options. One is to communicate through the local and/or state chapters of the National Education Association or the American Federation of Teachers. In many states, these associations are powerful precisely because they represent and speak on behalf of a large number of teachers, and policymakers are interested in hearing the views and opinions of their members.

A second option is direct contact with policymakers. Visits to legislators' offices at the State Capitol, particularly by a large group of teachers from the same legislative district, are very compelling. In many states, teachers can also request the opportunity to deliver testimony on relevant topics before a legislative education committee or state board of education. Testimony from individual teachers can put a "human face" on an otherwise technical policy issue, and thus elicit a strong response from policymakers.

A third option is to write op-ed pieces and letters to the editor. Although a letter to the editor may seem somewhat quaint and old-fashioned, a timely, well-written letter on a controversial topic can prompt additional letters (and, perhaps related news stories) and capture the attention of policymakers.
—*Jay Cole, Deputy Secretary, Senior Policy Advisor, Department of Education and the Arts, State of West Virginia, June 27, 2003*

Educators can share their ideas with the policymakers through personal contact (written or personal visit) with the Governor's office or legislators.
—*Governor, State of Arkansas, June 17, 2003*

In Washington we encourage everyone, including teachers, to share their experiences and ideas with their state legislators. As these representatives control the state budget, they are eager for new ideas and innovations to improve learning in a cost effective manner. We provide a toll-free Legislative Hotline, or citizens can send letters or electronic mail.

Teachers can also forward their ideas to the state elected Superintendent of Public Instruction through her website. She utilizes a supportive Senator or Representative to propose bills making changes in educational policy.

The Governor also proposes his executive request bills through a supportive legislator. In the past six years, many of these bills targeted education improvements. Citizens, teachers, school administrators, and others provide valuable ideas and experiences for his education proposals.
—*Constituent Services, Office of the Governor, State of Washington, June 18, 2003*

(continued)

It is very important for educators to communicate with policymakers. My wife teaches kindergarten, so I know first-hand that educators have tremendous knowledge and insights to share. Here in Maine, I encourage teachers and school administrators to communicate directly with me. That can be accomplished through meetings, letters, telephone calls, or e-mail messages.

Many other opportunities are offered here in Maine to seek input from educators and to invite their involvement in the policymaking process. Teachers can take part in Department of Education regional informational and training sessions, which we try to provide throughout Maine at times when issues or emerging guidelines dictate. These sessions are often made more accessible through use of the ATM system.

Teachers can also participate in Maine Educational Assessment scoring and/or get involved in Local Assessment Development task field testing opportunities. Beyond these avenues, educators can volunteer to serve on one of the Education Commissioner's advisory committees. They should also feel free to communicate directly with the Commissioner or Deputy Commissioner by e-mail, or ask regional representatives of the Department to convey perspectives and comments back to the Department.

—*Governor, State of Maine, September 26, 2003*

The Media as a Source for Professional and Public Opinion

Whether you are advocating for local, state, or national concerns, you will find that you frequently research media sources to get support for your ideas and to interpret professional and public opinion. Journals, magazines, and newspapers can provide you with valuable information for developing your ideas. Television and radio programs also are good sources of information and public opinion. Many of these media offer results of public opinion polls, as do some websites that are also introduced to you in this section.

Professional Journals and Popular Magazines

Every education-related discipline has a professional association that publishes a journal or newsletter for its members. Some associations report scientifically based research, while others describe classroom research or postulate theory. These journals provide substantiation for advocacy efforts on instruction or assessment. University libraries carry many of these journals, but usually the more specialized ones can only be obtained through association subscriptions and memberships.

Popular magazines, such as *Time, Newsweek, U.S. News and World Report*, and *Scientific American*, also frequently carry stories about education. These magazines are written for the general public, however, and may not provide information that is as technical as you need for your advocacy purposes.

Although both professional journals and popular magazines express viewpoints, there is obviously a significant distinction between their readerships. This is why advocates need to know to whom they are hoping to "sell" their ideas. If, for example, you want to convince parents that starting the school day later is a good idea for high school students, your advocacy focus and supporting evidence might be on such considerations as the late start's positive effects on academic achievement and family relations. Support for these ideas may be found in anecdotal stories in popular magazines as well as in interviews with psychologists and family members. However, if you were looking to convince teachers or school administrators of the value of a later start for the school day, you might shift your focus to its effects on motivation as well as academic achievement, and find it more useful to provide data found in journal articles.

Newspaper, Television, and Radio

These forms of media are perhaps the best ways to learn the pulse of the United States with regard to education issues. An increasing number of stories are appearing in daily newspapers, on television, and on local and public radio stations on such issues as high-stakes assessment, reading programs, funding for urban schools, international comparisons of student achievement, and home schooling. The stories are often informative and condense research findings into more understandable, briefer text. However, depending on the audience and the viewpoint of the writer or speaker, a given story may have a particular slant that may or may not serve your purposes.

One of the rewards of conducting research is that you may discover feature articles, op-eds, and letters to the editor that offer information you can use to your advantage. For example, you might read about a school that is losing funds for its football team and what this loss might mean to the community. Letters to the editor of one Florida newspaper increased when parents learned through a featured story that their local school district was considering implementing policies that would require parents to pay additional fees if their children participated in competitive sports. Other parents wrote to the newspaper out of concern that the school district might also consider charging fees for participation in other extracurricular activities such as music or drama. This example illustrates that by drawing parallels between your issues and more commonplace or high-profile issues, you can help the public or policymakers better understand your position and your concerns.

A careful advocate also will be able to identify public opinion from various parts of the newspaper. Letters to the editor and editorials are two obvious places where readers find comments about schools, teachers, boards of education, taxes, and so on. Other parts of a newspaper also can suggest the public climate and even directions that education policy might go in the near future. For instance, if the media report that the demographics in your community are changing and increasing numbers of a non–English-speaking people are moving in, you might anticipate that serving the needs of second language learners will become an important issue for your school district. Also, as obesity among U.S. children gains more media attention, health educators might use the opportunity to press for reforms in school curricula and for more attention to physical education funding. Education advocates who read or listen to the news critically will be able to assume a proactive stance in anticipation of the outcomes of some of these headlines.

When advocates examine the media to identify public opinion, they also look for evidence to support the expressed opinions. Charles Cummins (1998), author of a weekly column titled *Report Card on Education*, said about opinions in newspapers, "Without supporting data or references, readers have no way of knowing whether this is simply a noise-making gunshot to grab headlines and sell magazines or is actually something to be concerned about" (n.p.). If the authors claim that there are facts supporting their opinions, you should evaluate the information carefully. Remember the following ways in which factual statements can be distinguished from statements of opinion:

> Facts can be proved to be true.
>
> Facts are based on direct evidence or actual observation. Examples, statistics, original documents, reports from research experiments, or eyewitness accounts are used to verify them.
>
> Facts are things that have occurred. They are not predictions. (Lewis, 2003, p. 192)

Conversely, opinions cannot be verified conclusively, and they often express one person's values, beliefs, attitudes, and feelings. Opinions frequently are based on hunches, inferences, or guesses. You must find supporting research to document your opinions if you want others to accept them and to advocate with you for these ideas.

Two other sources for learning public opinion and where you will need to make distinctions between facts and opinions are radio and television talk shows. Radio talk shows are increasingly popular. Many include segments for listener call-ins. Careful listening may introduce you to individual supporters, supportive groups, and opponents whom you had not considered. The opposing ideas may be the most valuable as you learn what objections individuals have to what you want for education. Using the information you have gained from your radio and television research, you can begin to prepare your arguments against the ideas you have heard. In chapter 6, we offer more specific information on how you can use radio, television, and other multimedia to disseminate your advocacy messages to diverse audiences.

The vignette below tells a story of a parent-turned-advocate. Consider the sources of information made available to her during her journey. Also reflect on the benefits she might derive from some of the other resources discussed in this chapter and how she might use the resources in her teaching and in her work as an advocate for parents of special-needs students.

Tapping Into Talents

Avivah Dahbany
School Psychologist, Franklin Township Public Schools, New Jersey, USA

One of the functions of a school psychologist is to evaluate students to determine their need for special education and related services. Another function is to advise parents of the process and their rights.

Recently, a very quiet, unassuming parent had her child evaluated. Although this parent had an interest in the process, she was too polite and quiet to ask questions of the evaluation team. I offered her various materials to read, including newspaper accounts of special educational services that were available to parents of children in special education, letters to the editor in response to these accounts from parents complaining that their children weren't getting these services, and state documents about special education services the state was required to provide. I then arranged individual appointments with her to discuss these materials. I offered to answer any questions she had as a result of what she read. In these individual sessions, she demonstrated an avid interest, so I invited her to participate in a special education steering committee. Initially, she declined the invitation; she claimed she would have nothing to contribute. With encouragement, she attended the committee meetings and eventually became an active participant. As her confidence grew, she became a strong advocate for her own child and for other parents who are navigating the waters of special education.

This mother also expressed a desire to teach. She had her credentials but was too insecure to apply for a position. With advice and encouragement, and the confidence she developed as a member of the special education committee, she pursued her goal. Now she is not only an advocate for other parents with children who have special needs but also a teacher!

Sometimes people only need someone to help them advocate for themselves in order to realize their strengths and pursue their dreams.

FOR YOUR CONSIDERATION

• What advocacy resources mentioned thus far in this chapter would be valuable to parents of children with special needs?

• What other resources might be useful?

Public Opinion Polls

Public opinion carries great weight when it comes to education issues. After all, every taxpayer makes a contribution to public education, and every child is affected by decisions that are made. Therefore, if you are going to be an education advocate, you will want to learn as best you can what the public—parents, teachers, the business community, senior citizens, children, and politicians—have to say about education.

The difficulty with public opinion as a source of data, however, is that by its very nature it is opinion, not fact. But depending on how the opinions are obtained, and who is offering them, some opinions may be viewed as important sources of support for education advocates. Simply put, some opinions are more important than others. Although all opinions are subjective, differentiations can be made among different types of opinions. For example, expert opinion carries more weight than other opinions because the person expressing the opinion knows quite a bit about the subject. You may be an expert, or you may have an informed opinion, which means that you may have conducted research or sought information from other sources. Your opinions may be informed by statistical reference, historical reference, or even some relevant personal experience. These two types of opinions—expert and informed—are better for advocates to use than unsupported opinions, which often consist of sweeping generalizations and stereotypes. Unsupported opinions are even less reliable than opinions based on personal experience and should be avoided when arguing for a specific initiative.

Polling results often appear in newspapers and on television, but there are other sources that can provide you with data on public opinion. At Public Agenda's website, you can find recent education polls as well as suggestions for interpreting their results. One document available from this organization is titled *Where We Are Now*. Public Agenda defines this as a "survey of surveys" (n.d.) because it looks at more than a decade of public opinion polls on education to draw conclusions and to show shifts in thinking over time. It synthesizes polls taken by a number of organizations, both education-related and noneducation-related, and across the political spectrum. (See Figure 6 for a list of online sources of opinion polls.)

In some cases, portions of a website are restricted to members, but if you go to the organization's homepage and request research or publications, you will find useful information, including research reports and polling results. Some organizations will have polled only their members; others will have polled professional groups. A few organizations will have taken statewide polls across sectors. Some polls are issue specific, for example, about attitudes toward vouchers. Other polls ask more generally about a variety of school reforms that either have occurred or are under consideration. As mentioned previously, you should consider the source conducting the poll. What is its agenda? Look at the questions asked. Are they biased in any direction? Are there other conclusions that might be drawn from the data? These sources of information can be valuable, but the information also may be misleading.

If you want to take a poll to express your views on education, you can visit the American Education Association's website at http://amedu.com/polls.

Figure 6. Online Sources of Opinion Polls

American Council on Education
www.acenet.edu

American Federation of Teachers
www.aft.org

Americans for Better Education
www.bettered.org

Center for Education Reform
http://edreform.com

Committee for Education Funding
www.cef.org

Every Child Matters Education Fund
www.everychildmatters.org

National Education Association
www.nea.org

Phi Delta Kappa/Gallup Polls of the Public's
Attitudes Toward the Public Schools
www.pdkintl.org/kappan/kpollpdf.htm

Public Education Network/*Education Week* polls
www.edweek.org/ew/newstory.cfm?slug=
32pen.h21

Public Agenda
www.publicagenda.org

If education advocates become aware that a particular topic that concerns them also is evoking considerable public opinion in the media, they can use this situation to address the issue. The vignette below describes the start-up of an advocacy network, the formation of which, as Lesley Morrow notes, was precipitated by her awareness of mounting negative public opinion toward teacher education.

Forming a Dean's Network

Lesley M. Morrow
Professor of Literacy, Rutgers University, New Brunswick, New Jersey, USA

When I first took office in May 2001 as vice president of the International Reading Association (IRA), I began to think about what I wanted to emphasize during my term. The preparation of excellent teachers of reading and their ongoing professional development were high on my list. Teacher preparation was increasingly under attack in the popular media. IRA needed to take a proactive stance, addressing concerns and making recommendations. I consulted with Richard Long, IRA's Director of Government Relations, and we decided that creating an Urban Dean's Network could be one initiative to address teacher preparation.

The network would begin with an exploratory meeting to examine deans' ideas about excellent preparation of teachers of reading in urban settings. Invited deans would be from schools that were preparing future teachers to teach in urban communities. Although we didn't know what the outcome of this meeting would be, we had many possibilities in mind, and the meeting would help us set an agenda for the future. It was clear that whatever thoughts we developed concerning the excellent preparation of teachers of reading, we had to address practical issues and policy issues.

We decided to hold our first meeting in Spring 2003 at Rutgers University in New Brunswick, New Jersey, USA, a perfect urban setting. Fifty deans from around the United States were invited to participate in the conversation. In addition to deans, we wanted officials from IRA at the meeting so we could all work together. From IRA the invitees included the Executive Director, several staff directors, and selected members of the Board of Directors.

We wanted presenters who could speak about preparing excellent teachers of reading for urban schools. We were fortunate to have previous research to provide a foundation for our discussion and rich resources of experienced deans, literacy researchers, and state education officials. One dean provided a keynote address on the challenge of urban literacy education. A panel of four others discussed diversity in urban schools and how it affects learning, adapting instruction to meet many needs, reading and motivating the urban reader, and enhancing teacher education by linking the college of education to the K–12 system. A superintendent from a large urban district in New Jersey gave us the perspective of an urban leader in the schools. Small-group discussion extended these conversations.

In the afternoon, G. Reid Lyon, chief of the child development and behavior branch of the National Institute for Child Health and Human Development at the National Institutes of Health, talked about models of national reform of teacher education. William Librera, commissioner of education for New Jersey, spoke about the state's new successful reading coach program. Afterward, participants agreed that they wanted to continue to meet and plan for moving forward. The attending IRA board members and directors developed an action plan to present at our next meeting, which was scheduled for Fall 2003.

We are just starting; we have yet to decide policies to advocate, the target audience, or the advocacy process we will use. What we have done is select stakeholders who will help us make some of these decisions and set the stage for what is to come.

To be successful with policy, we need to deliberate about what we want to do and how we want to do it. We know our approach can't be to just get a group together and march on Washington. For lasting effects, there must be careful and thoughtful planning of the entire process and critical decisions made each step of the way.

Because of the stakeholders we have brought together and the time we are committing, I am confident that as we progress with this initiative, we will create a positive and forward-thinking action plan for schools of education and for the U.S. federal government. The momentum is in place for something important to occur.

FOR YOUR CONSIDERATION

• Do you think this network could provide the basis for an advocacy group on a wide range of education issues? Explain your reasoning.

• The author says this initiative would help to plan an agenda for the future. Is an agenda emerging? If so, what is it?

• How might some of the resources mentioned in this chapter be used to assist this group as it develops its agenda?

• If you were planning this initiative, would you do anything differently than these organizers?

Public opinion also influences policy initiatives. Education advocates must be mindful of what is happening legislatively at the state and federal levels so they will know when action is needed to support or oppose particular pieces of legislation. In the next section, you will learn how to monitor proposed legislation before it becomes law.

Monitoring Current and Pending State and Federal Legislation

Obviously, much of what schools do is the result of regulations found in U.S. state and federal laws. A critical role for education advocates is the ongoing monitoring of new and pending state and federal education legislation and regulations. Once a proposed piece of legislation becomes law, it is much more difficult for education advocates to get it changed. Therefore, education advocates need to know about pending legislation in order to attempt to influence its development prior to the possibility of it becoming law. Thus, education advocates need to know what proposals are being considered, and they need to find this out very early in the legislative process.

State Legislation

There are many sources of information to learn what your state legislature and governor are considering, such as the media resources previously mentioned. You will want to become familiar with your state legislature's website and how to retrieve information from it. Every state legislature has a website from which anyone with access to the Internet can obtain information about pending bills. Each state's website is similar; the universal resource locator (URL) follows a pattern. For example, Alaska's URL is www.legis.state.ak.us. To find another state's website, change "ak" in this example to the other state's two-letter postal abbreviation and keep the rest of the URL the same. From the homepage of a state's website, you can usually link to the governor's office, committees within the legislature, the state board of education, the state department of education, and other state offices. The calendar for the legislature is also usually there to let you to know when you could testify for or against a piece of proposed legislation. Contact information for further assistance is usually provided as well.

The routine to search for bills under consideration by the legislature varies from state to state, but there are some common strategies to all. On your state legislature's website, go to the section on bills or resolutions, and locate the ones that are in committee. At some state websites, you can link directly to the committee and read what bills are under consideration; when you click on the bill number, you obtain the content as well as where it is in the legislative process. At other state websites, you can type in a key word or phrase, such as *history curriculum*, and any bills that fall within that subject will appear, along with their status in the legislative process. At these same sites you can obtain bill summaries and, sometimes, numbers for other bills that deal with similar topics.

You also can easily locate your state government offices, including individual state departments, by going to www.statelocalgov.net/index.cfm. This valuable website will link you to your state's website and the webpages of any counties and townships that have information online. Additionally, the site provides a listing of every state's government constitutional officers, state legislatures, and state judiciaries and departments. You can choose *education* as a topic and then select a state to get up-to-date developments.

Another excellent source for links to state and local governments is provided by the Library of Congress at www.loc.gov/global/state/stategov.html. Here you will be able to connect easily to such resources as the National Conference of State Legislatures, the full text of state statutes, state constitutions and other legislative resources, and the state government website for each U.S. state.

Sometimes advocates are brought into the legislative process early and have an opportunity to perhaps influence—but certainly to see up close—how education policies evolve. The vignette below describes the experiences of one advocate who served on a panel charged by the state's board of education to set assessment standards. His analysis of what occurred offers insights into the kinds of things we should consider when we are monitoring policy developments.

Research-Based Assessment Derailed

Randy Overbeck

Director of Instructional Services, Xenia Community Schools, Xenia, Ohio, USA

Like other states, for more than a decade Ohio has maintained an accountability system that includes a set of high-visibility, high-stakes tests for high school students. Passing the tests became a requirement for earning a diploma. Calls for earlier markers of student progress soon gave birth to elementary proficiency tests in five core areas at the fourth- and sixth-grade levels, along with the requisite state accountability program.

Each new generation of state tests became more sophisticated and more challenging to younger students and served as more effective diagnostic instruments for most students. Test results were publicly released, published statewide, and used to compare one school against another.

The Ohio Department of Education contracted with a reputable testing company to produce reliable and valid assessments and set an appropriate passing score. Expert panels of educators, parents, and board members were assembled. In 1997, I served on one panel, dubbed the Standard Setting Committee, for the sixth-grade reading proficiency test. Our group consisted of 24 volunteers from school districts across the state, including one local board member and 23 educators. With the exception of two building principals and me, the educator group was comprised of language arts teachers with experience teaching intermediate grades.

To establish the state score, the Ohio Department of Education used the Modified Angoff process, a well-researched method to determine an appropriate passing score for a new assessment. This required that all committee members take a full-length prototype of the new test and make independent determinations of the appropriateness of each selection and question for assessing the literacy ability of a successful sixth grader. For each item on the test, committee members responded to questions such as, Is this selection/question one that a sixth-grade student who is successful in reading should be able to read and answer correctly?

Next, the entire committee reviewed the complete test, painstakingly analyzing each selection and question, debating individual judgments on whether particular test items fairly assessed the reading skills of sixth graders. After much discussion, the committee arrived at a consensus for a passing threshold for the new test. This formed the recommendation we then submitted to the Ohio Board of Education; the board would formally establish state passing scores for all the tests.

Here is where politics and separate agendas derailed the meticulously designed state standard-setting process. Because the sixth-grade reading proficiency test was one of the most challenging produced by the state, the raw score the Standard Setting Committee determined was appropriate for demonstrating sixth-grade skills was low, at least as a raw percentage—somewhere around 55%. Ohio Department of Education representatives presented to the state board of education the committee's recommendation for the passing score, as well as the research-based process used to arrive at the figure. A spirited, sometimes partisan, debate ensued between and among the state board of education's members.

Because a few of these board members did not grasp the concept of how a passing level was established, they easily—or deliberately—confused the raw score with an actual percentage of reading knowledge. How can we say students are proficient when they only got 58% of the questions right? was a repeated question, argued vehemently. In the end, the state board of education voted to reject the Standard Setting Committee's recommendation and chose, instead, to arbitrarily raise the passing score significantly from the recommended 200 to 222 scaled score points.

The outcome was, of course, predictable. Correlational research later conducted by school districts and test companies put the board-approved passing score for the sixth-grade proficiency test at approximately the 70th percentile nationally. In the ensuing years, it was hardly a surprise that thousands of sixth graders who in fact were successful readers and achieving at or above grade level were branded as failures. Many schools doing an effective job of preparing students were identified as failing schools by state report cards and state-released publicity.

In the end, students, teachers, and administrators in public schools across the state were given one more undeserved black eye, which may have been the ultimate political goal of some. Most important, students were poorly served by the very individuals voted to represent them.

FOR YOUR CONSIDERATION

- What role did "doing homework" play in this story? How did it affect the turn of events?

- What advocacy strategies might the Standard Setting Committee have used to work toward a different outcome?

- What changes in educational policy are now under consideration in your state that are of concern to you? How will you let your concerns be known?

- What efforts do your state's department of education and board of education make to seek information and opinions of experts for decision making? How has this affected outcomes?

Federal Legislation

One of the best ways to learn what is happening with U.S. federal legislation is to pay a visit to the U.S. Congress's website, www.congress.gov. To see the education bills and issues, click on *Issues & Action*. Then select *Education/Schools* from the box in the center of the page, and click *Go*. From the resulting page, you can then click on specific bills.

Another advantage of this website is that it posts news releases, alerts, and letters on education issues that have been authored by various education organizations. You also will find bill regulations here and a listing of some education organizations.

Another excellent source of information about federal legislation is the website Thomas: Legislative Information on the Internet (http://thomas.loc.gov), a service of the Library of Congress. At this website, you will be able to locate pending bills by bill number or by a key word or phrase. When you reach the page of a specific bill, you can choose to obtain a PDF file of the entire bill, the bill's status, sponsors, a summary of the full text, notices about the bill that appeared in the *Congressional Record*, and a printer-friendly text version of the bill.

Special interest groups that focus on education, including nonprofit or-ganizations and professional associations, often track federal legislation in order to inform their members and to promote advocacy for or against particular pending bills. For instance, the National Education Association has an online weekly newsletter, *Education Insider*, published by their Office of Government Relations. As is the case with many of these resources, you do not need to be a member to receive this publication that provides information on developments in the federal government that affect children and public education. You can sign up to receive *Education Insider* by going to www.nea.org/lac and clicking on *Subscribe to NEA's Weekly E-mail Action Alert*. Similarly, IRA's Government Relations Division sends a weekly legislative update to members on activities at the fed-eral level. You can join this electronic newsletter by following the directions at the E-newsletter area of www.reading.org. In addition to providing the most cur-rent information on legislative activity, these organizations often propose ac-tions they would like their members to take in response to pending legislation, such as writing letters to their representatives in Congress.

Not surprisingly, the U.S. Department of Education also makes web-based information available about pending legislation and new regulations. You can sign up for their biweekly newsletter, *Ed Review*, at www.ed.gov/news/newsletters/edreview/index.html. Additional online resources can be found in Appendix B.

As you no doubt realize, monitoring current and pending state and federal legislation can be very time consuming. If you have a single issue about which you want to advocate, it is easier to track developments. If you are working as an advocate for a professional organization and you have several concerns, then the task of monitoring legislation might be divided among several organization members, each assigned to monitor a different issue. The desired outcome is that you feel knowledgeable about what is happening and know where you can go for additional information to answer questions when others ask about further support for your views.

Conclusion

Obviously, there is too much information available for any single person to know everything about every educational issue. By working in collaboration with others, as discussed throughout this book, you will be able to pool your collective knowledge and selectively identify the data that best serve your purpose. Those who work with you will have ideas about how to best allocate responsibility. They might want to select specific websites they will monitor or specific subtopics of your larger issue that they will investigate. As you begin to develop your advocacy research skills, you will be able to recognize those sources that are most valuable to you and concentrate on obtaining information from them.

Once you have the data you need, you will be ready to take some concrete advocacy steps. In chapter 4, you will learn more about specific procedures for developing a detailed advocacy plan to help you reach your intended advocacy goals.

CHAPTER 4

Developing a Clear
Advocacy Plan

By now you are well aware that effective advocacy requires both commitment and preparation. Without commitment, most potential advocates will not persevere. When advocacy procedures are not going well, it is easy to become discouraged and to question whether time and resources are well spent.

The advocacy process is sometimes rocky. Successes may be few and far between. At times, progress toward desired goals seems minimal. Yet many of you keep going with your advocacy work because you care deeply about your issue. When your planned procedures are not going smoothly, you reevaluate and substitute alternate strategies for any that are not working. You put in long hours. You negotiate with others in order to accomplish as much of your goal as possible. You try and try again because you are committed to your cause.

The results of our labor may not become apparent for quite some time. The seed of an idea may take months—or even years—of continued nurturing in order to grow. Do you remember Dever's vignette (see chapter 2, pages 39–40) on defeating the statewide mandatory testing of kindergarten children? Dever and her colleagues worked on their advocacy issue for five years before they saw a change in a policy that they knew was detrimental to young children. At many points in those five years, it would have been easy for them to walk away from the issue, but commitment to the cause kept them coming back and trying yet another means for sharing their message with those who could make a difference.

But commitment by itself is not enough. You can have great passion for what you believe and the changes you want to make, but if you do not have a well-developed and well-implemented advocacy plan, your hard work probably will not reach fruition.

As you can see in the vignettes throughout this book, most of the advocates had plans. Whether they were advocating for a personal concern or on behalf of a group or organization, they did not act randomly. They started by articulating their concerns; then they devoted considerable time, effort, and, perhaps, expense to identifying information that would help them understand their issues. Many of them built their plans on extensive research from many sources. As you begin to develop your plan, information from the resources identified in chapter 3 will help you shape and refine your thinking for the many audiences you want to address. Chapters 5 and 6 will help you use specific tools to present your information to others.

This chapter focuses on possibilities to consider as you develop your advocacy plan. Whether you are working alone or collaboratively, whether you are advocating for a personal concern or for the concerns of a group or organization, you will go through similar procedures. We three believe that more is usually accomplished when you work with others. You are able to divide the workload and increase the chances for success. Thus, we urge you to work with an advocacy coalition whenever possible. Most of the information in this and the remaining chapters assumes that you will be working in this way to accomplish your advocacy goals.

As you design your plan, you and your colleagues will need to consider some specific actions, many of which will happen concurrently, although the sequence may vary depending on your particular advocacy issue. Each action will be considered in this chapter.

Clarifying Your Issue and Developing Your List of Priorities

Whether you are working alone or with others, you need to be clear about your issue and establish your priorities. Identifying your concerns may take extensive deliberation because your issue probably has many facets. Ask yourself, What are the most important and immediate concerns that have an impact on my issue? Is it really an issue? For whom? What are the implications for different stakeholders? How would different outcomes affect them? What are possible positions that individuals or groups might take on this issue? What are possible positions that I might take?

All the things you want to do cannot be accomplished at once. Deciding which objectives are most crucial and which can be set aside or handled at a later date may take considerable discussion if you are working with others. There may be extensive negotiation as you and your fellow coalition members try to agree on objectives and prioritize concerns. Many face-to-face meetings may transpire before you have consensus on a plan. At the center of your plan should be a strategic vision for where you want to be in the future. This vision will provide the framework for guiding your choices of activities and the direction of your work and will evolve from your purpose and your objectives. The success of a single advocacy activity may cause you to reprioritize. A modified vision, policy developments, or the addition of new members to your working group may affect your advocacy plan.

Whether you successfully develop your plan may depend on what you accomplish when you meet with others. Effective meetings do not just happen; they are well planned and well organized. Because meetings are critical to your advocacy efforts, let's review some of the attributes that make a meeting successful.

Planning, Organizing, and Conducting Meetings

The development and implementation of your advocacy plan will require you to meet frequently. Later in the advocacy process, you also might need meetings to disseminate information about your advocacy concern to a variety of public audiences. When you consider using meetings as an advocacy tool, remember that well-planned and well-organized meetings will help you accomplish your goals. Disorganized and unproductive meetings may thwart your progress, especially if participants believe that your meetings are a waste of time.

Few potential advocates have received formal training in how to conduct a meeting. This section will guide you on how to ensure a successful meeting, by providing you with tips on all stages from preparation through follow up and on how to handle challenging situations.

Planning the Meeting

As part of your advocacy planning, first determine who needs to be present at your meeting. At the initial stages, you may decide to involve a small core group of interested individuals and expand the group later as your plan takes form.

Decide how you will contact your group members. Will you call or e-mail them to invite their attendance? Will you send them written invitations? What might entice them to come to your meeting? Try to give your potential participants two weeks' notice for a meeting. People have very busy schedules and may need to rearrange commitments to be present. Of course, there will be times when your issue cannot wait that long and a meeting may need to be scheduled more quickly.

Be sure to keep records of contacts made with group members so you know whom to expect at the meeting. Write down any questions people asked when you contacted them that you might want to address to the whole group. During your initial meeting together, you can develop a strategy for communicating information to those group members who could not attend but need to know what transpired.

Organizing the Meeting

If you notify potential meeting attendees by e-mail or by regular mail, include an agenda for the meeting in your mailing. If you contact people by phone, follow up by sending an agenda. Knowing the agenda in advance will enable individuals to prepare themselves and to bring relevant materials for consideration. Typically a meeting agenda notes the date, time, and location of the meeting and includes the following topics:

    I. Introductions of New Members

   II. Approval of Minutes From Previous Meeting

  III. Old Business

       A. Formal reports

       B. Other updates

  IV. New Business

   V. Announcements

  VI. Determination of Next Meeting Date

Some groups also include "Approval of the Agenda" as a topic on the printed agenda. Other groups add "Summary of Decisions" after "Determination of Next Meeting Date." When such a summary is included on the agenda, all group members know they will leave with a common understanding of areas of agreement achieved during the meeting.

Having a prepared and disseminated agenda will help you manage your actual meeting time effectively. It will enable you to focus the group so that by the meeting's end, good decisions will have been made and meeting participants will know the next steps and when those steps need to be accomplished.

Objectives for each meeting should be reasonable and achievable. You cannot accomplish everything in one sitting, and most individuals cannot sit or focus for an extended period of time. Frequent, shorter meetings may accomplish more than those that are several hours long.

In addition to distributing the agenda ahead of time, it is also useful to let potential meeting participants know in advance the names of other people who also may be attending—and, if possible, their job titles and areas of interest—because that knowledge may affect what materials people bring with them. For example, if you learned that you were the only attendee familiar with prekindergarten programs, you might want to bring materials on the education of young children or the positions of various early childhood professional organizations that you could share with others.

Occasionally, you will send the potential participants materials for their consideration in advance of the meeting. Specify what you will want them to do with these materials. If you expect participants to be prepared for discussion, tell them in advance. If you want them to find supporting information, state your request clearly.

If your schedule permits, call or e-mail meeting participants a day or two before the meeting to confirm the date, time, and place. This reminder is also an opportunity for them to ask questions of you and to clarify what materials they might want to bring.

The success of a meeting is often determined even before the first participants arrive. The choice of time and place may be important for ensuring meeting success. Is the location convenient? Is the room you picked the right size for your group? Are the lighting and temperature appropriate? Can the furniture be rearranged to accommodate breakouts into smaller work groups? Can you purchase refreshments at the meeting locations? If not, can you or someone else bring them?

On the day of your meeting, check and double check that you have agendas, handouts, and all other relevant materials with you. Arrive early. Make sure that the room is set up to help you accomplish your goals. Consider having refreshments or candies available on the table. Verify that you have enough materials for everyone. It is a good idea to have additional copies of the agenda in case the participants have left theirs at their homes or offices. Bring supplies such as highlighters, self-stick notes, and markers, if you plan to use them. If you are going to do any brainstorming, chart tablets or self-stick chart paper that can adhere to any wall will come in handy.

Conducting the Meeting

Begin your meeting by reviewing the agenda. Request suggestions for any additional agenda items. If a member has a contribution to make but needs to leave the meeting early, move the member's request to an earlier placement on the agenda. You also may ask the group for permission to move the order of agenda items if a different order will facilitate discussion.

Because your participants may not know one another, begin your meeting with introductions, as suggested in the sample agenda. Welcome each person who attends. You also may indicate that other members may arrive late so the group will be accepting of any latecomers. Depending on the size of your group, you may wish to have name tags or to put name place cards on the tables. This introduction time will be well spent because individuals will learn a little about the backgrounds of their fellow meeting participants. When you introduce yourself, indicate any advocacy experience you have had, along with any successes, even very small ones. Mention what you have been doing to develop your advocacy skills. You want the group to have confidence in your ability to lead them through what might be a new experience for them.

Be sure to remind your group of the purpose for your meeting and the objectives you have in mind. Allow plenty of opportunity for clarification, reconsideration, and revision of these objectives as well as of the planned advocacy initiative. For group members to value the effort, they will need to recognize how participation will benefit them, their organization, or both. If there is a budget for your work, inform the group at the outset of the meeting so funds can be taken into consideration as you plan your advocacy activities.

It will be important to set time limits for discussing specific topics or ideas during your meeting. You may do so in advance or with the input of the participants at the beginning of the meeting. Having time limits may help you keep on task so that all of your agenda items can be considered.

Be enthusiastic during the meeting. If you are tired and unresponsive, what can you expect from the group? Also, be encouraging and recognize individual contributions. Participants will want to feel that their work is valued. As work is delegated, be sure that assignments are fair and reasonable, with consideration for each person's time constraints.

It is important that someone records the key information from the meeting and the outcomes of each discussion. With the group's permission, you also may want to tape record the discussion. Any written or taped record should be in addition to what your group records on charts or something similar during the meeting. If the notetaker is willing, he or she will edit the notes for a summary that can be disseminated afterward to the group. You as the meeting convener might also take the recorder's notes and prepare a summary of ideas. Notes that are sent to participants should include the gist of each meeting as well as clear statements of next steps. You should prominently list the names of who will do what and when. You also should specify the date and location for the next meeting. Prompt and efficient dissemination of the meeting notes to all participants will reinforce the information, so try to distribute your summary within three days of the meeting. Encourage the group to let you know as soon as possible if the notes do not accurately reflect their thinking or the meeting's developments so that clarifications can be sent to the group immediately.

Although a complete summary of the meeting will be forthcoming, it may be useful before leaving the meeting to agree on a "Summary of Decisions." Attendees might write these decisions at the bottom of their agenda sheet. This way, all attendees will leave with a common understanding of areas of agreement achieved during the meeting so there will be no surprises when they receive the completed meeting summary.

As you end your meeting, recap the key points and thank participants for attending. Spend a few minutes evaluating the meeting and the participants' interpretations. Ask for suggestions on how future meetings might be improved. A few minutes of wrap-up may provide valuable information for future meetings.

Handling Challenges During a Meeting

Although your meetings will usually go well if you follow the procedures recommended here, occasionally you will face some difficulties that will require your attention. You may need to deal with mildly disruptive behaviors. For example, perhaps some attendees are continually late to meetings. You may have others who want to dominate the meeting or who nay-say, negate, or put down the ideas of others. Some attendees may perseverate with certain ideas, returning to points that are already covered or dwelling on minutia that are minimally relevant to the discussion. Some may want to complain or tell "war stories," rather than moving on to the considerations at hand. Still other attendees may bring up peripheral issues or personal agendas that are not related to the central advocacy focus.

For many of these situations, you will need to be the mediator. You may be able to prevent difficulties via modeling: If you are seen as a good listener, showing interest in and appreciation for the ideas of others, other attendees may follow suit. However, consider appointing a facilitator who can help you keep the meeting focused and moving forward. The facilitator also may help you with involving all participants and keeping any one participant from dominating the meeting. He or she may help you tactfully end discussions that are going nowhere or becoming destructive or unproductive.

As part of your deliberations, your group should consider the logic of each idea proposed and any problems that might arise from suggested courses of action. Be certain than any individual's questions are answered. Now is the time to clear up any misunderstandings or uncertainties. If participants share common understandings at this point, fewer problems will develop.

Many meeting difficulties can be prevented by establishing ground rules at the beginning. If the group agrees that comments will be nonjudgmental, that all attendees will participate, that all ideas will be accepted, and that all attendees will listen carefully and not interrupt each other, the facilitator may not need to intervene. You may need to revisit ground rules established by the group, speak with a troublesome attendee individually, or suggest that certain ideas be tabled for later discussion. Sometimes putting a peripheral issue on a chart where it will be remembered and dealt with at a later time will diffuse the problem.

If a particular participant is argumentative and not willing to work with the group, you may need to invite the person to leave. It is important to hear minority viewpoints and to discuss them and try to resolve them so that consensus can be reached. However, if compromise is not possible and the individual is not open to group suggestion and alternative viewpoints, the best option may be to have him or her leave the group.

When you are working together for an advocacy goal, you need group members to feel that a positive outcome is the goal and that this will require all members to work as one. They may need to be reminded that some of their ideas may not be adopted by the group. Other ideas may be decidedly changed from the way they were presented initially. If the advocacy plan is to be a group effort, members will need to understand the necessity of coming to an agreement. Your skills as mediator may help the group identify and evaluate potential solutions so that consensus can be built. Your facilitator may help you move the thinking of the group as a whole by asking strategic questions or by synthesizing the group's different viewpoints. Facilitators might also speak privately to specific individuals or subgroups to resolve areas of disagreement.

Following Up After the Meeting

Once your advocacy issues, objectives, priorities, and strategic vision have been articulated, responsibilities have been delegated, and work groups have been established, your responsibilities as a meeting convener are not over. You will need to follow up with individuals to see how the ideas are implemented. You will need to identify impediments to the process and ways to resolve them. You may need to reconvene the group for a periodic review of strategies and plans. And as you find materials or identify resources related to particular tasks, you will need to send them to the individuals responsible for those tasks. Frequently, you will find that you need to be both coach and cheerleader. Most important, the group members need to see the issue as their issue, rather than as yours. If all along you have honored individuals' opinions, encouraged group discussions, and enabled groups within the larger group to compromise and coalesce, you will generally have consensus and your group members will willingly work toward the accomplishment of group goals.

Let's look at what one group learned from its experiences in organizing parent–staff meetings for a school. Your meetings may be more formal and have more participants, but we can learn practical pointers from this story on what worked well and where the group encountered obstacles.

Building Positive Home–School Relationships

Lisa Gonzon
Teacher, John S. Charlton School, Dover, Delaware, USA

Staff morale was low at our school for children with developmental disabilities. Only a handful of parents had shown up for the annual open house, and just as few communicated regularly with us about their children's out of school activities. This perceived lack of parental interest and involvement led to staff resentment and created an overall adversarial atmosphere between home and school.

However, the teachers in the preschool and early grades didn't want an "us versus them" relationship with our students' parents. At the next monthly staff meeting, we brought up the idea of forming a parent information and support group. Several teachers, including myself, and the principal expressed interest. Three of us volunteered to take on the task of contacting the parents and organizing the group.

We sent home a friendly introductory letter and a checklist to the parents, asking them to rate the topics they'd be interested in, with several blank spaces to add their own suggestions in addition to supplying the days of the week and the times that they thought would work best for meetings. If we didn't get a response in two weeks, we made follow-up phone calls. We also put posters in the school halls for parents to see when they picked up their children.

After three weeks, we set dates, times, and topics based on the returned information, sent a newsletter home, and got started.

We found out that meetings could turn into gripe sessions, or go way off topic, without a good meeting facilitator. We asked our school psychologist to step in and help us. We invited experts from local universities and various state departments to conduct question-and-answer sessions so the teachers could learn right alongside the parents.

Some meetings were packed, some had two parent attendees, and some had to be rescheduled. We learned not to take things personally, to be flexible, and to listen to parents' concerns and interests. In short, we became better teachers through our efforts to reach out and work with our students' parents.

FOR YOUR CONSIDERATION

- How might you use these teachers' experiences and this book's tips for planning effective meetings to prevent any sessions you conduct from derailing or moving in opposite directions from your goals?
- What additional strategies might you recommend to staff members in this vignette for attracting more participants to their meetings? What strategies have you found effective for recruiting participants for your school activities?
- How would you describe the relationships between parents and education staff at your school?
- Are there ideas that you can borrow from these advocates and their experiences that might help you further home–school relationships in your community?

Perhaps you wonder why we have given so much attention to running a successful meeting. Simply put, we believe that meetings are essential to good advocacy campaigns. As long as you work with others, meetings will be a necessity. If your meetings are not well planned, positive outcomes are unlikely.

Evaluating Your Strengths and Limitations

As mentioned previously, many of your planning actions will happen concurrently. They also will happen recursively because you will return to earlier considerations from time to time. As you plan, you should consider all the strategies that are available to you. You should evaluate your strengths and limitations and, based on them, determine which strategies are best to try. When working with others, analyzing group members' collective talents also will be crucial. Mapping your own assets and the assets of the group is a wise and useful procedure.

All group members will need to devote much enthusiasm and energy to the advocacy goals the group has set. Upon evaluation, you may decide that you need to narrow these goals and to refocus your activities depending on everyone's time, talents, interests, and experience. You also may want to build on your past advocacy successes, directing your efforts to extensions of earlier activities and using previous positive results as stepping stones for new ideas. You also may need to reevaluate your goals because your plans to achieve them are too expensive. Your group may have to downsize its plans to work within the limits of available funds, or find new funding opportunities. We have included information about locating funding sources and grant writing information in Appendix C.

Considering Your Available Time

Certainly, you cannot implement every strategy that is suggested in this book. You will need to evaluate how much time you have available for advocacy. As you consider possible strategies, which can you use right now? Which might you have to defer to later or assign to others who may have more time than you can spend? Be mindful of what are reasonable and achievable goals. Trying to accomplish too much may result in overall ineffectiveness. Identify what you can manage, and pour your energies into accomplishing those activities well.

Considering Your Talents

As part of your advocacy planning, take a serious look at your personal strengths. Which of the possible activities can you do well? Which might be too difficult for you at this moment? Where might you have to invest so much effort in becoming knowledgeable that you would leave little time for actually engaging in the advocacy? Choose those initiatives that you will be able to accomplish. Find others who can help you with areas in which they feel confident. Forming partnerships and coalitions broadens the array of possible activities you can consider because they expand the skills and strengths that are available to you.

Consider, too, that working with others provides opportunities for you and other group members to develop new skills. For example, some group members may be reluctant to take on an assignment such as meeting with a policymaker. You may feel the same about other necessary tasks. Suggest that group members mentor each other so that everyone learns a new advocacy skill while also utilizing the talents he or she already possesses.

Considering Your Interests

Plan initiatives that interest and excite you. Your enthusiasm is important in showing others that your cause is important. If a given advocacy task is not one that interests you, you may not do it well, so plan other advocacy activities instead. If you have formed a coalition, distributing responsibilities according to the interests of the participants will strengthen your approach. Let participants volunteer for the activities that they find personally motivating. There is more than enough work to keep everyone involved.

Considering Your Experience

As you examine your strengths, you may feel that the demands of being an advocate are beyond your background and experience. Others working with you may feel they have no talents to offer. Do not allow yourself or others to underestimate all your group can do. Collectively, you have many skills to bring to advocacy initiatives. Remind yourself that, as educators, you have many years' experience in management and organization.

Take stock of your experiences. Many of the skills you have developed over time, such as those listed in Figure 7, are foundational skills for advocacy work. Our list could be longer, but we hope you can see that you have many relevant experiences and personal strengths to bring to your advocacy plans. Determine which skills might be most appropriate for meeting the advocacy goals you have set.

Figure 7. Things Educators Know How to Do Well

- Organize and prepare agendas for meetings
- Arrange rooms so that all can see and hear
- Run a meeting and keep the majority of attendees on task
- Stick to a schedule and start and end something on time
- Work under tight time constraints
- Listen to people's arguments and concerns
- Use effective strategies for communicating with others
- Respond to people with differing viewpoints
- Defuse an argument and get people to work together, rather than in opposition
- Negotiate in difficult situations
- Build consensus among people of differing opinions
- Work well with committees
- Negotiate through proper organizational channels
- Use public speaking skills developed through extensive practice in speaking in classrooms and at educational meetings
- Motivate others and keep them involved in diverse tasks
- Prioritize tasks
- Delegate responsibilities to other individuals
- Write reasonably well and develop arguments or summarize divergent ideas
- Self-evaluate and be evaluated for personal strengths and weaknesses
- Decide when things need to be redone or altered
- Multitask

Considering Past Advocacy Successes

As you plan your strategies, it will be helpful to consider where you have been successful in past advocacy efforts and when these did not go as planned. Reflecting on past activities will help you plan new approaches more successfully. What worked well for you before? Which of your past activities would be useful for your new plan? Celebrate past successes and incorporate winning ideas into your new advocacy campaign.

Sometimes achieving the goals of school-based advocacy initiatives depends entirely on teacher talents. The following vignette offers such an example.

School Size, Community Development, and Student Performance

Elizabeth Lokon

Professor of Education, Miyazaki International College, Miyazaki, Kyushu, Japan

Heritage School is a relatively large urban high school in the midwestern United States, with mostly poor, underachieving African American and Appalachian students. I studied this school as a graduate student and volunteered on a daily basis for two years. California Achievement Test scores show that approximately 75% of Heritage School students are below the national norm in reading and 82% are below the national norm in mathematics. Of its approximately 600 ninth graders in any given school year, only about 100 (16%) eventually receive their high school diplomas.

Within this context, eight teachers advocated for and created a smaller school of 150 randomly selected students. They met in an abandoned building in the back of the existing Heritage School campus. They called themselves the Heritage Interdisciplinary Team. Their primary goal was to address the above problems. They received no additional funding or administrative support.

The principal's laissez faire approach gave them the freedom to experiment with various innovative practices such as team-teaching, block scheduling, and using interdisciplinary projects. However, none of these practices became routinized. In fact, the only factor that distinguished the Team from the rest of the school was its smaller size and a sense of community that resulted from it. As one student put it,

> It helps [being in a team] because we see the same faces every day. We know each other well. So, when someone is capping [teasing], we know it's just capping. We don't fight because we know each other. We're making friends because we see each other not only one year, one hour. We're making friends for life.

The sense of community created by the reduced number of students and the daily contact with caring teachers altered the students' performance. When compared with randomly selected students in the rest of the school, the students in the Team had a higher year-to-year retention rate (87% vs. 54%), a higher passing rate of core courses (61% vs. 34%), a higher attendance rate (85% vs. 78%), and a lower rate of reported disciplinary cases (36% vs. 52%).

Although these percentages could be better, they showed the beginning of real change. The momentum behind these changes was supplied by the commitment of the Team and their advocacy for building an interdependent community of teachers and learners who shared a sense of moral obligation to each other.

FOR YOUR CONSIDERATION

- The Heritage Interdisciplinary Team received little or no support from their building administrator. Advocacy work under such conditions is difficult. Think about how you might support your fellow advocates when you experience difficulty achieving your goals. What might you do?

- Advocacy work by educators often grows from personal beliefs, as it did for these Heritage School teachers. Are there inequities in your school that you feel strongly about? Are you willing to advocate on behalf of the problems you identify? How might you begin to do this?

Education advocacy takes a great deal of time and energy, and working together may help you reach a wider audience. Previously, we suggested special interest groups you might seek out. We also encouraged you to consider working with people representing different perspectives, such as health care professionals, members of the business community, and senior citizens. Bill Hammond's vignette illustrates how powerful individuals of differing perspectives can be when they are working together for issues of common concern.

Lobbying for Child Care

Bill Hammond
Lobbyist and Child-Care Advocate, Black Child Development Institute,
Atlanta, Georgia, USA

I have served as the legislative lobbyist for a child-care organization for a few years. One of the major goals of the organization is to receive funding through the

Governor's Child Care Initiative to provide training and assistance for small child-care programs seeking accreditation from the National Association for the Education of Young Children (NAEYC).

The governor had a group of "field advisors" and assistants in the House and Senate who advised him and made recommendations for legislation. After developing a strong association with a key African American member of the governor's advisory group, members of our child-care organization introduced information on the importance of these small child-care centers in the African American community. We attended information sessions set up by these advisory group members and also by members of the Legislative Black Caucus to provide input and to establish our organization as a reliable source of information.

With the help of our Director of Education, we met individually with key members of the Appropriations Committee, the Education Committee, and selected key members of the House and Senate to brief them on the significance of our proposal and how funding would affect child-care programs in their district.

We also asked child-care center operators within each member's district to contact their elected representatives in person about a month before the beginning of the legislative session. Careful planning and regular contacts with their representatives seemed to have a positive impact on the legislative process.

At all of our informational sessions, we emphasized the service that child-care centers provided for single parents who desperately need affordable child care to keep their jobs and remain off welfare. We also conveyed to legislators the impact of our proposal on their constituents, especially the positive effects of child-care centers within their district.

As a result of these efforts, the governor set aside $350,000 to be used by our organization for assisting these small child-care centers in attaining accreditation. After the proposal was funded, we prepared and distributed to all legislators (supporters and nonsupporters) the benefits that their district received. We will use this information to lay the groundwork for the next legislative session.

To date, through their participation in our training program, more than 30 small child-care centers in the African American community in Atlanta have received NAEYC accreditation. Our program has just received another $350,000 in funding to continue this training in three additional communities for the coming year. We've also received assurance that funding will continue as a budget item into the future.

- This activist encouraged child-care providers to meet with their elected representatives or representatives' aides on a regular basis. Are there groups of individuals you can mobilize to make similar legislator visits on your advocacy issue? Who are they? How will you work with them?

- This vignette suggests the importance of building on past successes. Information and results from one advocacy success led to funding to establish additional training sites. What are some previous successes you can build on as you plan additional advocacy initiatives?

- This advocate reminds us of the importance of personalizing the issue for elected representatives by giving examples of how their constituents will be affected. How can you use a similar strategy in your advocacy efforts?

Finding People to Work With You

How do you find like-minded people with whom you might work? Again, begin close to home. You might start your search for individuals who will work with you at your local building level, just as the Heritage School teachers did. Share your concerns with fellow teachers and administrators. Use conversations with your colleagues as times to share your concerns and to promote advocacy. See if your colleagues feel similarly about your issues and would like to work with you to try to bring about change.

Ask your school administrator if you can present your ideas at grade-level or department meetings. Request time on the agenda of the next faculty meeting or at a meeting of the board of the Parent–Teacher Association. When you share your ideas at these meetings, others may express interest in working with you on your advocacy concern.

If you represent your school building on any school district councils or at functions, ask the moderator or presiding school district official if you may have time to speak to the group. Again, you may find others who will approach you after the meeting, willing to advocate with you.

Speaking to members of civic and fraternal organizations also may be useful. Identify organizations that might be interested in and concerned about education. Contact their officers or program chairpersons, and see if you can speak to the board or if you can present at a meeting of the membership.

Consider also contacting religious groups. Many may share your concern for students and will welcome you to speak at a service, class, or meeting.

Do not be shy at social functions. People will be interested in hearing what you have to say about education and sharing their thoughts with you. In the process, you may find new education advocates.

If part of your goal is to influence legislation and education and public policy, you will need to identify policymakers who might be open to your issues and willing to work with you toward change. You may need to do considerable investigation before your can identify the individuals you might want to approach. The professional organizations to which you belong may have government relations specialists who know the special interests of individual officials or groups and can help you network with their representatives.

Identifying key legislative staffs with whom you can work is important to your success. Regularly reading newspapers and watching newscasts may alert you to people who may be supportive. As discussed in chapter 3, you can identify past voting records on legislation that might be related to your concern. Your school district may have someone in its central office who regularly works with state or national legislators and who can suggest specific legislative aides to approach to begin the process of working with a legislator. Once you have identified specific individuals to approach, you can use many of the strategies suggested in chapters 5 and 6 to further your cause.

Do not forget one of your most valuable resources: Your own students and their parents may be some of your strongest supporters and the best spokespersons. When they speak to members of the school board and the school district administration, their voices are heard. Some of the most powerful voices in opposition to many of the practices associated with high-stakes assessment have been those of students and parents who were concerned about the numbers of hours spent in test preparation, the diminished time for classroom instruction, or the number of school days spent in testing. Many of these advocacy efforts are chronicled on websites such as www.arlingtoncare.org or www.caremass.org. Additional sources are compiled on the "Featured Resources" webpage at www.susanohanian.org, where you can read about other opposition movements to state testing practices. Organized efforts such as these often get local and state board of education attention.

Is your issue one that would galvanize students and parents? If so, consider what roles they can play in your campaign and how you might get them involved. You may want to start with a well-conducted meeting where you lay out your concerns and the options that might be possible. Then you might recruit participants to help you implement your plan. You may need to work with the students and parents to prepare their information and testimony so that their messages are effective. If you do, your results can be highly rewarding. One of this book's authors remembers a meeting of her state board of education at which four students from her school district's communications arts high school so impressed the board members with their testimony that the members gave them a standing ovation when they were finished. When the students talked about their programs and the value of the activities they were engaging in, they spoke eloquently about the advantages of the proposed state language arts curriculum and the problems associated with an alternative curriculum document that was proposed by a specific group of citizens.

Depending on the nature of your advocacy issue, there is one additional group of individuals you might want to contact: ombudsmen and community liaisons. In the United States and Canada, ombudsmen usually assist individuals who want to address their concerns confidentially. According to the Office of the University Ombudsman at Washington State University, Pullman, Washington, USA, "the ombudsmen function has been utilized in state and federal agencies, prisons, hospitals, nursing homes, child protective services, industry and higher education colleges and universities" (n.d.). In a school district of any size, there may be one or several people holding this type of role. These individuals are advocates for the students and the programs of the school district. They are fair and impartial individuals who often serve as sounding boards for members of the community. Frequently, they are called on to resolve conflict and dissent.

Because ombudsmen and liaisons work with many individuals and organizations, they will know of resources both within and outside the school district that will be helpful to you and your cause. They may help you with coalition building. They may be able to suggest appropriate legislators to approach. Ombudsmen also may assist you at the personal level if your advocacy work puts you in difficult positions in the school district. For example, sometimes advocacy work jeopardizes your relationships with coworkers and administrators. Ombudsmen can assist in calming these troubled waters.

Outside the school district, community ombudsmen and liaisons play similar roles. They often are the go-betweens, linking individuals and organizations that share similar interests and concerns. It is their job to know individuals and to know agencies. They may be able to help you cut through organizational red tape to get to the individuals who might offer you the most help. See if there are ombudsmen or liaisons in social service agencies who can help you make contacts with people outside your profession who share concerns similar to your own.

Creating a Reasonable Timeline

As you develop your advocacy plan, set some realistic targets. What are your windows of opportunity? By what dates must specific tasks be completed? When do materials need to be submitted? What are the dates of school board meetings or meetings of important educational committees? What did you learn about the legislative calendar?

Once you know some of the time parameters that will govern your work, set some deadlines. If you are working collaboratively, decide who is going to do what and when the group will meet to provide input and feedback. Schedule specific times for debriefing. Although much of your group work may be conducted via telephone calls or e-mail messages, you need time to get together for face-to-face meetings.

Planning for Ongoing Evaluation of Your Advocacy Efforts

As part of the planning for your advocacy, also determine how you will evaluate whether you are successful. Discuss what you will consider as evidence that your strategies are working and your advocacy is making a difference. Remember that many small steps may be necessary before accomplishing larger goals. With your colleagues, establish some realistic expectations for what you hope to accomplish.

Bring members of your group together to share their progress. Each individual needs to be informed of what others are doing and what they are encountering as they put their strategies into operation. We suggest that you designate specific times when the group reflects on its collective efforts and determines what is and is not working effectively. Putting these meetings on the timeline will keep them visible and in the minds of the group members.

At these sessions, plan for reports from individuals and subgroups. Look carefully at what has already transpired and look forward to the logical next steps. These debriefing occasions may also be necessary to lift lagging spirits and cheer members on toward success. Celebrate small accomplishments that build group morale and keep members working toward their established targets. If some members are discouraged, these meetings may provide help and support.

Chapter 8 suggests more specific possibilities that you might consider when assessing the effectiveness of your advocacy activities.

Adjusting Your Strategies if They Are Not Helping You Accomplish Your Goals

As part of your overall planning, consider the possibility that all may not go well and your strategies may not work as planned. Debriefing meetings may be the times when the group decides that there needs to be some adjusting of strategies and plans. If the group initially establishes the expectation that plans will be monitored and adjusted as they go along, there may be less confusion and less tension when other ideas need to be considered and pursued. Even the best-designed plan can go awry. Group members need to be prepared to redirect their efforts and try different ideas. Planning for this very real possibility is wise. When you read chapter 7, "An Advocacy Tale of Success," you will see how a team of advocates constantly monitored and adjusted their plans and procedures as they discovered the need for additional or replacement strategies.

Conclusion

Recall this chapter's basic premise: Successful advocacy work requires clear objectives, a vision, and careful planning. When you consider all the options that are available for your use, make deliberate choices. Which strategies will most likely help you meet your goals within the time limits you have allocated? In chapter 5, we'll provide many guidelines that will help you use print media for effective dissemination of your advocacy messages.

Print–Based Advocacy Strategies

S uccessful education advocates realize that it is critical for their messages to reach a wide audience—not just policymakers, but others whose opinions are shaped in part by information that they receive from other sources. This is true whether you are advocating on behalf of parents, teachers, or students, or for libraries, equipment, or school construction. Almost every education issue that you want to affect will require public support.

This chapter will show you how you can use printed media to accomplish your advocacy goals. You will read stories from other advocates about strategies that they used successfully as well as some pitfalls you will want to avoid. As you read this chapter, think about which strategies will work best for you. Your choices will rest in part on the outcomes you can expect if you are successful. Your choices also will be influenced by

- your personal connections,
- your financial resources,
- your manpower resources,
- your personal creativity, and
- your relations with the media and other sources of information that reach wide audiences.

The more you have of each of the above items, the easier it will be to get started. Once you learn to use the media effectively, the strategies will become familiar to you and you will experience greater satisfaction and success.

Remember, too, that the bottom line in education advocacy is that what really counts is what is good for the children. Advocacy is not just about high-quality teachers, more libraries, a different curriculum, or assessments. These things are important, but they are important because of the bearing they have on students' achievement and well-being. If you lose sight of this, your message may not be heard. As J.B. Buxton, Senior Education Advisor for Michael F. Easley, Governor of North Carolina, reminded us, teachers and other educators need to "anchor their advocacy in the goal of improved student achievement" (personal communication, July 30, 2003).

Using Print Media Effectively

To the title of this section, we should add the words *and Honestly.* So often you may see or hear something and think, "That is not true! That is so dishonest!" It is our belief that education advocates can be as effective, and perhaps even more so, by being honest as we can by being dishonest. Consider some of the recent reports about dishonest news reporters, misleading claims by pharmaceutical companies, and inaccurate accounts of war events. What were the consequences? How skeptical are you of advertising and news accounts you now hear or read? You should expect that others will question any claims you make. Only by being honest will you earn the respect of your audience.

Some advocates suggest that initiating a media campaign is the most important thing they do to affect public thinking and, ultimately, policymaking decisions. The media have the ability to set the public agenda by highlighting some issues and repressing others. For instance, although school construction is of critical concern to most educators, it has not received the same media attention as other education issues such as school violence and student achievement. Your goal in working with the media is to affect what issues will take on importance by keeping them in the public eye.

As you plan your media strategies, you will want to think about media in the broadest sense possible. Do not overlook any of the multiple ways in which you can communicate your message to large numbers of people, such as newsletters, newspapers, and press releases. Each media type offers various communication formats, and each has unique considerations that are explained in this chapter. In addition, you should adhere to the general guidelines in Figure 8 for dealing with all types of media.

There are also some specific guidelines for each type of print media you might consider using. First, you will want to investigate what resources are available to you, and then you will want to familiarize yourself with the particular

Figure 8. Guidelines for Working With Media Sources

- Get accurate contact information for each source—including name, affiliation, phone and fax numbers, and e-mail addresses—and keep this information up to date.

- Find out as much as you can about each media outlet. Who is its audience? Does it usually take any particular stance on education issues? Does it tend to be conservative or liberal?

- Make initial introductions to your media contact people even before you ask them to work with you. Let them know who you are, what your interests are, and something about your organization, if you are representing one. Be certain you are talking to the person who will determine if your material will be used. You also can develop more personal relationships with your media contacts by paying visits to their offices. Call ahead to make appointments.

- Offer assistance. Although your specific issue might not be of immediate interest to your media contact person, perhaps you can provide other information and develop a working relationship with him or her.

- Pay attention to deadlines; these vary for each media source.

- Be prepared for requests for additional information, and follow through with these requests. For example, a reporter may request more information before your story can be published. Provide the information immediately.

- Be sure the information you provide is accurate. If you are announcing an event, it is critical that the date, time, and location are specified and are correct. Make sure any research you cite is presented accurately and that you have provided correct citations.

- Get any necessary permissions beforehand to use materials that others have developed.

- Know your opposition. If you can neutralize their arguments through repudiation with sufficient facts, your cause will be given more serious consideration.

- Double-check for spelling and grammatical errors in any written material you are submitting to your media sources.

- Stay on top of your product. If you were told that an interview you have had or an op-ed piece you have written will appear "soon," follow up for more specific information and confirmation.

- If you are representing an organization, be sure you have confirmed with its decision makers that what you are submitting for publication or broadcast has their consent. You would not want to require a public retraction of something you have said.

- If for some reason you are quoted inaccurately, or if later you find that information you provided is incorrect, issue a public retraction as quickly as possible. Newspapers issue these every day; it is when they do not issue retractions that they have problems. If you misquoted someone, let him or her know personally that you have taken steps to correct the misinformation that was circulated.

requirements to which you will need to adhere for each resource. The next several sections provide information on these topics.

Let's start with materials that may be readily available to you or to most members of an organization with which you are advocating. The following sections begin with possibilities close to home and move outward to your community and beyond. As you develop your plan, consider if these resources will be good places for you or your organization to disseminate your information or to recruit individuals to join you in your advocacy efforts.

Newsletters

School Newsletters

Many schools publish newsletters that are distributed to students' families. Often, these newsletters also are sent to businesses in the school community and to real estate agents who are brokering homes or apartments for sale or rent in the area of the school campus's boundaries. These newsletters usually are issued monthly, but occasionally a school sends out a special edition or publishes its newsletter more frequently.

The contents of school newsletters differ, but newsletters usually publish information of concern to students' family members, such as upcoming events or meetings, school awards or recognitions, student or teacher successes, and requests for volunteers or specific resources. In many newsletters there is a featured article, usually written by a building administrator, explaining a policy or asking input from the newsletter's readers.

Is it possible that you might write your ideas into an article for the newsletter? Make an appointment to speak with your administrator and find out. Perhaps your administrator would be open to publishing your ideas and then encouraging responses from parents, teachers, or school district personnel. Discussion of the concern might continue over several newsletter issues. Note, however, that if your issue or concern is perceived as controversial, your administrator may turn down your request. School administrators generally see the school newsletter as a place for sharing information, rather than a place for fueling controversy.

Some specific school-related organizations also may publish newsletters for their members. These organizations frequently distribute their newsletters to other community members as well. Check with the presidents of such organizations as the Parent–Teacher Association, the Band Boosters Association, or the Athletic Boosters Association if you feel that your message would be appropriate for their groups. Perhaps a strategic paragraph or two in one of these special publications will be helpful in getting your message to those who might be called to action. Consider, for example, the issue of school district budget cuts for specific programs in the arts. Parents of students who are interested in drama or music might be eager to read your comments about how the programs at your specific school will be altered as a result of declines in budget appropriations. They might be interested in reading your possible alternatives to solutions that are being proposed at the school district level. The home school district of one of this book's authors, for example, has proposed a plan to eliminate all funding for busing students from their home campuses to special programs at the various magnet academies. The parents of students currently enrolled in magnet programs might be very interested in reading alternate solutions to this proposal. Therefore, an article on this transportation issue might be welcomed by the magnet program's newsletter editors.

School District Newsletters

Beyond the building level, many school districts publish a districtwide newsletter that goes out to every taxpayer and business located within the school district's geographical boundaries. In most school districts, this newsletter appears on a monthly or quarterly basis. Additional issues, or even a separate publication, may kick off the new school year or the new semester. From time to time, a special newsletter issue focuses on a specific school district program, policy, or concern, such as an upcoming school board election or a school bond issue.

Check with your school district's office of communications or media relations department to determine the school district policy for submitting information for possible publication in the districtwide newsletter. Each school district has its own policies about what types of information are disseminated, and there may be a section of the newsletter where your materials could be published. In this or in any print resource, your likelihood of publication will increase if your issue is presented clearly, your material is tightly written, and your ideas are presented in an objective manner. Your ideas also will be more likely to be published if you go beyond the discussion of the problem to laying out some possible solutions.

In addition to a general newsletter, some school districts also have newsletters for specific audiences such as parents of special needs students; English-language learners; and Even Start, Head Start, and Title I participants. Depending on your issue of concern, these specialized newsletters may be more appropriate for your message than the school district's general publication. Also, newsletter editors of these specific publications may welcome contributions that address the needs and interests of their targeted readers.

If you are unfamiliar with all of the print information resources that are available in your school district, see if information is offered on your school district's website, or again, consult the office of communications or media relations department. Usually there will be several staff members who may provide you with the information you need. In the school district of one of this book's authors, for example, eight people work to handle the school district's communications with the public.

Even if your material cannot be included in school district publications, you may find that members of the office of communications or media relations department will agree to work with you as you prepare your ideas for wider publication. They may suggest places to disseminate your ideas because they have extensive files on where they send their information briefings and on the names of key informants or lead personnel at each of the organizations or agencies.

Community Newsletters

Once you want your information to reach a wider audience than an individual school's or district's boundaries, you may continue to work alone on your writing, or you may find yourself working more closely with others who have similar concerns. Although the school district might be reluctant to print anything from a nondistrict employee, community organizations may have a looser publication policy. See if there are community publications that you can use for sharing your information. It would be easy to overlook these publications; however, they may be one of your most appropriate targets. For example, many home-owners' associations have monthly or quarterly publications they distribute to all the households in their communities. Often, these publications have featured sections about schools. Contact the editors of such publications and see if your ideas would be welcomed and what procedures you would need to follow for submission of your information.

Many real estate agents also send out newsletters to current homeowners and potential homebuyers in the community. Check with the real estate agents or their agencies to see if your information might be appropriate for their publications. These people and groups know the link between strong schools and housing market value. They may be eager to publish your information, especially if it advocates for a change that may put the schools in an even more positive light.

Medical personnel in your area, such as pediatricians or dentists, also may distribute newsletters or bulletins to the homeowners of your community. Contact these professionals to see if you might write a column or a letter to go out in their next publications.

Consider approaching social and fraternal organizations. Space may be available in their newsletters for information about schools, students, and education needs. Often, members of these organizations engage in community service activities. Perhaps your ideas might be just what they are looking for in terms of finding a project for their members and toward which they can volunteer their time and resources. Many mentoring programs for students have started because teachers or administrators advocated for more adult involvement in the schools and then reached out to community organizations to see if members would donate their time to work with students. One author of this book remembers that in two communities where she served as reading supervisor and university department chair, members of Kiwanis and Rotary groups volunteered to mentor students in schools after she spoke at one of their organization's scheduled meetings. Also, the volunteer coordinator for the district regularly sought these and other groups' support through letters and telephone calls that she and her staff made to organization leaders. Articles in newsletters and presentations at meetings of these organizations have helped many school-based people find possible mentors for their students.

Do not forget your city officials. Your mayor or city council members frequently publish newsletters or bulletins that are distributed to all households in the community. These may appear quarterly or on a semiregular basis, so you may need to make some phone calls to find out whether you can submit materials for possible publication and when the deadlines might be. The likelihood of publishing in such publications might be small, but if your issue is one of importance to local schools, your elected officials might be eager to disseminate your information.

Newsletters From Your Elected State and National Officials

Your elected senators and representatives, particularly those at the national level, frequently send newsletters or mailings to the constituents in their home districts. Although many elected officials have created and rely on websites, most still disseminate printed materials. Contact the offices of the elected officials representing your school district, and see if you might provide information about their mailings.

Professional Newsletters

As you widen your consideration of possible places to disseminate your information or to find people who will join you in your advocacy concern, remember your professional associations. You probably belong to several state and national professional organizations. Some of your organizations may have local chapters as well. Almost every professional organization has some kind of a newsletter or bulletin that is distributed to all its members. Although some organizations are now relying on online bulletins, most organizations still send regular mailings to their membership. Often, these are sent on a monthly or quarterly basis. Most feature information about the organization and its issues, but many also have featured articles, guest columns, letters to the editor, and surveys of the membership. Perhaps your issue lends itself to one of these formats and you can negotiate with newsletter editors to submit something for publication consideration.

Newspapers

Nearly every town, large or small, has a newspaper. Some newspapers appear every day and cover several communities; others may appear only weekly and possibly cover only a single town. Some newspapers, such as *The New York Times* or *The Washington Post*, have a large circulation outside their home areas, but the readership of most newspapers is confined to the communities whose news the newspaper covers. You will need to identify the newspapers that are available to you on the basis of the audiences that you believe they will reach.

Check out all the possibilities. Because their circulation is usually concentrated, community newspapers frequently want information about the schools that are within their distribution boundaries. Some of your best opportunities for publishing your ideas might be in these weekly or biweekly editions. Is there a community newspaper in which you could publish a letter to the editor or an op-ed piece?

If they find out that you write well, editors of community newspapers may invite you to submit copy to them on an ongoing basis. Perhaps they will want you to write a featured column. Or they may call on you for information if they find you a valuable informant.

Bonita Wilcox approached the newspaper in her local community. The following vignette describes how she approached the newspaper's editor with a plan for presenting information to parents. Perhaps such an approach would also work in your community.

Writing Articles for Your Local Newspaper

Bonita Wilcox

Adjunct Professor, Duquesne University, Pittsburgh, Pennsylvania, USA

As a teacher and parent, I think that a student's parents ought to be the first to know if their child is failing in school. If the teacher is the first to know, the teacher needs to inform the parents so they can work with the school to solve the problems and get the student back on track.

As I thought of what I could do to help other parents and perhaps prevent some students from failing, I decided it might be useful to write short articles and try to get them published in my local newspaper. These articles would offer suggestions for parents on how they might help their children benefit more from their school experiences.

First, I made a list of all the topics I could think of that related to parents, students, and school success. Then I contacted the editor of the local newspaper to explain what I wanted to do and to see if she thought articles for parents would be a worthy endeavor. She was interested, so I started writing. I submitted initial drafts of each article to my professor, Allen Berger, at the University of Pittsburgh. He would read each draft and make suggestions about what I had written. I would then revise and rewrite. Sometimes, little of what I originally wrote could be salvaged, but as time progressed, more was left than was deleted. Finally, one by one, I submitted 12 articles to the paper for possible publication. Nine have been published so far. Titles of two of them are "Parents Are The Best Teachers When They Take the Initiative" and "Learning Through Questions Can Be Fun and Effective." Perhaps the rest of the articles I have written will be published in the future.

FOR YOUR CONSIDERATION

• What guest columns are carried by your local newspaper? How many of these seem to be written by individuals from your community?

• If you were going to write a series of articles in support of education for your local newspaper, what topics might be of interest to your community?

• How might you use the print media in your community to assist parents in advocating for the needs of their children?

If you are uncertain of what community or regional newspapers exist in your area, usually a quick reference to your phone book, a search on the Internet, or a phone call to your chamber of commerce will guide you to all the community or regional publications. As previously noted, your school district's department of communications staff also may furnish you with contact information for a variety of community publications. Another source of information is www.capitaladvantage.com/data_media.html. This site will help you identify useful local and regional media, reports, and agencies.

In addition, remember the free advertising fliers that are widely circulated. These publications, usually weekly, often have short articles as well as the information on apartment rentals and items for sale.

Newspapers include several possibilities for education advocates to offer comments, such as the options described below. Again, you will need to decide which possibilities best meet your needs.

Letters to the Editor

Probably the best way to begin communicating through the newspaper is by writing succinct letters in response to articles, editorials, or letters that have appeared in your local newspaper. Your letter may concur with or dispute what was said. The important thing is that the material you are responding to is providing an opportunity for you to advocate for your position. Most newspapers explain how to send letters to the editor—either by e-mail or fax. Follow the newspaper's rules and state your points carefully and clearly. Identify the material you are responding to by including the title, date, and page number from the original publication, and be sure to add a sentence or two about the content for the benefit of those readers who may not have read the original material. Be certain to send your response within a day or two of the original material appearing in print because you want the original article or letter to the editor to be fresh in the minds of the newspapers' readers. If you wait too long, your letter will not be pertinent, and it probably will not be published.

Your letter is more likely to be published if you follow the conventions of the paper and if you are concise in what you write. Know the one message you want to get across to the readership and stick to that message. Write a compelling first sentence and then use short, concise paragraphs. Avoid any defamatory or obscene language, no matter how angry you might be. Remember, your letter will have more impact if you can provide local examples and local statistics to illustrate your viewpoint.

If your letter is accepted to appear in the newspaper, you may receive a phone call or e-mail from someone on the newspaper's staff. Why? Many newspapers have had bad experiences with people sending letters in other people's names. Newspapers now tend to verify that you are the one who wrote the letter that they plan to publish. They also want to be certain that you did not write your letter out of anger and would regret having it published. In other words, they want your permission to disseminate it.

Many newspapers have a limit on how often letters from the same person can be published. Find out if such a limit exists at your local newspaper and then space your letters accordingly. Also, bear in mind that most newspapers do not accept letters on behalf of a group. Write your letter as an individual who is expressing personal views, rather than the views of an organization or association. If you need to write a longer piece, consider writing an op-ed instead.

Editorials

One of the most powerful ways to reach many people is through the editorial. After the front page, and perhaps the sports section, readers most often turn to the editorial pages to see what other people are thinking about the topics of the day. Once you have written a letter to the editor, you may want to write an editorial or op-ed piece. Such a piece is longer than a letter and gives you more opportunity to express your viewpoints.

First, plan what you want to write. Identify the three or four most important points you want to make. Sometimes advocates are angry about some turn of events or a policy under consideration, but they are unable to get beyond the anger to explain their feelings in a reasoned way. By forcing yourself to think beyond the emotional level, by analyzing your feelings logically, you will recognize the strength of your argument and know whether you need to find more support for your ideas. Accentuate the local angle in your op-ed. Distinguish your submission with local anecdotes, statistics, or stories. Show that you have experience in the area you are writing about, and personalize your piece. Remember that editors have access to lots of op-ed pieces from news services. Adding local stories may make the difference between publication and rejection of your writing.

Once you have outlined your points and are satisfied that they are justified, relay your ideas within the word limit set by the newspaper. The range for most newspapers is usually 500–700 words, which is not much space for you to express your views. A double-spaced page of word-processed text is approximately 250 words, so you can only write approximately two-and-a-half pages of text. We want to emphasize that staying within this limit is crucial. You may write the greatest op-ed in the world, but if it is too long, it may not be published.

As you are writing, think about your audience. They most likely value plain English, so respect this value. You might be surprised to learn that most newspapers are written on a fairly low level. *The New York Times*, for instance, writes most of its news stories on a ninth- or tenth-grade level. Be sure your pronoun references are clear, and avoid technical language that a general readership would not know. Your local bookstore will have a number of good publications that can help you to develop a clear writing style.

Close your op-ed with a short and powerful last paragraph that will keep your issue in the mind of the reader. Personalize the message, and indicate the relevance of your issue to local concerns. If you are responding to an earlier issue, explain how your suggestion or recommendation makes a more powerful contribution to the solution of the problem than does the original piece. Indicate what might be the consequences if your issue is ignored or only partially implemented. In addition, you might urge readers to engage in a specific action on behalf of their schools or their wider community.

Once you feel that your op-ed piece is close to finished, usually after several hours of work and a number of revisions, show your material to at least one other person who is not in education—a friend, spouse, son, daughter, or neighbor. Ask this person if everything you have written is clear: Are your arguments logical? Have you used terms that people outside the education field would not understand? If the person points out something that should be changed, consider whether the suggestion makes sense. If it does, make the change. Remember that things that may be clear in your mind may not be clear to the rest of the world.

When you are ready, call the newspaper to ask which way they would like to receive your op-ed piece. Find out to whom you should send the material, and send your op-ed directly to that person. Be certain to include your own contact information with your mailing. Consider including a cover letter with your submission explaining why your piece is timely and why it is important to the newspaper's readers. Your comments in such a letter may increase the likelihood of someone at the newspaper reading your piece and considering it for publication. Be sure to include your job title beneath your signature.

Responses From the Newspaper

A newspaper might have one of three responses to your submissions: outright rejection, outright acceptance, or something in between.

Do not get discouraged if your submission is not accepted for publication. There are many reasons a piece might be rejected—space (or lack thereof), previous op-ed materials on the same topic, and so on. If you don't hear from the paper in a few days, follow up to determine the status of your submission and whether changes need to be made to get it accepted for publication. For example, Allen Berger wrote a long op-ed and submitted it to a newspaper. After a few weeks, he phoned the newspaper and inquired about the status of the piece. He was told that it was too long—twice as long as the word limit, in fact. Allen asked if the piece might be published if he cut the word count in half. The newspaper staff person's response was positive, so Allen made the revision. His op-ed piece appeared in the newspaper soon afterward.

It is important that you do not take any rejections personally. Continue to send in your work. The newspaper staff will become familiar with you, and after a while you may develop a positive working relationship with the newspaper's editorial department.

Sometimes you can be pleasantly surprised by the results of your letters to the editor. Jill Lewis read a newspaper story on an education issue that prompted her to write a letter to the editor, turning the readers' attention to another issue that concerned her. Her local paper mentioned that there was statewide concern about uncertified teachers teaching in special education classes. She knew that individuals seeking certification as special education teachers in her state did not take sufficient coursework in how to teach reading. She used the newspaper story as a lead into her issue, and her letter to the editor became an op-ed piece with a byline and a drawing. (See Appendix A, page 240.)

Final Considerations When Writing for a Newspaper

Most of us are so busy that even if we read something in the newspaper that provokes us to want to respond with a letter to the editor or op-ed piece, we do not write down our ideas even if we compose the perfect response in our heads. However, if we do not take these opportunities for expressing our ideas, we miss the chance to share our research, experiences, and viewpoints with large audiences. Newspapers are vital for disseminating our advocacy messages, so use them well. The article "Writing About Reading for the Public" (see Appendix A, page 242) contains some additional strategies for communicating your ideas through the newspaper.

Note also that you are not limited to sending pieces to your local newspapers. If you issue is one that has statewide or national relevance, do not hesitate to reach beyond your community's or school district's borders.

Press Releases

Another effective way to reach a large audience is to prepare a press release, either to stand on its own or to be used in conjunction with a specific press event. When a press release is used in conjunction with a press event, the event's purpose needs to be well defined and the who, what, when, and where need to be explained thoroughly.

Press releases provide excellent opportunities for groups and organizations to share information with the general public. At the district level, for example, press releases might share news about student, teacher, or district accolades. They could present information on changing district demographics or the need for redistricting boundaries or building new schools. Press releases might highlight recent test scores or report on district testing trends over a period of years. They might share concerns about the impact of recently passed state or federal legislation on current district policies. Beyond the district level, press releases also may share information about state or national reports or their implications for local and state education policies. For example, many states issued press releases about their responses to and their concerns about specific provisions of NCLB. Press releases also can highlight new initiatives. Organizations, such as the International Reading Association (IRA), use press releases to feature specific initiatives, for example, IRA's upcoming programs and projects in the areas of urban education and adolescent literacy.

When you write a press release, keep your material brief and factual. Also keep in mind the following points as you prepare your press release:

- At the top of the page, have a news-capturing headline that conveys the essence of the press release. Be sure that it is newsworthy.

- At the top of the page, also put the date and time of the press release. The date can be the same day as when you are sending it to media sources, or you can state that the press release is embargoed, or deferred from publication, until a specific date and time to protect it from early release.

- In the upper right-hand corner of the page, provide sufficient contact information, such as your name, title, address, cell phone and fax numbers, e-mail address, and website URL.

- The body of the press release should include the pertinent information.

- Include quotes in the press release if they help to convey the importance of the news to the media's audiences.

- Conclude the press release with a boilerplate mission-based statement of your organization, a statement that has been developed carefully by your organization to be used for any formal communication describing the organization.

See Figure 9 for a sample press release.

As you write the press release, ask yourself, What are some purposes for the event that might attract attention? Reporters keep a busy schedule and often are required to write 10 or more news stories each day. Your event will need to be unique enough to attract their attention. Remember that the event itself is not the

---

Figure 9. Fictitious Press Release

Contact: Jane Smith
Public Relations Officer
Education for Children
123 Education Way
New York, NY 10000

Date: Embargoed until (date and time)
Teachers Plan March on Washington

New York City—In an effort to stem the tide on unfunded education mandates emanating from the White House, teachers and administrators from across the United States will converge in front of the White House on Sunday.

Republican as well as Democratic leaders will address the crowd, which is expected to swell to a million strong, according to Alice Roberts, spokesperson for Education for Children, the organization that is sponsoring the march on Washington.

Ms. Roberts, who used to teach in Washington, DC, schools, said, "We need to go beyond artificial boundaries for the sake of our children and America."

Ted Kennedy (Democrat, Massachusetts) and Orin Hatch (Republican, Utah) will give the keynote addresses beginning at 2 o'clock.

People of all religious backgrounds will be boarding buses leaving from their churches, synagogues, and mosques in a display of unity. Further information is available from local houses of worship as well as from your school board.

Education for Children is an organization founded in 2004 for the preservation of public education in the United States.

---

primary reason you are holding it; the underlying purpose is to get your advocacy message to the public. For example, a Legislator of the Year award is given each year by the New Jersey Reading Association to a legislator who has done something significant for literacy. The carefully chosen recipient is also someone whose achievement supports issues that are valued by the association. The award is presented at the annual banquet that is part of the association's spring conference. Recently, the state's governor received the award because he had often spoken on behalf of literacy programs and had stressed the need for parents to read to very young children. The association was concerned about the recent emphasis on phonics instruction in schools, at the expense of good literature. By giving the award to the governor and recognizing the type of programs he had supported, the association showcased him while also sending an important message to anyone who read the press release that reading experts believed learning to read involved much more than phonics and valued the contributions parents could make to developing their children's literacy. Because the press release announced an award to the governor, it also attracted the attention of the press.

Although it is not always possible, we suggest that you send your press release at least a month in advance of the event. If you have access to a news bureau at a college or university, give your press release to someone there. If your event is newsworthy, and if the bureau has the manpower, it will do its best to get the event covered.

Delivering the press release in person is the best way to ensure delivery. However, usually this method of delivery is not possible. Alternatively, at some statehouses there is a mailbox for every newspaper and radio station; you can leave your message there. You also can send your press release by fax. Some associations have complete listings of media sources' fax numbers and may be willing to share this information with you. If you do not want the information released until a specific date, you need to indicate this on the release by saying it is "embargoed until (date and time)."

The choice of location for your event is also important. It should be centrally located for the individuals you are hoping will attend. The room should be large enough to accommodate any speakers as well as members of the press. Be sure there are sufficient electrical outlets for the variety of equipment that any newspaper, radio, or television reporters might bring. Your event should be held on time and in the morning to ensure sufficient time for each media outlet to prepare and present the story before the day's end.

On the day of your event, bring briefing packets for your guests. These packets should provide the basic information about your program, including the names and affiliations of presenters, questions that reporters might have and the corresponding answers, and background information on your group or organization. You might consider including photographs of key people, along with their names and contact information, as well as any other visuals pertinent to the event. A briefing packet will make it easier for reporters to write a story about your event. You also should bring a camera so the event can be recorded and included in promotional materials that you might develop later.

Be sure you and any guest speakers are available to the press during the event. Seek out the reporters to determine if they have any questions or need additional information from you or other members of your group.

Stories about your event may appear relatively soon afterward on television and radio, and in local newspapers, but stories in association newspapers may appear in issues a couple of months afterward.

One caveat: If for any reason your event is cancelled, it is critical that you notify all the people whom you originally invited. They will appreciate the courtesy, and you will avoid phone calls from individuals who showed up in response to your original press release.

If you are making an announcement, but not scheduling an event, send a press release to the same sources. You also can submit news stories to your sources, with photos; it is possible you will be contacted for an interview or additional information.

One advantage of the press release is that you are in complete control of what message goes out. You also may learn about media outlets you had not even considered as communication possibilities. Although you will not know who actually reads your press release once it has been published, there will be individuals getting your message who otherwise might not have heard from you at all.

Other Methods for Getting Your Message Into Print

In the first part of this chapter, we focused on ways to share your ideas through newsletters, newspapers, and press releases. The following sections offer additional strategies for sharing your ideas through print, including fliers; position papers and resolutions; themed journals; e-mail messages, letters, and postcards; and T-shirts. The following vignette describes one individual's unique approach to disseminating printed information to a large audience.

Disruption: Nonviolent Civil Disobedience Through Fliers

Richard J. Meyer

Associate Professor, University of New Mexico, Albuquerque, New Mexico, USA

A group of my university colleagues and I have been involved in informing teachers, parents, legislators, and anyone else who will listen about some of the facts within the present educational climate. One of the most powerful ways of doing this, we've found, is by using a flier. You might remember fliers from recent elections or rallies. We've found that most politicians rely on their office staffers for in-depth information on an issue. As a result, if we can tweak the politicians' interest or curiosity with a flier, we know they'll ask their staffers for more information.

A good flier does two things: (1) It presents information in a concise fashion, and (2) it lists specific questions that you want addressed. Flier information should be printed on a distinctive color of paper and in a font that is easy to read.

We knew that our state department of education was bringing speakers to our town to promote the report of the National Reading Panel. On the first day, one of my colleagues and I brought fliers printed on fluorescent green paper. When most individuals were seated in the room that held 500 teachers, two of us sat in the back, opened our backpacks, took out the fliers and said, "Someone said to take one and pass the rest." A sea of green soon filled the auditorium. On the second day, the room was much smaller and the presentation was to administrators, legislators, and university faculty and deans. We passed out white fliers before the attendees entered the room, instead of the distinctive green. This time we also chose not to put any contact information on the fliers.

Each time, the flier changed the atmosphere of the room by letting people know they were not hearing the whole truth but only a narrow interpretation of a limited number of studies. For those curious about the content of our flier, here is the essence of our message:

> The research you are hearing about today views reading narrowly, and such views are not particularly useful to teachers, administrators, and policymakers. The views you are hearing are not addressing the issues that make our schools a "battleground for opposing philosophies and prey for purveyors of quick fixes." The National Reading Panel did not rely upon classroom-based research or the realities of classroom life. As such, Panel findings are resulting in mandated instruction that is difficult if not impossible to implement. In short, the Panel's report is unbalanced and detrimental to education.

FOR YOUR CONSIDERATION

- What kind of impact might the flier have had on those attending the presentations?

- How might these advocates use a meeting such as this as an opportunity for developing an advocacy team?

- What additional suggestions would you make for preparing advocacy fliers?

Position Papers and Resolutions

An organization or group working with you on education advocacy may wish to share its views by writing a position paper or resolution. These issue-focused statements often are developed in response to ideas under consideration by policymakers that the organization wishes to support, refute, or clarify for policymakers or its own members before policy decisions are made. These papers make clear the organization's position on the specific issue and the rationale for the organization's views. Position papers and resolutions also often define steps that policymakers and education advocates can take to achieve the goals outlined.

Most often, position papers and resolutions are developed by a small committee; both papers involve similar writing processes and can be used for similar purposes. Position papers usually are reviewed by an executive committee or board, approved by a board of directors, and then distributed to the organization's membership. Resolutions are voted on by delegates of the full membership of the organization. Position papers might lead to resolutions or vice versa.

A well-planned position paper has three major components: (1) It defines what is needed, (2) why it is needed, and (3) what those who agree with the position can do to ensure that the outlined goals are achieved. When explaining why something is needed, writers of position papers include research-based evidence to support the viewpoints.

Resolutions usually contain a statement of concern, preceding statements of action. Resolutions also may contain research-based evidence, although this is not always the case.

The information in either a position paper or a resolution must be accessible to your readership. This means that you do not want to use jargon (e.g., "educationese"). Use terms that the general public will understand, and make each point clearly, perhaps using major headings for each of the key sections and bullet points within each section so your specific recommendations and supporting research are identifiable.

Writing position papers and resolutions has advantages for your organization or advocacy group. By talking through the targeted issue and determining what outcomes you would like to see, you will find where your group members agree and where they do not. It may be that some group members have made incorrect assumptions about how other members feel about certain issues. The opportunity to discuss these concerns can yield positive results. Discussion will allow you to find areas of agreement, and these should become your talking points when you meet with policymakers. This way, no matter who is representing your group, the points will be the same. However, if group members' individual ideas also are expressed during meetings with policymakers, the group's representative should be certain to identify them as such and not leave the policymakers with the impression that these ideas are the group's.

Position papers and resolutions become useful conversation starters for meetings with policymakers. They also are a good way to introduce your organization to others, such as to members of a newly elected state legislature or state board of education. If you strategically distribute the papers, they also may attract new members into your organization.

As you begin to plan for your position paper or resolution, clearly identify the issue. It should be something that has attracted considerable public interest, such as issues surrounding teacher certification, assessment, or special education. Next, you should find others in your group or organization who want to work on the advocacy issue with you and encourage them to learn everything they can about the issue, especially the basic arguments used for the various positions one might take on the topic. Group members not only should look for evidence to support your organization's viewpoint but also must be familiar with opposing views in order to refute these when the resolution or position paper is shared with others.

Once you start writing, be sure to consider your intended audience of policymakers. Also, as with writing for the newspaper, keep it short and simple. Briefly make the case, and then make a reasonable request. Be accurate and include sources of information for any research you have cited. Before completing the position paper or resolution, consult with noneducation stakeholders such as parents or members of the business community; you might share a draft with them and obtain their input. Proofread your writing carefully and then print copies for your board to review. Find a printer who is willing to work with you on the layout of your position paper or resolution. You may also want to add appropriate clip art that will make the publication's message immediately evident to readers.

In the vignette that follows, Allen Berger describes the process of drafting a resolution from start to finish. As you read it, think about how the process worked with this organization and how it compares to the suggestions we have made in this chapter for writing resolutions.

Drafting a Resolution: One Organization's Story

Allen Berger

Heckert Professor of Reading and Writing, Miami University, Oxford, Ohio, USA

After serving as a member of the Resolutions Committee of the National Council of Teachers of English, I was invited to chair the five-person committee one year. The work of the Resolutions Committee is considered so important that committee members arrive, expenses paid, a few days before the official start of the organization's annual convention to examine the resolutions submitted. While the committee reworks submitted resolutions, an employee of NCTE is in the room word-processing the committee's work in process so everything moves along smoothly.

During the meeting, individual NCTE members stopped in to drop off more resolutions. We on the committee lived the writing process: We did a lot of prewriting and thinking, we did a lot of writing, and we did a lot of revising.

Much of the revising came about all day Thursday and Friday morning. Hundreds of copies of the final drafts of the resolutions that we had put together were made available at large evening meetings on Thursday. Attendees of the meetings could pick up drafts of the resolutions to read carefully. Those attendees who had strong feelings about the resolutions had the opportunity to meet with our committee on Friday morning.

Around noon on Friday, we had a short time to put the finishing touches on all the resolutions because hundreds of the final versions had to be copied before the board of directors meeting that afternoon.

An interesting thing about the whole process is how attached each committee member became to the resolutions. It's understandable, of course: We all worked extremely hard for three days on the phrasing of each resolution. When I realized how strong the feelings were of the committee members with regard to the resolutions, I shared my thoughts with them about the process.

Essentially, what I said was that once the resolutions are out of our hands, they are totally out of our control. I likened it to having a child: We nourished these resolutions, we did the best we could, and now they were going out into the world—at least the world of NCTE members attending the meeting that afternoon.

The meeting was set up for approximately 600 people to attend in the ballroom of a hotel. The meeting agenda was the same as in previous years: There was a laundry list of items, near the bottom of which were the resolutions. The five of us on the Resolutions Committee had crystallized everything into three resolutions, and I had asked three different committee members to present one resolution each to the assembled audience.

What was interesting to me at this point was the fact that it's hard to gauge which resolutions will pass with little or no discussion, and which will cause controversy. I had thought that there would be little discussion on any of our three resolutions that year. The first one, "On Continued Government Intrusion Into Professional Decision Making" passed with ease. The second one, "On Testing and Equitable Treatment of Students," also passed handily. It was the third one, "On Certification for All Teachers," that provoked much discussion, drawing many people to the floor microphones to express their views for or against the resolution with suggested modifications. It seemed that in some locales the original wording would have undercut English teachers by loosening the requirements for paraprofessionals to work in English classrooms.

Eventually, all three resolutions were approved by the membership, and NCTE now has these resolutions, among others, to send to state and federal education agencies, professional education associations, teachers' unions, the media, parent groups, and other appropriate organizations.

FOR YOUR CONSIDERATION

• What did the author foresee, and what surprises were there, as he chaired the resolutions committee?

- How did the process used for writing this resolution compare to the suggestions made in this chapter? Read the resolution in Appendix A (see page 251). What guidelines that we have suggested does it follow?

- If you were going to write a resolution, what would you do to begin the process and see it through to its conclusion?

In Appendix A, pages 251–255, you will find an example resolution from NCTE and an example position paper that was developed collaboratively by the New Jersey Reading Association, the New Jersey Association for the Education of Young Children, and the New Jersey Association of Kindergarten Educators.

Themed Journals

If you are advocating for a professional organization, it may wish to have a themed issue of its journal on a topic of critical importance. These themed issues can make an impact because they focus the readers' attention on specific areas or problems that need their concern and attention.

First, get the advocacy concern clear in your mind. As an education advocate, you can explore the topic with the publication editor and your organization's board of directors. If they like the idea, you might be invited to guest-edit the journal issue. Editing the issue would take some effort, but it would give you the opportunity to network with individuals who share common concerns, and they would appreciate your interest in their work.

Next, either you or the journal's editor should identify appropriate authors and invite them to write articles for the journal. Consider inviting people with varying views so you will have a balanced perspective within the journal issue. Remember, also to try to have a balance of genders and geographic areas represented by the invited authors. When you contact the authors, be specific about the topic, and let the authors know that you are willing to accept a shorter piece if they cannot provide a full article. Be very clear about the format, style, and length of the articles you want. If you want authors to use a particular style manual, inform them at the outset. Invite more individuals than your themed issue will be able to publish because some will be unable to accept your offer. In cases where you know someone's specialization, be sure to indicate if this is the topic on which you would like him or her to write.

When you have an issue you are proud of, print sufficient copies to send for free to political leaders and educators in key positions. Also, send complimentary copies to newspaper editors and others in the media.

In 2001, one state's reading association developed a themed journal issue on advocacy. The editor of the journal invited the chair of the association's legislation committee to be guest editor. She contacted individuals from around the United States whom she knew had been ardent advocates and successfully produced a journal issue that had wide appeal. It was sent to state legislators and members of the state board of education and is still distributed at professional meetings because the topic remains timely.

E-mails, Letters, and Postcards

Many professional education associations encourage their members to write to their legislators, asking them to vote for or against some piece of legislation or to consider initiating new legislation to meet a specific need. You can use letters, postcards, or e-mails for this purpose.

If you decide to write a letter, there are some basic guidelines to follow that will leave a good impression with the legislator who receives it (see Figure 10). The vignette below describes one advocate's results from sending a letter to her local board of education.

Challenging a Public Initiative

Anita Hernandez
Assistant Professor, California Polytechnic State University, San Luis Obispo, California, USA

In California in 1998, an initiative with the misleading name of English for the Children—Proposition 227 was placed on the ballot. The proposition called for second-language learners, most of whom were Hispanic, to be enrolled in a structured English-language immersion program for nine months and then placed in a mainstream English classroom, even if they needed additional English-language assistance. The underlying agenda of the proposition's authors was to limit, or even eliminate, bilingual education programs for immigrant children in public schools.

Figure 10. Guidelines for Letter Writing

- Put the date above the inside address. Then skip four lines before beginning the address.

- Be sure your letter is addressed correctly. This refers to both the address and the opening that you use. The conventions for addressing the envelope and inside address for local and state officials is as follows:

Local officials

"The Honorable" (Mayor's full name) / "Dear Mayor (last name)"

"Councilman/Councilor (full name) / "Dear Mr./Mrs./Ms. (last name)"

State officials

"The Honorable (full name) / "Dear Governor/Senator/Representative (last name)"

When writing to the chair of a committee or the Speaker of the House, it is proper to address him or her as Dear Mr. Chairman or Madam Chairwoman, or Dear Mr. Speaker.

- Put the topic of the letter beneath the address as RE: _____ (topic). If you are writing about a specific piece of legislation, identify it accordingly. For example, if it is a House Bill, write H.R._____. If it is a Senate Bill, write S.B.____.

- Keep your letter to a single page that contains only the essential ideas. Your key points should be easily identifiable and specific (e.g., "I support ____ because"), and you should give two or three reasons for them.

- Write (or type) legibly, grammatically, and with correct spelling and punctuation.

- Be polite and to the point. Avoid explosive expressions such as "I'm outraged," or "Your idea is ludicrous."

- Explain your background and that of your group, if you are writing on behalf of an organization. What makes you qualified to write about this issue?

- Provide evidence for your opinions. Policymakers are seeking reasoned arguments that they can use to help them make their points when they argue for or against a policy.

- Be sure to include a way for the legislator to respond to you. Include your name and address on the letter, along with your legislative district (state or federal) when contacting a legislator. If you are in the legislator's voting district, what you say will carry more weight.

- Use a formal closing such as "Respectfully," or "Yours truly."

- Sign your letter. Beneath your signature, type your name and position.

This proposition incensed many advocates for immigrant children, including this writer, because we believed at the time, and still believe, that bilingual education allows second-language learners to acquire a high level of English, which is needed to succeed academically. Two of the ways that I opposed the proposition were by joining an advocacy group in Palo Alto, California, USA, and writing letters to public officials, asking for their support of bilingual education. In particular, I wrote to the Palo Alto school board members, asking them to oppose Proposition 227, and I received positive letters from several members of the board.

In the end, the board as a whole passed a resolution opposing the proposition, which aligned the Palo Alto school district with more than 200 other school districts in the state of California. The Palo Alto school board's resolution had more than symbolic importance because one of the two principal authors of the proposition owned a business in the city. Unfortunately, however, the proposition passed statewide by a margin of 60% to 40%.

Since the proposal's implementation, a number of research scholars (e.g., Patricia Gardara, Eugene Garcia, Kenji Hakuta, and Russell Rumberger) have continued to study the academic achievement of second-language learners. Many teachers and university professors, including myself, continue to read the studies (see, for example, www.lmri.ucsb.edu) that discuss second-language learners' academic achievements in structured English-language-immersion and mainstream classrooms.

FOR YOUR CONSIDERATION

- What might this vignette writer have included in her letter to the Palo Alto school board that influenced the school board members' decision to pass the resolution opposing the proposition?

- The author says that the "resolution had more than symbolic importance" and gives as a reason that "one of the two principal authors of the proposition owned a business in the city." Why did this give the resolution more than symbolic importance? What is an issue that concerns you that might spark interest in your business community?

- How might you use information from the website Hernandez cites to help you in advocating for second-language learners in your community?

- Although this advocacy group was influential in shaping the Palo Alto school board's opinions on the second-language issue, the public was not as easily influenced. What strategies suggested in this and earlier chapters might this advocacy group try the next time they wish to influence a large number of voters? What other strategies can you think of that might also work?

When policymakers receive correspondence from large numbers of their constituents, expressing the same viewpoint on an issue, it often can swing the vote. To make the job of writing to your legislator easier, associations often provide a letter template. However, legislators easily recognize these form letters, which are not as impressive as mail that has been individually crafted. As a result, postcards and e-mails also can be effective advocacy tools. For writing either a postcard or e-mail, use guidelines similar to those for writing letters. Note, however, that not all legislators will respond to your e-mail messages personally. If you send an e-mail message to President George W. Bush at president@ whitehouse.gov, for instance, you will get an immediate reply that says the president will not be able to respond personally to all messages. Further, you will learn that the White House has "developed White House Web Mail, an automated e-mail response system" where you can submit comments on a specific issue.

One other way to get your message noticed should not be overlooked. If you are mailing something, choose your postage stamps carefully. Postage stamps convey messages, so if you know the person to whom you are writing has a favorite issue or is strongly opposed to one, take this into consideration when choosing your stamps.

In the following vignette, read how one education advocate is using letters and e-mails to further her advocacy efforts.

The Power of Letters and E-Mails

Eileen Diamond
4-Blocks Literacy Coach, Cincinnati Public Schools, Cincinnati, Ohio, USA

I encourage my urban middle school students to voice their opinions. The students write letters to the editor of their local newspaper or to their state or national representatives. It is helpful for the students to research a topic, gather facts, write their messages, and then have someone respond to their concerns in a thoughtful manner. The newspaper publishes excerpts from their letters, and students are amazed when readers respond to their thoughts. This activity allows students to understand how powerful words can be.

On the other hand, as a teacher, I felt frustrated by the lack of information on education issues that was provided to me by my teachers' union, my professional organizations, and by the media. Although my students and I are often affected directly by these laws, I am not consulted when they are under consideration. I reflected on this problem with several school district colleagues, and we decided to do something about our dilemma.

We started communicating via e-mail with our state legislators so they could keep us informed about education issues. Even though we have not yet heard from our legislators, I feel more empowered because I am voicing my opinion. I am hopeful that the lines of communication will continue to grow. Perhaps my ideas will be listened to in the future.

FOR YOUR CONSIDERATION

• What frustrations does this author share with district colleagues? What does she do about these frustrations?

• The author refers to a lack of information provided to her by her teachers' union, professional organizations, and the media. How much information do these groups provide to you about your educational concerns?

• How might you involve your students in advocating for their own areas of concern?

Other Types of Printed Messages for Advocacy

Printed messages advocating for specific ideas can be found nearly everywhere: billboards, T-shirts, mugs, keychains, and even store receipts. Think about the many ways print has been used to inform you about the views of groups or individuals.

We have already had one story from Richard Meyer who distributed colored fliers to disseminate ideas about the National Reading Panel report. The following is another story that further illustrates his creative talent as an education advocate.

Using T-Shirts to Send an Antitesting Message

Richard J. Meyer

Associate Professor, University of New Mexico, Albuquerque, New Mexico, USA

Every year our city and state succumbs to March Madness—not the madness about basketball, but the one about standardized testing. Local newspapers remind the citizens of just how poorly the students in certain schools continue to perform on these tests. Each year teachers and parents write to the newspaper, protesting the overemphasis on testing and explaining why a standardized test is not a good way to demonstrate what children know. Each year the protests of these writers are ignored as families are reminded that their children should eat well and get to bed early the night before each test. My friends and I tease each other about never sending our children to bed at a reasonable hour except during March Madness. During March Madness we are also sure to give our children wholesome breakfasts.

Driving home from the university, having read recent e-mails from colleagues around the country, an idea struck. The next morning I went to the local T-shirt printing business and paid $400 to have 50 T-shirts printed. On the front they read, "Raise a child, not a test score." On the back was a red circle with a line through it and in the circle were the words: "High Stakes Testing."

I used savings to pay for the shirts. I sold them at cost, and in two weeks they were gone. When I wore mine, people stopped me in stores to talk. Most wanted to buy one. One teacher said she was told she could not wear her shirt to school, but a call I placed to the person who was then president of the Albuquerque Teachers Federation reaffirmed her First Amendment rights and she wore it once a week for the remainder of the school year.

The T-shirt helps teachers know they are not alone and reminds families that their children are not just numbers.

FOR YOUR CONSIDERATION

• Was the strategy used in this vignette successful? Explain your reasoning.

• Throughout this text there have been several vignettes from advocates concerned about high-stakes assessment. How would you determine that the advocacy strategies they implemented were successful? Which of the strategies these advocates used seemed to have the greatest success? Which of their strategies might work for you if you had similar concerns?

• What other types of material could you use to print an advocacy message? What would your message be on each type of material you would use?

Conclusion

In this chapter, we have offered many ideas for reaching the public through print, along with pointers for using each medium effectively. We have shared these many examples with you because we believe that for your advocacy efforts to have impact you must use different approaches for different audiences. In chapter 6, we carry this theme further, moving beyond the use of various print media to the use of multimedia, especially radio and television. In addition, we show the importance of personal meetings and telephone calls to policymakers and discuss how to best conduct these. Because advocacy work often involves giving testimony before important committees, we also share our insights on how to testify effectively.

CHAPTER 6

Multimedia and In-Person
Advocacy Strategies

In the previous chapter, we offered suggestions for getting your message into print through newsletters, newspapers, position papers, resolutions, and so forth. This chapter offers audio, visual, electronic, and in-person advocacy strategies you might use for disseminating information and ideas. Here you'll find suggestions for using radio and television for your advocacy messages, including use of public service announcements, underwriting, commentaries, newscasts and interviews, and talk show appearances. Perhaps you will also consider creating videotapes, DVDs, and CD-ROMs. We'll give you some helpful pointers. Because the Internet is so widely accessible, we'll also suggest strategies for using it to disseminate advocacy messages.

Much of the chapter will focus on specific strategies for influencing policy. We'll present techniques for effective phone calls, office visits, and writing and presenting testimony for individual policymakers, and members of legislative committees. We'll suggest the value of forming Legislative Action Teams for uniting advocacy efforts and the usefulness of events such as policymakers' breakfasts for getting your messages to the people who can influence policy. Finally, we'll try to entice you to run for political office—an advocacy adventure you may not yet have considered! Some of the methods may already be familiar to you, and others you might not have considered yet. As the vignettes in this chapter illustrate, education advocates have been successful with many of these strategies. As you read through this chapter, think about which ones might best serve your purposes.

Creating Public Service Announcements
to Convey Strong Messages

Lucille Davy (2003), an attorney and certified math teacher who has worked on education policy for the governor's office in New Jersey, reminds us that advocacy often requires educating the public and raising awareness. She suggests that one of the most effective ways to reach a large number of people, to influence opinions, or to engage people in behavioral changes is the use of public service announcements (PSAs). This section offers Davy's advice on how to design PSAs that convey strong messages and how you might get them aired.

Broadcast networks, cable television stations, and radio stations air PSAs on a regular basis. Sometimes they are aired without cost; in other cases, there is a charge for air time. PSAs can impart powerful visual and/or auditory messages to an intended audience. Two recent examples immediately come to mind. One is an anti-drug PSA that shows an egg frying in a cast iron skillet as a symbol of a person's brain on drugs. The other is a series of PSAs featuring aging and out-of-shape adults participating with great difficulty in high school activities such as gym class, competitive basketball, and cheerleading. The message of those PSAs? Stay in school. Don't drop out because it is hard to return at a later time. In both these examples, the images are quickly implanted into the audience members' minds and are difficult to forget. In addition, the PSAs' repeated airings with widespread audience exposure may help to ensure the desired result, keeping kids off drugs and urging potential dropouts to stay in school. Davy's suggestions for creating effective PSAs are as follows: determine the message and audience, use media consultants, plan the content, and choose a method of delivery.

Determining the Message and Audience

Before you begin to create your PSA, it is important to determine both the message you seek to convey and the specific audience you want to reach with it. These determinations may sound easy, but they require careful consideration because they will have an impact on the effectiveness of the PSA. You should listen carefully to several television and radio PSAs and note their lengths. Listening to and viewing other peoples' PSAs will provide you with a better understanding of how the message needs to be simple and how the contents can be shaped to reach a specific audience.

Keep your PSA's message simple and short. Most PSAs are 15, 30, or 60 seconds long. These timeframes are much shorter than you may think. However, because you want your message to be remembered by the viewer or listener, it must be brief and easily understood within the specified timeframe.

You also must decide exactly what group you are targeting. It could be all viewers and listeners of the television or radio station that will broadcast your

PSA, but more likely you will have a specific subgroup in mind, such as parents, mothers, working adults, or the business community. The intended audience will influence the content of the PSA. Airtime costs will vary depending on the television or radio station and the time of day. Further, larger audiences mean higher broadcast charges, so it is important to choose the radio or television station that (a) provides the greatest number of listeners in your desired audience group and (b) is within your budget to maximize the opportunity to reach your desired audience.

Using Media Consultants

If your budget permits, hire outside media consultants to create and produce the PSA. Media consultants will provide you with information about your intended audience and the message you seek to convey, and with concepts for your review and approval. Once you have settled on a concept, they will prepare the PSA using professional speakers or actors. You will have an opportunity to review and approve the finished product and to make changes if you are not satisfied. Media consultants also will help determine which radio and/or television stations you should choose for airing your message, based on your intended audience as well as the broadcasting costs.

The costs of hiring media consultants will vary depending on the complexity of your PSA and the time required to create it. The decision as to whether you want to invest in professional expertise is one that you should make on a case-by-case basis. Where the spot will be aired and your budgetary constraints will likely affect this determination.

Regardless of whether you hire media consultants, you probably will need some professional assistance to tape, mix, and edit the PSA, unless you can prevail upon local professionals or friends to donate their services. You also might consider engaging the assistance of local high school or community college students who may be enrolled in radio and television production courses, and who may be willing to assist you as a community service.

Planning the Content

It is important to provide a reason for your advocacy in order to persuade your viewers and/or listeners. Therefore, it will be helpful to do some research and data collection regarding the content of your PSA. For example, in the case of early literacy, there is much research and ample statistical information available to support the claim that reading to young children is important. If the PSA seeks to persuade parents to read to their young children, it is important to tell them why and how taking that action will positively affect their children's development.

Whether or not you use media consultants, the PSA's content is extremely important. Common sense should govern, so ask yourself, Is the message appealing? Is it clear and easily understood? Does the viewer or listener know what I am asking him or her to do? Will the PSA have an impact on the viewer or listener? The best way to know if your message is effective is to have several people review it and provide feedback. Of course, these must be people who will be honest and provide constructive criticism if necessary.

The most common pitfall to avoid is a message that is too broad or overreaching, or one that simply contains too much content. One of the best ways to learn how to craft a message is to listen to and view other PSAs and consider which ones have had the most impact on you and why you think they were effective.

Deciding How the Message Is Delivered

Your PSA's delivery can be as simple as a single speaker making an announcement or delivering the text. This is probably the least expensive production, but it may not be as effective as incorporating multiple speakers and using appropriate background music. For instance, you might consider including soundbites from classroom lessons or discussion with students, teachers, parents, or administrators to add rich context to your advocacy message. From time to time, including excerpts from a policymaker who supports your views might be useful as well.

You also should consider providing your message in multiple ways to broaden its reach and to reinforce the message you are trying to convey. For example, if you wanted to develop PSAs on dropout prevention, one message might focus on the impact of dropouts on families. Another message might feature the impact of dropouts on the available workforce. A third message might present the possible impact of dropouts on larger social problems, including health care and crime.

Few of us education advocates have Davy's experience with developing a strong PSA from start to finish. Her expertise and guidance can help us enormously. In the remaining sections of this chapter, we offer several other ideas for using radio and television effectively for advocacy and for working more closely with policymakers.

Using Public Radio to Convey Your Advocacy Message

The five most common ways to get your message on public radio are (1) commentaries, (2) PSAs, (3) underwriting, (4) news and interviews, and (5) talk shows. As you consider these alternatives, think of the big picture. What is your overall marketing plan for your ideas? Select the way or ways to present your message that are best for your group or organization.

Commentary

Radio stations tend to have a group of commentators who express opinions in ways that provoke thought and reflection. Find out the rules for presenting commentary by calling your public radio station. Generally, commentaries run between two and three minutes in length. They have a distinct viewpoint, are interesting and entertaining, and meet reasonable standards of fairness. Sometimes they are repeated throughout the day on a radio station; at other times, they are played only once, on one program.

PSAs for Events

PSAs also can be used to announce an event such as a performance, lecture, or conference. In these cases, prepare a PSA that includes the name of your organization, the title of your event, a brief description of it (which may also appear on the radio station's website), contact name and information, dates and times, and ticket prices, if applicable. If there are any hard-to-pronounce names, be sure to spell them phonetically because radio station personnel will be delivering the PSAs and may need assistance in announcing the names correctly.

Find out if the radio station prefers to receive PSAs that announce events by letter, e-mail, fax, or website form. Also, ask how far in advance the station needs to receive your PSA. Most radio stations want them at least two weeks ahead of the event.

The competition to get this type of PSA on the air is enormous. Most radio stations receive hundreds of them each week. Your PSA must stand out for its clearness and crispness. A good format is to have a column on the left-hand side of a sheet with the words *who, what, where, when,* and *why,* with the explanations of each of these words in a second column on the right-hand side of the sheet. In addition, include a copy of the PSA written in the continuous text form that the reader will use for delivering the message.

Underwriting

Getting your message on radio via commentaries or PSAs is free; underwriting costs money. However, the cost may not be as much as you expect, so call your local radio station and find out what it charges. When you underwrite, your financial support is frequently mentioned on the station. Your message is value neutral with a simple mention of your group's name, location, phone number, and Internet address. Although you will not have the opportunity to express your organization's views, public perceptions of your organization and its concerns may be enhanced as the public repeatedly hears your organization's name and becomes more aware of your organization's commitment to the community.

News and Interviews

News and interviews provide the content for most public radio programs. News, of course, is the factual reporting of events or trends that affect or interest listeners. A good news story would include one or more elements such as focus, impact, proximity, quirkiness, timeliness, and ease of understanding.

If you can detect or reveal a trend, new development, or story behind a story, contact your local radio station. Send a news release that is clearly marked to distinguish what you are sending from a PSA. Make your main point prominent in the first sentence of your release. If you have "spot news" to share, that is, news that is extremely timely, phone the radio station immediately. Follow up with a second phone call or e-mail if you do not get on the news with your first attempt at contacting the station.

Whether you are focusing on news or interviews, remember that it is vital to be honest and available. Provide the radio station with your phone number so you can provide additional information promptly if you are asked.

Talk Shows

Most public radio stations have talk shows. The guests for these shows are usually lined up at least a month ahead of each broadcast. Let your radio station know your availability or the availability of someone else from your organization who has the credentials and reputation to speak publicly for your organization. That person should also have strong opinions, a sense of humor, intelligent insights, and responses to many questions and issues.

As you think about these ways to share your message through your public radio station, consider these statistics. Public radio stations tend to have fewer total listeners than commercial radio, but they have more listeners who have earned advanced degrees and have higher incomes than the general populace. Their listeners also tend to be quite active and influential, with a major interest in schools, education, and their communities.

In the vignette below, one advocate shares his experience using radio to make his message public.

Using Radio to Make a Message Public

Michael P. Ford

Advocacy Liaison, Wisconsin State Reading Association, Wisconsin, USA

One morning I discovered a fairly short article about education in my local paper. However, despite its brevity, in its four short paragraphs the article managed to question the reading achievement of Wisconsin students, the techniques of their teachers, and the decisions of their administrators, while simultaneously advocating for a single, cost-effective alternative. Within 24 hours, I was also listening to local talk radio hosts embracing the reported results, with one of the article's authors given an hour on Wisconsin Public Radio (WPR).

As the Advocacy Liaison for the Wisconsin State Reading Association (WSRA), it was easy for me to realize that what I was encountering were press releases from a local conservative think tank based on a non–peer-reviewed study commissioned from like-minded researchers. For most others, however, the released information would seem credible. These releases often get shared with local educators, becoming catalysts for discussions related to policy and pedagogy.

Knowing the potential impact of this so-called study and its spin from the think tank, WSRA put in place a recently developed organizational response process. After obtaining the original document and critically analyzing it, we secured an hour forum on WPR to question the study's findings. We prepared and made available to WSRA members a background paper on the study, a set of blackline masters addressing the political and profit-driven motives of the think tank, the credentials of the study authors, the content of the study, a bibliography of additional resources that could be consulted, and a two-page talking points paper that members could use as a handout or guide in discussing the study with constituency groups (accessible at www.wsra.org/fordDirectInstruction.html). We wanted this think tank to realize that WSRA will mobilize its resources to critically examine any position they or other similar groups take denying teacher voice and choice in reading practices in Wisconsin.

FOR YOUR CONSIDERATION

• The author makes a distinction between his own reactions and those of other readers. Is his comparison valid? Explain your reasoning.

• What strategies not mentioned in this chapter were used by the author and WSRA? How effective do these strategies seem to be? How do you know?

• Use the Internet to find out what WSRA is currently doing to advocate for public education. What strategies do you find particularly interesting and effective?

Appearing on Television Talk Shows

One way to go public with your ideas for education is to appear on a local television station's talk show. Should you be working on a special project or directing a grant-funded program that reflects your thinking about education, the station may well be interested in having you on as a guest. The television station might reach out to you directly, especially if your project has received some newspaper coverage. If this does not occur and you work for a university or a larger school district, you can talk to your office of communications or media relations department. Let the staff there know that you want and are available to appear on television. Many such offices keep a list of people who are ready, willing, and able to be available for such appearances at a moment's notice. If you don't work for a university or a school district with such a department, call or visit a local television station and make the same offer.

When invited to appear on the talk show, remember that you are not making a speech. You may have certain ideas you want to get across: Try to do so in response to the moderator's or host's questions. If you are asked a question, respond briefly so the show can keep moving. If there is a slow spot, use it to get a certain point across. But remember, you are not there to proselytize or propagandize. You are there to convey honest information. If you are not appearing to do so, you may not be invited back for future appearances.

If your organization is invited to appear on television, pick your most articulate speaker to be your representative. Specifically, you want someone who combines the talents of a sales person, an entertainer, an informer, and a storyteller. Ahead of time, provide the television station with a one-page background sheet of information about your organization, along with some suggested questions. The person who is invited should practice the most important thing to say and how to say it most effectively. Your speaker should be able to anticipate questions and practice answering them, making sure to include the name of the organization, its purpose, and the reasons for being on the program.

Using the Internet to Disseminate Your Ideas

As you plan your advocacy efforts, consider Internet resources you might use. A large percentage of world homes now have Internet capability. Recent surveys of how many people are online worldwide estimated that as of September 2002, a total of 605.60 million people had online capability. In Canada and the United States, there were 182.67 million Internet users. In Europe, the number reached 190.91 million, while in Asia and the Pacific the number was 187.24 million. The remainder of Internet users—44.78 million people—are located in the Middle East, Africa, and Latin America (Nua, 2003). In many of these homes, the Internet might be the preferred tool for receiving information, and print resources might receive less attention than those delivered online.

Websites have become familiar tools for education advocates who want to both receive and send information. You have a number of possibilities to take advantage of these advocacy tools—school, personal, school district, community, and organization websites. Using these tools will help you disseminate information. If you include as part of each advocacy message a call for like-minded individuals to contact you, you also may find others with whom you share interests and concerns, and who might be interested in forming coalitions. Your Web message might be the start for organizing others around your issue.

Using Websites

SCHOOL WEBSITES. Begin with your school. Does it have its own website? If so, contact the administrator and the webmaster, and find out if you might submit information for consideration. Ask in what form the materials need to be submitted. You may need to work closely with your webmaster or with other teachers to get your materials in a suitable format for uploading to the website. Do not be discouraged if you do not have the skills to do this yourself.

PERSONAL WEBPAGES. Many teachers create individual webpages that are linked to the school's website. These webpages become important tools for parent-teacher communication and for displaying student work. With your administrator's permission, you might use part of your personal webpage to disseminate information to your students' parents and to advocate for your education issues. You also may lay the groundwork for later advocacy efforts. Posting your students' writing, for example, will help parents see the value of specific curricular activities and strategies. At a later time, when program cuts suggest the need to diminish resources or to eliminate materials, parents who have seen the quality of your students' work might be your program's strongest and most vocal supporters.

SCHOOL DISTRICT WEBSITES. Your school district probably has a website, too. Just as you would contact the school district's office of communications to see if you could put any of your ideas into newsletters or other print matter, you could make an appointment with the school district's webmaster. If school district policy allows your contributions, work with the webmaster to get your information into the appropriate format so it can be considered for posting on the website.

COMMUNITY WEBSITES. There also may be many community websites to which you can link your information. Go online to locate local neighborhood associations that have websites through which they communicate with their members. See if there is a specific webmaster listed on a given association's homepage. Contact that individual or the association office to find out if you can supply the association with information or link your own website or the website of the organization you represent to the association's website.

Earlier, we suggested that you contact dentists, pediatricians, realtors, and elected officials to see if you could publish information in the newsletters they send to their patients, clients, and constituents. Determine whether these individuals have websites. Study each website to see if there would be a place where you can include the information you want to share. If there is, contact each person individually and ask if he or she would be open to your contributing information that could be posted on the website. Then, work with each person to get your information posted online.

ORGANIZATION WEBSITES. Just as you previously think about writing for the newsletters of organizations to which you belong, think about submitting information to their websites. Contact each organization's webmaster or president to investigate the possibilities. If your advocacy concern is one that will affect many of the organization's members, the likelihood is higher for your material to be accepted and posted online than if your issue is narrowly focused.

If you or your organization already have a website, you could ask other organizations that share similar concerns and have their own websites if you can link your website to theirs. Then, interested individuals could be connected quickly.

The potential for reaching a large audience will be enhanced when individuals learn that your website or the website of your organization can be a helpful source of information, one they will want to bookmark and access on a recurring basis. If your website has a "Contact Us" capability, visitors can send e-mails with comments, questions, or concerns. Finding like-minded individuals may help you begin the process of coalition building.

LISTSERVS AND CHAT ROOMS. You may want to participate in education-related listservs and chat rooms; both are forums that provide opportunities for you to express your opinions and disseminate information to other educators. Many professional organizations have set up websites for these forms of teacher communication. Usually, you need to be an organization member to participate in them. Several educational publishers who publish materials for the K–12 school market also have allocated portions of their websites for listservs and chat rooms. On these sites, enrollment is usually open to anybody who is interested. You may need to sign on with some sort of identifying password or code to participate, but information for signing up for the listserv or chat room is usually available at the website.

Once you are officially signed onto a listserv, you will receive all the messages that are disseminated to the list's members. On most listservs, you can choose to respond to individual messages or to the group as a whole. Some lists offer the option of receiving messages in a daily digest format instead of one by one. If your list is an active one, you may want to use the digest format because otherwise you may receive 50 or more individual messages a day.

When you log into a chat room you usually find yourself participating in a more focused discussion than you would find on a listserv where concerns or comments may range over many issues. Often, organizations will designate certain times when a chat room will be devoted to a specific topic and publish the topics and the date and times for discussion in advance. They may also send reminders to all registered individuals, inviting them to join the conversation at the specified time. A chat room may be devoted to a specific topic or to generic issues. Often, organizations will designate certain times when a chat room will be devoted to a specific topic or to generic issues. Frequently, the chat room will have a designated moderator who keeps the discussion going and monitors individuals' participation. This is especially true when the topic is designated, but monitors may be present at other times as well. The monitor's responsibility includes keeping the discussion focused on the assigned topic or topics. This may include redirecting responses if a participant seems to be introducing information that is not pertinent to the discussion or if a participant uses inappropriate language or examples. In an open chat room, where there may be less frequent monitoring, the conversations are much more free flowing. Participants respond freely to the comments or questions of others, there may be several concurrent threads of discussion, and individuals may switch back and forth between threads.

In addition to their value as forums for information dissemination, listservs and chat rooms may be excellent places to identify individuals who might want to assist you with your advocacy issues.

Creating a Website

Now that you have seen how much information is available on the Internet for researching issues and learning about other viewpoints, if you or your organization does not yet have a website, you might consider designing a website as one of your advocacy goals. Your website could be an important vehicle for keeping members of your organization informed about progress in your advocacy efforts. It is also a way to disseminate huge amounts of information to very large audiences, especially if your website is designed so that it is easily navigated and information can be found readily.

Many individuals have the technical expertise to put up a website for you. If you have access to someone with such talents, or if you have sufficient funds for someone to maintain the site for you, consider creating a website. You could post information about your organization, such as its mission statement; officers; organizational structure, including committees; meeting information; contact information; conferences; membership benefits; and how to join. For advocacy purposes, you could include your organization's position on critical issues, position papers from the organization, written testimony from organization members, and talking points for education advocacy. You could also use your website for conducting surveys and polling your membership on issues.

Your website could inform your membership and other visitors of pending legislation and of advocacy success stories in your organization or state. You could include action alerts and samples of letters or e-mails that visitors might send to elected officials. You might have examples of information to use in testimony before legislative committees, state boards of education, textbook committees, and the like. If your website becomes a source for dependable and reliable information, you may well increase your organization's membership and, in turn, your capacity for advocacy.

You may want to look at a few examples of education organizations with strong advocacy components on their websites to give you useful suggestions for strengthening your organization's online advocacy approaches. See, for example, the advocacy portions of the Wisconsin State Reading Association website at www.wsra.org/advocacy.html, the Reading Recovery Council of North America website at www.readingrecovery.org/sections/home/advocacy.asp, the National Association for Secondary School Principals website at www.nassp.org, the Learning First Alliance's website at www.learningfirst.org/issues, or the National School Public Relations Association website at www.nspra.org.

If you are considering website development on a tight budget, you might want to look at website hosting opportunities and website building tools at http://geocities.yahoo.com or www.tripod.lycos.com. Both of these websites will give you valuable pointers and walk you through establishing a website for your personal use or for your organization's use. Once you have your website established, see that it is listed on all the major search engines. To do this, contact each search engine to find out its policies for including your URL. For example, see www.google.com/addurl.html for how to list your URL in the Google search engine. Then, when people are searching the Internet for information, your website might come up in their search.

You will want your website to have links to like-minded associations, your state legislature, and the U.S. Congress. Having these links will provide your members with quick access to relevant and important information. To include these links, contact each website's webmaster. Usually that person's e-mail address can be found on the homepage. If there is a "Contact Us" capability, you may click on it and be connected directly to the organization or its leaders instead. Frequently, organizations also list specific e-mail addresses for organization officers whom you might contact. Request permission for reciprocal linking; you want your organization to be listed on their website and their organization to be listed on yours. If they agree with your request, you are ready to establish the appropriate links.

Should you decide that you want to learn how to create a website on your own and you do not currently have the skills, consider enrolling in a professional development course that will help you learn. Perhaps your school district publishes a professional development catalog of all the workshops and courses that are available to school district personnel. If the Information and Communications Technologies staff offers courses on website development, you might find that this hands-on approach helps you acquire the skills you will need to create effective websites and to link your website to those of other individuals and organizations. You also can check for courses at community colleges and technical high schools in your area that offer noncredit courses to the community.

Writing E-Mails to Organize Protests and Disseminate Information

A recent edition of the *Wall Street Journal Reports* column on technology (Carlton, 2003) notes the value of using organized e-mail messages to rapidly disseminate information and to plan active protests related to your advocacy cause. Carlton recommends a focused e-mail list as a way to target messages to specific individuals, coordinate information that is disseminated, and organize protests. He gives several noneducation advocacy examples to show that Internet communication helped galvanize support for an array of causes, including the release of jailed farm activists, a stop to logging of virgin forests in northern California, protests against military actions in the Middle East, and grass-roots coverage of the protests against the World Trade Organization meeting in Seattle, Washington, USA. For each organization he cites, e-mail messages were indispensable tools for coordination and outreach. Distilling information from several activists, he suggests the following guidelines for using focused e-mail for effective advocacy:

- E-mails need to be short and to the point.
- The subject line needs to clearly state the desired action—what you want readers to do.
- The e-mail should conclude with some sort of closure such as a slogan or a positive statement.

Carlton notes the importance of following up with phone calls to ensure that your messages have reached your desired audience. Because most people receive a great many e-mails each day, these phone calls may confirm the importance of your message.

Creating Videotapes, DVDs, and CD-ROMs

If your group has sufficient funding, another effective way of disseminating advocacy materials is by creating a videotape, DVD, or CD-ROM for distribution at meetings and conferences, or directly to policymakers through the mail.

If you are not adept with technology, perhaps a few of your students are. You also could talk to someone who teaches technology at your local school or college. If you are at an elementary school, your community's high school might have a video production class. Seek help from these sources, and involve other personnel from your school, too. Students and teachers who are active in music, drama, athletics, or creative writing are among those who might be able to help with various facets of such a project. Making this type of media involves the time and coordination of many talented people. Make a judgment as to whether or not you have the resources to pursue this avenue to reach policymakers.

If you are a more independent person, get access to a video camera and browse through the instructional booklet or visit www.videomaker.com. This website provides tips on shooting videos and recording audio. You also will find detailed information on preproduction, production, postproduction, business and distribution, and legal issues. In addition you can consult *Digital Video in the Classroom* for suggestions and examples. This online magazine is available through techLearning, The Resource for Education Technology Leaders, at www.techlearning.com/digitalvideo. The article "Meaningful Digital Video for Every Classroom" (see www.techlearning.com/story/showArticle.jhtml?articleID= 18700330) may give you ideas for your own videos, DVDs, and CD-ROMs.

If you choose to develop any or all of these three advocacy tools, you many find that your featured audio and visual messages are especially effective for showing instruction or assessment strategies or the application of specific curriculum materials and tools. Through videos, DVDs and CD-ROMs, you can bring policymakers into actual classrooms and schools. With these tools, they may see your concerns and perhaps, depending on the content of your messages, have a keener appreciation.

Making Phone Calls to Legislators

If you plan to call an elected official, follow guidelines similar to the ones in chapter 5 for writing letters. You might call ahead to schedule a time to speak directly to the legislator. Let the receptionist know whom you represent and why you are phoning. If it will be a week or more before you actually have the conversation with your legislator, you can send materials ahead of time that clarify who you are and the concerns you have. It is also perfectly reasonable to ask to speak with the legislative assistant for education if the legislator is not available.

Keep in mind a few general guidelines. First, you will want to time your call advantageously. This means you should have an idea of the legislator's meeting schedule as well as whether your issue is timely. If for any reason you plan to tape the conversation, you must let the other party know, so ask permission at the start of the conversation. Also at the beginning of the conversation, you should be sure to identify yourself, your organization, your issue, and your viewpoint. If you are phoning about a particular piece of legislation, you should identify it. If you are unfamiliar with the legislator's viewpoint, you should ask what it is. During the call, be brief and courteous. If the call is interrupted, wait patiently. Try to sound relaxed and positive. Remember that you are the authority on the subject and one of your reasons for phoning is to share what you know while making a persuasive argument for your viewpoint. Do not speak too fast, and be sure to use a professional tone of voice. Give your listener time to respond and also to ask questions. Offer to meet with him or her, to send information, or to find answers to questions you could not answer during the conversation. At the end of the call, be sure to thank your listener for providing information and listening to you. Provide your contact information, and reiterate your offer to send any materials relevant to your issue and discussion.

Presenting Your Case in Person to Local, State, and National Policymakers

Working with the media and using technology are, perhaps, the most effective means for getting your advocacy message to a wide audience. However, it will ultimately be the elected officials whom you will want to influence because they decide what bills to draft for consideration and what policies should be implemented. Obtaining the support of these influential individuals requires approaches beyond those of mass appeal that were discussed in the previous section of this chapter and in chapter 5. In fact, there is a saying that all politics is local, and, indeed, to influence policy at the legislative or state board level, you will need work face to face. These next sessions will show you a variety of ways to get in closer touch with your legislators. They include giving testimony at scheduled hearings, arranging policymakers' breakfasts, visiting elected officials and policymakers in their offices, and acting as part of a legislative action team. We also provide suggestions for holding rallies and marches. All of these strategies may help you get the attention of your legislators and other policymakers.

In-Person Strategies for Influencing Policy

GIVING TESTIMONY AT HEARINGS. Education advocates who routinely monitor the activities of their state legislature or their state or local boards of education will know that there are hearings at which you can testify to let these groups know your or your organization's viewpoint on an issue. Each body of policymakers has its own set of rules for how and when you can offer testimony. In the case of the state legislature, you would probably appear before the education committee of the state assembly or state senate. For most governing bodies, you will need to alert the group ahead of time that you would like to be included on the list of those giving testimony at a particular hearing. In some cases, this means calling at least a week before the scheduled hearing. In other cases, you can sign in on the day of the hearing, just before it starts.

There is usually a time limit on testimony, ranging from 2–5 minutes, with the board or committee members having time to ask questions afterward. Prior to your testimony, you will need to provide each member of the board or committee who will hear your testimony with a printed copy of it. Obviously, then, you will need to write your testimony in advance, and your appearance may be mentioned in the public record, depending on the procedures used by the particular group to whom you are presenting testimony.

As with every advocacy strategy discussed thus far, when you are writing testimony, it will be critical for you to have done your homework. This might include reviewing the literature, consulting with others, and knowing all about the organization you are representing. You also will want to be familiar with positions on the issue that differ from yours so you can refute their claims.

Your audience is expecting you to present a point of view that may differ from theirs. Prepare your argument logically with as much supporting data as time will allow. In addition to the statistical data that is increasingly being sought by policymakers, boards and committees sometimes enjoy hearing true stories that make your case real. If the story is memorable, it will help your cause.

In the example testimony in Appendix A, page 256, note that the advocate has followed some specific guidelines. She identifies herself and who she represents. Her language is very simple and she only makes a few points. These points are numbered for easy reference by both policymakers and the advocate during the question phase of her testimony. The speaker cites research and stays on the subject. She knows her time is limited, so she avoids including extraneous material.

Like this speaker, you also will want to know as much as possible about your audience as you can before you present. Who are they? What constituents do they represent? If possible, make reference to them during your testimony. If you can anticipate their objections ahead of time, such as costs associated with your proposal, address these criticisms in your testimony. Do not dismiss their importance.

Also, notice in the example testimony that at the beginning the speaker thanks the committee chair and members for giving her the opportunity to speak. You can thank them again at the end of your testimony if you have time, although this is not necessary.

Before you give testimony at the hearing, it is a good idea to share it with others for practice and feedback. If your practice audience is unclear on a point or raises good questions, make revisions to what you have written. When you practice, also be sure that you have stayed within the time limits set by the board or committee. If you have not, at the hearing they may stop you the second your time is up, even if you have not completed your testimony. In addition, make sure your tone is appropriate; it should not be negative or personal. Finally, double-check your written testimony for proper grammar and spelling. Such errors can leave a bad impression, even if your ideas are wonderful.

When you prepare copies of your written testimony for distribution, be certain to use good quality paper and ensure that the copies are neat. If you have supporting documentation that you would like to include with your testimony, check whether this is permissible before distributing it.

Before you deliver your testimony, you should become very familiar with its content. Even if someone else has written it for you, as in the example in Appendix A, you must know the material so you can answer questions and even rephrase some of the ideas during the question period.

On the day of the hearing, be sure you dress professionally, even if the meeting is in a casual location, on a weekend, or after work hours. If you are very familiar with your testimony, you might be more comfortable speaking it rather than reading it. Speak or read at a moderate pace and loud enough to be heard not only by the board or committee but also by others in the room.

Your responses to questions should be polite and reflect that you have sophisticated knowledge about the topic that extends even beyond your testimony. Your answer to each question should be brief but must address the question. If you do not have an answer, it is acceptable to say that you do not know but will research the inquiry and provide your findings to the board or committee in a timely way.

When you have completed your testimony, you should ask to have your comments and any supporting documents included in the record of the meeting. Others reading this record may be influenced by what you have said, even if they did not hear you speak.

There may be many individuals who have come to the same hearing, all planning to give testimony. Sessions may be long to accommodate everyone; in some instances the board or committee may be divided into several rooms, with testifiers being assigned to one of them. You may feel that this reduces the impact you are making, and you may be correct. However, remember that you are providing a written copy of your remarks to all board or committee members for their consideration.

Sometimes after a hearing, like-minded individuals will approach each other to form temporary support coalitions, a real benefit of participating in hearings. For this reason, you should not leave the hearing room until after all speakers have given their testimony.

There are opportunities to present testimony at local board of education meetings, city council meetings, and before other formal groups. Most board meetings include a time during which members of the community can share their concerns and ask their questions. The procedures and rules for participation in these meetings may vary slightly, but generally speaking the strategies to use will be similar to those already suggested. Read the vignette that follows to learn how one group of interested advocates used the meetings of their board of education to protest policies that they felt were inequitable in their school district.

Hollister Parents and Students for Educational Justice

Marian Cruz
Retired Teacher, Hollister, California, USA

Approximately two years ago a group of students, parents, and community members began meeting because of their concerns about the treatment of some students in our public schools. We called ourselves the Hollister Parents and Students for Educational Justice (HPSEJ).

It was brought to our attention that a female student with a 3.4 grade point average went to a school function and was stopped at the door because the chaperone suspected she had been drinking. The student admitted to having had one beer. Subsequently, the student was suspended from school. She was told that she would not be able to return for the remainder of the semester. This meant her chances for applying to colleges would be in jeopardy. Her mom, a single parent, discovered that the rules for suspension and time away from school were not consistent for all students. In some cases, if one student were well connected in the community, the student's punishment appeared less harsh.

Our group continued to hold meetings, and parents and students came forward with their specific issues. It was apparent that the school administration was not consistent and that special treatment was given to certain students. The HPSEJ made sure to get on the agenda of the high school board meetings, where the students and parents aired their concerns. Members of the board and many faculty members were not receptive to our group. In my opinion, they were hostile to those of us who spoke at the meetings.

We did not give up. The group continued to meet and to speak out about our concerns. Each time we attended a school board meeting, another parent or student told about another example of inconsistent treatment. During this time, the teachers' association was out talking to people they thought would be good replacements for members of the current school board. The HPSEJ got involved with the teachers and invited school board candidates to come to our meetings and respond to questions we had. Two of the three people we supported were ultimately elected to the school board. The current superintendent retired and a new superintendent was hired. The new superintendent has a totally different approach to managing the school district and has been well received by the community.

The HPSEJ believes we accomplished what we set out to do. The school board and administration have rewritten many of the rules for suspension and expulsion, there seems to be a more equitable treatment of students, the new board is more receptive to the concerns of the parents, and there appears to be a more open communication between the school and the public. It was a very time-consuming endeavor for the members of the HPSEJ, but we feel our efforts had a positive impact on how the parents and students are treated in our school district.

FOR YOUR CONSIDERATION

- What prompted the concerns of parents and teachers in this high school community?
- How did they mobilize their concerns toward a desired outcome?
- What similar concerns have you experienced that might lead you toward action?

After you have testified at a hearing or meeting, be sure to follow up with a thank you note or e-mail to the board or committee chair. Send responses to questions you might not have been able to answer at the hearing, and offer to provide additional information should it be needed. Of course, you also will want to follow developments on your issue. What course of action is the board or committee considering? Have you had an impact? It might be necessary for you to make some office visits to follow up on your testimony. Office visits are a topic of a later section of this chapter.

The idea of presenting testimony can be a little unnerving. But if you organize your testimony well, make your points clearly, and allow yourself enough time to practice your statements before the hearing, you should have no difficulties in presenting your case. This does not mean that your audience will accept your viewpoint, but at least you will have made cogent arguments and will have been a part of the process of deliberation.

FORMING LEGISLATIVE ACTION TEAMS (LATs). Legislative action teams are composed of individuals within groups or organizations who have volunteered to contact policymakers whenever the group feels it is necessary to address a particular issue. When the group or organization alerts its membership about the urgency of responding to a certain piece of legislation or policy under consideration, it may call on LAT members, in particular, to write letters, send e-mails, or make phone calls in support or opposition to the policy. Many LAT members agree to also visit their legislators in the capital or in their local district offices. In response to requests from their group or organization, some LAT members are willing to send information to their legislators or to present testimony at hearings. They know the importance of rapid response and are eager to spring into action on short notice when they receive an education alert.

To form a legislative action team (LAT), you need one person who has political savvy and others who are passionate about reform. The team initiator might invite others from different areas of education (e.g., inside and outside your school district, a university, or children's hospital) to join. If you have about 20 people on your team, then you can form subgroups for certain issues about which people care deeply. One subgroup, for example, might focus on funds for professional development, another on credentials for paraprofessionals, and another on obtaining more current books and magazines for school libraries.

Each subgroup could become an entity unto itself, with its own chair or cochair. Each subgroup also would decide how often and where it should meet before reporting progress to the meeting of the entire team. Following a subgroup's report at a whole-group meeting, the entire team should support the subgroup's next steps (e.g., preparing position papers, phoning political aides to inform them and arrange visits, or posting information on a website your team has created).

Keep in mind that one of your many goals as an LAT member may be to influence the budget. Because much money for education is funneled through the states, it is important to focus your attention and direction toward your state representatives. If your state's governor shows little interest in education, work with the state legislature. If the legislature shows little interest, work with individual legislators who have positive education track records.

You can obtain additional, specific information about how to form and maintain legislative action teams to promote education from professional education organizations such as the National Council for the Social Studies, National Council of Teachers of Mathematics, International Reading Association, and National Council of Teachers of English.

In the following vignette, Michelle Cardaronella describes how her professional association's newly formed Legislative Advocacy Committee mobilized for action under difficult time constraints. Their advocacy actions made a significant difference in the thinking of members of their state governing board for education.

When Teachers Use Their Voices

Michelle Cardaronella
Chair, Legislative Advocacy Committee, Louisiana State Reading Association,
Louisiana, USA

Recently our association's newly formed Legislative Advocacy Committee was thrust into action. Our committee, reflecting the desire of our state reading association membership, decided to focus on quality professional development. We collaborated with our local affiliate of a national staff development organization and created a joint position statement about what constitutes quality staff development. While these efforts were under way, a larger issue arose.

Five years earlier our state had moved to use a uniform reading assessment for all children in grades 1–3. This action was controversial and not accepted willingly by many of the state's educators. Children's scores on the reading assessment were to be reported to our state department of education. The children's scores determined whether they were reading below, on, or above level. After several years of administering this assessment, teachers have now embraced it as a good instructional tool.

Our state has an 11-member governing board to oversee all education decisions. Of the 11 members, 8 are elected by the public and 3 are appointed by the governor. This board meets monthly to review information provided by our state department of education and make decisions. Last spring I received information that our state governing board would be making a decision the next day to eliminate the state reading assessment. This information came from a reliable source, so our advocacy network sprung into action. Starting at 10:00 p.m. of the day we first heard the news, we began contacting members of our reading association across the state, urging them to reach their board member and the state superintendent of education.

The next morning I attended the board meeting. There had been a flurry of activity prior to my arrival. Members of the reading association had flooded the state superintendent's office with phone calls and faxes. They also had contacted their board members, many of whom appeared unaware that a vote to eliminate the reading assessment was scheduled. Before the start of the meeting, I was introduced to the chair of the committee of the state governing board looking at this issue. She was explicit: She wanted me to know that her committee would receive information regarding the state reading assessment but that no action (vote) would be taken. Our efforts were successful that day!

Our state reading association continues to develop advocacy skills and to network. For the first time in the history of our association, we are being asked to serve on state education committees and have our voices heard.

FOR YOUR CONSIDERATION

- What steps would you take to form a legislative advocacy committee or legislative action team if you do not have one already?

- Who might want to be members of your legislative advocacy committee or legislative action team?

- On the Internet, locate your state's board of education or governing board for education. What conclusions can you draw about the members' backgrounds and possible interest in issues that are important to you?

HOSTING POLICYMAKER BREAKFASTS. Members of your state legislature usually serve on several committees that may be quite diverse in scope. For example, one member might serve on the transportation, education, and budget committees all during the same term of office. The same is true for the various assignments that might be held by members of your state board of education and those in leadership roles at your state department of education, such as a commissioner of education. It is impossible for these individuals to be fully informed on every issue for which they have to create a policy or cast a vote. As an education advocate, if you are working with a professional association, you can host an informative breakfast for these policymakers.

Although planning a policymakers' breakfast can take considerable effort and some funding is needed, much can be accomplished at such an event. Your goals during the breakfast are multiple: (1) You want your invited guests to get to know you and your organization, (2) you want to provide your guests with research-based information that supports your interests, and (3) you want your guests to perceive you and your organization as having the potential to assist them with deliberations and policy development in the future. Therefore, it is critical that your policymakers breakfast be well planned.

There are three popular formats for policymaker breakfasts. The first format does not appear to involve much planning, but this impression is deceptive. The format calls for a casual breakfast without formal presentations. However, the room must be filled with knowledgeable and like-minded individuals from your organization and, perhaps, other stakeholder groups, who can informally discuss issues with the policymakers in attendance. These organization representatives should be familiar with and in agreement with your group's viewpoints on key issues. Your guest list should include all members of the state legislature and state board of education, all directors in the state department of education, and others who you believe might be influential in determining education policy in your state. You would not ask individuals to RSVP. However, you need to keep careful track of who attends, what issues they discussed with your group members, and what their particular concerns might be with regard to your group's viewpoints. This will be useful information for follow-up visits to these policymakers' offices. To accomplish these goals, have blank name badges available, perhaps with your organization's logo, so policymakers who attend can let you know who they are. You will need name badges for your organization's attendees, too.

The menu for the breakfast might be light (coffee, tea, juice, bagels, etc.) and you can expect that most people will stand during the time set aside—usually no more than one hour—for this meet-and-greet occasion. Policymakers may come to the breakfast for just a few minutes to say "hello." A photographer from your organization can take photos for your group's newsletter or website. You should have handouts for your guests to take with them, including information about your organization and perhaps a position paper or a letter to the editor that someone from your organization published. Your guests will appreciate whatever you have to let them know who you are and how to contact you.

A second policymaker breakfast format is more formal. For this type of breakfast, you could arrange to have speakers who will discuss a particularly hot topic with the policymakers, such as the need for more health education in schools, concerns about school violence, or the achievement gap. Your invitations should let your guests know the topics and the times that your speakers will make presentations. You should include postcards or e-mail addresses for RSVPs with your invitation and prepare name badges for those who will be attending so you can address your guests by name. Also prepare badges for your organization's attendees. Your room set-up should include chairs, tables, a podium, a microphone, an overhead projector or other projection device, and—if there is more than one speaker—a speakers' table at the front of the room. The same literature that you should have available for the casual breakfast should be available to the attendees of this type of breakfast as well. Because this should be a sit-down event, you might have a slightly more elaborate breakfast, although this is not necessary. Be careful about spending too much money on food because education nonprofits should not give the impression that they have a lot of money.

A third format used for policymaker breakfasts involves a set of roundtables, each focused on some aspect of your organization's work. If your organization concerns itself with literacy, your roundtable topics might be high-stakes testing in reading, the role of phonics in reading instruction, reading specialists in schools, teacher preparation to teach reading, and middle school and secondary school reading issues. Well before your event, assign one or two members of your organization to sit at each roundtable to lead the discussion on the topic. Your invitations will let the guests know the topics and that this format will allow each attendee to sit at two roundtables for 30 or 45 minutes apiece. You might invite those who RSVP to submit questions that they would like the roundtable members to discuss. Again, you should supply name badges for all attendees, literature from your organization, an appropriate room set-up, and a less-than-elaborate simple breakfast. This format will require that your organization's members do more in preparation, and those chosen to lead the discussion at each roundtable must be absolutely committed to attending the event.

Whatever format you choose, you will need to plan the policymakers' breakfast a few months before its scheduled date. Determine the date and time to hold your event by looking at the calendar for your state legislature. Usually specific dates for meetings of the full assembly or senate are available through the state's Office of Legislative Services or on your state legislature's website. The time you pick should make it possible for members of the legislature to be at their scheduled meetings after the breakfast. You also need to pick a location for your breakfast. Meeting at the statehouse would be very convenient for members of the state legislature. If you hold your breakfast at the statehouse, you may need to use the statehouse caterer or you might have to hire one from outside. You will need to send your invitations approximately six weeks in advance. Request the RSVPs at least two weeks prior to the event date, realizing that not all who are invited will respond. Legislative calendars can change, and some guests who say they will attend will not show. Someone will need to assume responsibility for receiving the RSVPs if they are requested. Depending on your breakfast format, you will need to determine who the speakers or roundtable hosts will be, and you will need to plan an appropriate set-up for the room. You also might need to arrange for a photographer from within your organization to attend the breakfast. You should keep in mind that some members of your organization may need substitute teachers for their classes; perhaps your organization can pay for these so that classroom teachers can more easily attend the breakfast.

At least 10 days before your breakfast, you should send out a media advisory and press release. A few days before, call the education reporters at newspapers in the vicinity of the breakfast to remind them of your event. Some members of the press might attend and subsequently feature pictures of the breakfast participants along with descriptions of the event in their papers or on their newscasts. This publicity will help your organization disseminate information to a larger public than those people attending the actual event.

There also is work to be done following a policymakers' breakfast, including developing and updating your policymaker database, sending thank-you letters to attendees, and sending photos to the press for possible publication. In addition, keep your organization's membership informed of the ideas generated at the breakfast so they can make reference to them when they meet with policymakers and other stakeholders on future occasions.

HOLDING RALLIES AND MARCHES. Rallies and marches can be extremely powerful ways of conveying your message to the public because they attract a great deal of attention from the media. Although we usually think of these as protest events, they also can be used to highlight positive occurrences. For instance, you can have a rally or march to honor teachers who have volunteered time in after-school programs in your school district or state. You can hold a rally to recognize school administrators who have demonstrated strong leadership and managed to craft school budgets that recognize the importance of school libraries, paraprofessionals, or professional development for teachers.

For both rallies and marches, you need to prepare well in advance. Once you have identified a group of like-minded people to undertake and oversee the work required, you will need to contact city, county, and state officials to be sure you are adhering to all the rules and regulations for public gatherings. One of these rules is to obtain a permit for such an event. Next, check to see whose responsibility it is to inform the police and public safety offices. You will want to work with these officials to guarantee a safe parade route for all march participants. Request police escorts. For marches more so than rallies, you will need to estimate the number of people who will participate as well as discuss with authorities the planned route so that decisions can be made as to temporarily closing off streets to traffic. If you anticipate a large crowd of observers, you might also want to request officers for crowd control. You also need to make arrangements for a sound system and contact the media in sufficient time for them to prepare to cover your event. For both rallies and marches it is helpful if you have signs (which may end up as part of newspaper photographs) and slogans that encapsulate the essence of your organization's message.

Try to hold your rally or march on the last day of a professional conference. For example, school superintendents in Ohio held a rally on the last day of their Ohio School Boards Association annual conference in Columbus, the state capital. They, along with teachers and students, expressed their displeasure with the inadequate funding of the public schools in Ohio with a rally in front of the state capitol. Although the rally did not have the effect of changing the political landscape relating to the funding of public schools, it did receive media coverage and encouraged some legislators to engage in conversations with the superintendents. It is imperative that marches are peaceful and the event is accomplished through responsible, easily identifiable leadership.

Read the vignette below and consider whether a rally or march might have been useful for helping Juanita Doyon and Jen Hewett in their advocacy efforts against the Washington Assessment of Student Learning. If Hewett had organized tenth-grade students and they had participated in a rally or a march, would their issue have received more attention? Would more have been accomplished than what was achieved by working within the district for change?

Challenging Authority

Juanita Doyon
Public School Advocate, Spanaway, Washington, USA

When high school student Jen Hewett contacted me by e-mail, she not only planned to boycott the tenth-grade Washington Assessment of Student Learning (WASL) herself, she also wanted to organize a statewide group of students to join her efforts. As the organizer of Mothers Against WASL, I offered her buttons, shirts, and printed information, and I offered to meet with her.

In August I met with Jen, bringing her the promised "de-testing" materials. Jen set up a website and began an all-out protest at her school, passing out buttons and information and encouraging her fellow students to opt out of the test, which is administered in mid-spring. It is legal for students to opt out in the state of Washington, but schools discourage students from doing this because for each omitted student a zero is averaged into the overall school test score. In my opinion, much coercion takes place and, in some school districts, outright lies are told to students and their parents.

By October Jen had been "dragged into the vice principal's office about five times" and labeled "the instigator." The vice principal and the school district superintendent in charge of curriculum and assessment called for a meeting. Jen invited me to attend.

The control tactics the vice principal used were unsettling. When asking if I would like a cup of coffee, she condescendingly offered Jen one, too, with a smirk.

Jen remained calm. When the assistant superintendent arrived, it was immediately evident that no middle ground would be found, but the administrator was courteous and honored Jen's right to free speech and protest. Jen held her own, calmly making point after counterpoint, standing up for students who were not succeeding on the test for one reason or another, even students enrolled in school districts beyond her own.

When we were clear of the administrator's office, Jen's anger came out as she said to me, "I HATE it when they get like that!"

Don't we all?

FOR YOUR CONSIDERATION

- If you were in the position of the school district administrators, what might your perspective be in this situation?

- If Hewett had approached you with her concerns, what additional strategies would you have suggested that she try in order to change school district and state policy? Would you have suggested either a rally or a march?

- What are ways to be the loyal opposition and remain on cordial relations with those with whom you have different viewpoints?

ATTENDING PUBLIC HEARINGS. Many policymakers and policymaking bodies, including elected officials and boards of education, hold hearings that are open to the public and at which public citizens have a chance to speak. You might attend such public hearings first as an observer to see how they work and how public citizens participate. Once you are more comfortable with the hearings, you can begin to make public statements yourself. Doing so offers you a chance to interact with policymakers, express your opinion about pending legislation, mention your organization and its mission, provide information that can help policymakers make wise decisions, give feedback on enacted policies, and raise questions to determine future policies that might be under consideration. If you attend these hearings with some frequency, you may become recognized as an education advocate and be sought after for participation in policymaking activities at the local or state level.

VISITING WITH ELECTED OFFICIALS. Elected officials enjoy meeting concerned educators, especially if they are constituents. Sometimes those meetings are planned; other times they may be by chance. Occasionally, such visits may be initiated by others who have already established good communication with an elected official whom you would like to meet. These individuals might make phone calls, arrange appointments, or send e-mails of introduction on your behalf.

As you read the following vignette, consider how informal encounters between an educator and a legislator may lead to later advocacy opportunities.

Imagination to Legislation

Douglas M. Brooks
Professor, Miami University, Oxford, Ohio, USA

In 1994, my Partners In Learning project at Miami University had submitted a successful Ohio SchoolNet Prototype application. Partners In Learning/SchoolNet was selected as one of 14 Ohio prototypes to advance the full application of the Internet in every K–12 classroom in Ohio. Then-governor George Voinovich had successfully passed legislation supporting the installation of hardwire Internet drops in every classroom in Ohio.

A mutual friend introduced me to Senator Mike Fox, then-chair of the Ohio House Education Commission, at a dinner party. I expressed concerns about the direction of the Ohio SchoolNet Project to the senator. I was told my concerns would be addressed. They were. In return, Senator Fox asked me to come to his office in Fairfield, Ohio, for a one-hour briefing on the evolution of the technology agenda in Ohio schools. This visit turned out to be the most significant 60 minutes of my professional career in public education.

Senator Fox explained that he had been unsuccessful in passing legislation that would have put a computer on the desktop of every elementary school student in Ohio. I discovered that he was unaware of the Ohio SchoolNet Project and even less aware of how classrooms, teachers, and schools operated as a cultural reality.

I began by reviewing with him the current trends and projected realities of technology integration in schools. We discussed how to shape his proposed legislation into something that would be more acceptable to his legislative colleagues and more useful to Ohio schoolteachers. I found myself describing how elementary classrooms actually operated, based on my years of personal experience, direct observation, and research. We agreed that a computer center in every classroom was more consistent with how most elementary school classrooms operated. Clustering four or five computers would let the teacher introduce computer skills to small groups, let the students work with selected software programs, and complement the existing procedures and organization of the classroom. We agreed that the proposed initiative should complement the governor's current agenda. We decided to call this proposed legislation "SchoolNet Plus."

Every K–4 classroom in Ohio's 611 school districts now has a SchoolNet Plus computer center. Having the right time, right place, right people, and some imagination affected legislation in Ohio.

FOR YOUR CONSIDERATION

• In this vignette, how did a conversation turn into a political reality?

• What did the educator and the politician have to teach each other in order to work together effectively?

• Are there some existing successful initiatives that you can put together and build on as you advocate for education in your community?

Your legislators usually will welcome your visits to their offices, especially to their district offices in your home community. Setting up such visits is relatively easy to do, but some work also is required ahead of time. Before you schedule a visit, find out something about the legislators who are in important positions in either your state legislature or in Congress, especially those who serve on education committees. Be sure to see at least these influential policymakers. If you are a member of a national professional association that has a government relations office, that office may be able to assist you with scheduling an appointment and providing information on your representative's voting record on education issues.

Prior to your visit, find out what you can about the legislator's areas of interest and voting records, especially votes that, from your perspective, have been positive. You can thank the legislator for some of these at the start of your visit.

Plan carefully what you want to say at your visit. Your purpose might be to introduce yourself and your organization, as well as to lay out your concerns about education, policy, and perhaps some specific pending legislation. Recall the fictitious office visits made by organization representatives to Assemblywoman Pritchard in chapter 3. The second scenario in that chapter shows some key components of a successful visit to an elected official. Figure 11 contains some specific suggestions from the Office of the Governor of Florida, Jeb Bush, for visiting elected officials.

In addition to these suggestions, you should pay attention to the calendar when scheduling your visit. If it is during the period when a budget is being negotiated, you will have less success making your appointment. Holiday periods also are difficult. Begin by contacting the legislator's district staff. If you have a policy concern and the district staff feels it is warranted, they can alert the Washington, DC, staff to your concerns and assist you with scheduling a face-to-face meeting with your legislator.

When you make your appointment, state the reason for your visit and offer to send materials ahead of time. On the day of your visit, be punctual, but

---

Figure 11. Suggestions From the Office of Florida Governor Jeb Bush for Education Advocates' Visits to Legislators

• Make sure you understand the legislative process. Even the most basic understanding of the process will help you effectively express your ideas.

• Don't just drop by your legislator's office and expect him or her to drop everything to see you.

• Prepare a one-page fact sheet concerning your issue to give to your legislator. This will help him or her better retain what you present.

• Tell your legislator what effect you think a particular bill, if it becomes law, will have on you, your children, business, or community. Be concise, but specific.

• Be polite. Even if you disagree strongly with the legislator you are addressing. Lawmakers cannot please everyone. Your communication will be more effective if you are reasonable in your approach.

also recognize that although you have an appointment for a specific time, you may be kept waiting, especially if you are scheduled to meet personally with the legislator.

You might find that although your appointment is with the legislator, an aide meets with you instead. Do not be discouraged; aides have the important job of conveying your message to the elected official. They often are quite knowledgeable and professional and can provide an important link between you and the legislator. Be certain, however, that the aide meeting with you is the one who is assigned to education issues.

During the visit, you may be asked to provide your legislator with further information or research about your issue. Do not expect that he or she will make a firm commitment to your advocacy wishes at the time of your visit. A legislator often needs to confer with others who have a stake in decisions made on the issue that concerns you; for example, perhaps constituents with opposing viewpoints to your own also have made visits to the legislator's office. Be sure also to explain how your ideas connect to the interests of the legislator's constituency. In addition to stating your concerns, offer recommendations or a course of action. This provides the legislator with something tangible to do in response to your visit.

When you meet, be aware of how long your visit is taking. In Washington, DC, you may be given less time for your visit than if you visit your legislator's home office. As a guideline, figure that the legislator will have about 15 minutes to see you in Washington, DC, and perhaps 30 minutes at his or her home office. Because the time you may have is relatively short, be organized and have a specific message. Leave the legislator some supporting material, such as a research study supporting your views, and information about your organization.

Visits may take on a different emphasis if you are representing a professional organization than if you are advocating for a more personal concern. When you are working with an organization, all the people designated to make visits to legislators need to be speaking with one voice. Your organization's credibility is at stake, so develop an agreed-upon outline or set of talking points that each visitor will use. Include a set of recommendations or a course of action that your organization proposes. Each visitor also should be articulate and knowledgeable about the topic and able to respond to questions that might arise. You and your colleagues may choose to make your visits individually or as a small group. When visiting in groups, we recommend that at least one group member be a constituent of the legislator. Legislators know to be concerned about issues of their constituents. Representing their constituents well is their responsibility. They also know you vote!

After the visit, send a thank-you note to the person who met with you. If you met with a legislative aide, be sure to send a copy of your thank-you note to the legislator. In your note, you can summarize the meeting content. If you were asked to do some research on your issue, include it if you have it or indicate when it might be sent to the legislator. Make sure your contact information is included in your note.

Some time after the visit, you can phone the legislator's office to inquire about the status of any requests you made and what has occurred since your meeting. You might offer to meet again, although if you have had a successful meeting the first time, this should not be necessary.

Even if you feel your meeting did not go well and that the legislator will not support your views, remain optimistic. Pressure from others on the same issue, or facts that emerge after your visit, may cause some change in the legislator's position. As new issues evolve and other legislation is under consideration, you might find yourself seeking support again from this same office, sometimes with positive results. The least effective approach to advocacy is to write off an influential person as a lost cause.

ADOPT-A-LEGISLATOR PROGRAMS. As we noted earlier in this chapter, all politics is local. Your school district is situated in a community represented by particular elected officials who introduce legislation, vote on bills, and can be message carriers for constituents who let their views and needs be known. By initiating an Adopt-a-Legislator program in your school or school district, you can establish a close, ongoing relationship with these elected officials and can call on them to, at a minimum, listen to your concerns.

Starting such a program is fairly easy. Your primary activity will be inviting your local legislators to participate in some of your classroom, school, or school district's events. Begin by considering some of the special events you hold, such as open houses, special assembly programs, Read Across America Day, or science fairs. Add to your list the more common activities in which adults might participate, such as reading to children in classrooms, sharing stories about their work, assisting with textbook selection, and providing computer training to children.

Any of these events could be appropriate for an invitation to a legislator, but decide which events might have the greatest appeal. If you are a classroom teacher, first check with the principal about policies related to such visits as well as guidelines for the invitation. Then you can place a phone call to the legislator's office. If your request for the legislator is granted by phone, definitely follow this up with written confirmation of details and a request for an RSVP. If the event is newsworthy, be sure to let the press know that the legislator will be attending. Also, let the legislator know that you have invited the press; this might be a further incentive for him or her to keep the appointment with you. Regardless of whether the press can attend, have your own camera ready for photos, too.

Plan a schedule for your event and stick to it. Be sure the legislator who will be your guest knows ahead of time the schedule for the day and what his or her role at the event will be. Offer to answer any questions at any time before the visit. On the day of the legislator's visit, greet him or her at the front door. Even if the visit is to a single classroom, stop by the principal's office for quick introductions. If your event is large, next introduce your guest to the organizers. Do your best to avoid interruptions, such as public address announcements or fire drills, during the event. If your visitor is late, make adjustments to your event schedule that still highlight your school's best features.

Be aware that this visit is not the occasion for you to have a serious discussion about issues that are uppermost in your mind. Your goal is to get to know the legislator and vice versa. Afterward, send the legislator a thank-you note, photos of the event, any news clippings, and, if appropriate, an indication that you are hoping you can meet with him or her soon to discuss some education issues. Once you get to know your representatives, you can begin to discuss some of your issues more seriously. In her article "Taking Stock: Knowing What's Worthwhile and Advocating for It" (see Appendix A, page 259), Jill Lewis suggests some questions you might encourage your legislators to consider after they have visited your classroom a few times and have gotten to know you and your students.

Continue to send the legislator invitations to school and school district events, and share this advocacy strategy with other members of professional associations with whom you work. Every school district has its own legislators, and each legislator has a vote on state education legislation that is under consideration.

Several Florida schools tried a variation on the Adopt-a-Legislator program. They wanted to show their state legislators many of the good things that were happening in their schools because the press seemed to focus only on students' scores on Florida's Comprehensive Assessment Test. These teachers and their students established an ongoing relationship with elected representatives for their geographical area. Their approach was multifaceted. Students in the class wrote letters to the legislator on a regular basis. They included their stories and their artwork. Often, the teachers included photographs of student activities. These legislators had an open invitation to visit the class whenever they were in their home district offices. Often, the legislators stopped in for a few minutes to chat with the students and teachers or to read a story to the students. Not all legislators were responsive, but some conferred with the children and the teachers on a regular basis. These teachers felt that their legislators better understood the classrooms and the school activities as a result.

In Ohio, the legislative aide to Allen Berger's congressional representative visits college classrooms. The vignette below describes student reactions to a few of his visits. Although the aide's visits are worthwhile educational experiences in that students learn how to communicate to politicians, many students are upset by some of the views expressed.

Inviting Political Aides to Class

Allen Berger
Heckert Professor of Reading and Writing, Miami University, Oxford, Ohio, USA

A wonderful way to reach politicians is through their aides. And a wonderful way to engage their aides is by inviting them into your classroom.

To illustrate, for each course I teach at the university, I phone a politician's office for a representative to come and talk to my students. My congressman, John Boehner, chairs the U.S. House of Representatives Education and Workforce Committee. Because he spends much of his time in Washington, DC, one of his aides comes in his place.

Prior to the aide's visit, I explain to my students that an aide is very important because he or she is the conduit to the politician. One of my purposes for the visit is to alert students to ways they can communicate with an aide or a political leader about their community and educational concerns. (I also urge my students to write opinion/editorials or letters to the editor of the local newspapers about education issues or their personal concerns.)

My students are surprised at how young an aide is. They are also surprised at some of the ideas the aide may express. On one visit the aide was discussing high-stakes testing and expressing his view that all children must be tested and that there must be consequences for low performance. This upset some students who asked questions such as, "What about children from broken homes? What about children who go to school without breakfast?"

On another visit the congressional aide shared opinions about the separation of church and state, educational vouchers, and the teaching of evolution that upset many of the students.

What did these students learn about advocacy? They learned some important lessons. Advocacy does not always go smoothly. Your views may differ markedly from the views of the political aide and the representative he or she works for. The person seated near you may or may not be interested in what you have to say. How you present and support your ideas with well-thought-out arguments and research may make a difference in whether the ideas you are advocating are heard or dismissed.

FOR YOUR CONSIDERATION

- How knowledgeable are you about your elected officials? Can you give the names of your state and Congressional representatives? Do you know the representatives for your school district, if it is different from your home district? Do you know the issues that are important to these legislators, or their voting records?

- The author of this vignette explains, "One of my purposes for the visit is to alert students to ways they can communicate with an aide or a political leader about their community and educational concerns." From this classroom visit, what do you think the students learned about communicating with an aide?

- What could have been done before or during the visit to produce a more satisfying outcome for all who participated?

Other Ways to Develop Relationships With Legislators

Through school visits, frequent communication, and information updates, your legislator will develop a relationship with you and other members of your school or organizational community. Over time, he or she will begin to know you and your organization on a personal level and develop a better understanding of your education-related interests and concerns.

Earlier you read about a Legislator of the Year award some organizations give to honor a person who had made significant contributions to education or worked with the organization on behalf of a significant issue of concern. You or your organization might present similar awards to legislators at the local level, and your organization might consider honoring school board members, your school district's central office personnel, or local government officials who made important contributions to education in your community.

Still another way to build relationships with different legislators is to work on their reelection campaigns. Whether your legislator is a precinct captain, a city council member, a local school board member, a state board of education member, or a state or national legislator, he or she is usually concerned about reelection and is either planning or conducting a reelection campaign. If you agree with your legislator's views, support him or her by volunteering to help. You may be able to show your appreciation during election periods by helping to get out the vote, organizing meet-the-candidate breakfasts or teas, writing letters to the editor on behalf of the legislator's reelection, or holding a public debate that gives the legislator an opportunity to bring your issue and others into the election debate. It is best that you volunteer as an individual constituent, rather than on behalf of your organization, because you do not wish to jeopardize your organization's status and independence. If you are a school employee, you also may need to check your school district's policy on what you can and cannot do during school board campaigns.

What else can you do? Contribute financial resources if you are able. Election campaigns always need more funds. More important, contribute your time, energies, and talents. You can volunteer at many levels. Consider ringing doorbells and distributing campaign literature to members of the community. Help with information tables at festivals or fairs or in your local mall or shopping center. Fold and stuff envelopes with campaign circulars. Distribute supporting posters or signs. Assist those who are working with the policymaker's website. Offer to call or e-mail potential voters, reminding them to vote and asking them to consider your candidate as they mark their ballots. Speak at meetings of professional, civic, or religious organizations on behalf of your candidate. The policymaker's campaign committee may suggest other activities that will be supportive of their candidate. Help out where you can. Your work on behalf of the candidate will build good will with him or her. You also may meet and network with other people who you may later want to contact about your or your organization's advocacy issues.

It is important for our officials to know that when they take positive steps on our behalf by giving our issues more than lip service, we have the capacity to publicly acknowledge their contributions. Although your organization may not wish or be able to endorse specific candidates, you can encourage your members to volunteer for the individual candidates of their choice.

Running for Office

After participating in a variety of education advocacy activities and working with policymakers at many levels, you may consider further involvement, such as running for an elected office in your local school association—such as your parent–teacher association or the school board in your local district or state. Because running for election may require a considerable commitment of your finances and time, you will need to think carefully before taking on this project. Your passion for education must be strong. You must feel that you have important ideas to offer and that your candidacy might make a significant difference.

The decision to run for office is not an easy one. Talking with others may help you decide. Find out as much as you can about the position from former and current office holders. Interview officials about the job and what it entails. Research the individuals with whom you might serve and what concerns and issues they frequently represent. Consider your own stances on many issues.

If you are leaning toward running for office, think about forming an exploratory committee. Members of this committee will help you assess the situation by talking to board members, to community organizations, and to community representatives. They may conduct informal polls about current office holders to determine degree of support for them and the likelihood of reelectibility. Often they approach potential donors about the possibility of contributions for your campaign. What you all learn may help you make your final decision about whether to run for office. Perhaps you will learn that you have little opposition and your candidacy is encouraged. You may learn that the opposition is so strong that your success is unlikely. Even then, you may choose to run on principle or beliefs, deciding that your campaign is a way to get your ideas to the public and perhaps begin some much-needed change.

Sometimes, you may be surprised at the outcome of your candidacy. In the following vignettes, two educators share their personal stories of what happened when they decided to run for office. The first educator, Judie Thelen, ran for her local school board. The second educator, Jay Blanchard, ran for his state senate. Both moved beyond criticizing existing policies to working for change.

From President to School Board

Judie Thelen
Past President, International Reading Association, Newark, Delaware, USA
Vice President, Allegany County Board of Education, Maryland, USA

How do you facilitate change at the state and local levels when you are retiring from the university and can no longer inspire young teachers who pass through your doors?

In her 1996 publication *Literacy at the Crossroads*, my dear friend Regie Routman implores her audience to become political, to share beliefs and clarify issues. With Regie's encouragement I filed for and won a seat on my county's elected school board. I am now serving my second four-year term.

During my first term I realized that literacy instruction is but one part of the whole picture. School board members do not create curriculum but influence it by their votes on the budget and policy. When it comes to issues related to literacy, the other school board members have looked to me for direction.

In my role as a school board member I have had entry into arenas I never would have had, even as president of the International Reading Association or as a citizen. Most state board committees are composed of members of other state groups such as the PTA, teacher's groups, school boards, and so on. Because of my background, I was asked to serve on literacy-related state committees and thus have been able to influence the development of state reading standards and other literacy issues.

When my term is up on the school board, I am seriously considering running for the state legislature.

FOR YOUR CONSIDERATION

• Has Thelen's term on the school board been satisfying to her? How do you know?

- Is running for office an appropriate act for an education advocate? Explain your reasoning.
- How can the structure of a local, county, or state school board affect its members' effectiveness as education advocates?

As you read Jay Blanchard's vignette, note the similarities and differences in Thelen's and Blanchard's experiences.

Making a Difference: One Reading Teacher's Story

Jay Blanchard
Professor, Arizona State University, Tempe, Arizona, USA

My story is simple. I went from classroom teacher to Arizona State Senate member. How did it happen? I ran for the state senate as a protest candidate in 2000 with little hope of winning, but a strange thing happened—I won!

I was motivated to enter politics because at the time Arizona had (a) old buildings and no money to fix them, (b) a need for new buildings and no money to build them, (c) low teacher salaries and no inclination to increase them, (d) a legislative distrust of public education, and (e) the idea that state control of education is superior to teacher control. I had watched as the crisis in education grew with no leadership in sight. So one day I decided to run. I believed it was time to stop complaining and do something.

Unfortunately, I had little chance of getting elected to the senate because my party was outnumbered in the district almost 3 to1. I was also running against one of the most powerful men in the state—the former Speaker of the House of Representatives. From any vantage point, my run for office was dark and gloomy. But I ran anyway. I hoped to give the voters a choice.

As fate would have it, just before the election my opponent was caught up in a scandal. It promised to cost the state millions of dollars. The scandal grew in size, and suddenly overnight my opponent's sure victory turned to sure defeat. I won in a landslide.

The victory meant that the Senate would have equal representation from both parties—a first in history. This fact forced a bipartisan spirit. As a result of one teacher's almost crazy attempt to make a difference, it happened. The moral of this story is clear: You need to think about running for public office if you are unhappy with your elected officials. Only good candidates can lead to good elected officials. Regardless of your political party, we need caring, compassionate candidates who understand there are few easy answers to our problems and everyone must be at the table and involved in the discussions.

FOR YOUR CONSIDERATION

- Using the Internet, find out what you can about this elected official's performance while in office to confirm or reject your answers to the following questions: (1) Was he an effective education advocate? Explain. (2) What special skills might an educator bring to a statehouse environment?

- How would having an equal number of Democrats and Republicans push legislators to engage in more bipartisan activities?

- Blanchard listed five issues that motivated him to campaign for office. What do you see as the dominant education concerns in your state? Are your state's needs similar? Use the Internet to learn if your state legislature is addressing these issues and, if so, how.

Informing Your Membership

If you are working as an education advocate representing an organization, it will be critically important to keep your membership informed of your activities, to call on members for assistance, and to include them in some of the decision-making processes that can have long-term consequences for the organization's reputation. For example, if you are putting together a coalition, the membership, or at least the board of directors, should approve the coalition and suggest members. If you are hosting a policymaker breakfast, invite your board of directors to attend. When you have letters to the editor published that you have written on behalf of the organization, or when you are interviewed by a radio station as an organization's representative, let your membership know of your successes.

Once you are familiar with the tools for advocacy and have tried using some of them, consider conducting advocacy workshops for your membership. Many members may be intrigued by the new possibilities that advocacy opens for them to get their ideas to policymakers. They may want to join your Legislative Action Team, your committee, and your effort. This increased capacity will multiply, as will your success stories.

Conclusion

During a full-court press in a basketball game, each team member applies pressure to an individual player on the opposing team to regain possession of the ball; individual team members work separately yet are unified by one desired outcome. In a similar manner, you and your group should strive for a full-court press in your advocacy efforts. For example, while you are in touch with your policymaker or a legislative aide, a colleague may be writing op-eds. Another colleague may be focusing on conveying your group's advocacy message through radio or television. Other group members may be organizing breakfasts for policymakers and educators. Still others may be appearing at hearings. Students may be making videotapes, DVDs, or CD-ROMs.

And bring in with a crescendo your professional organizations; encourage officers or selected LAT members or individual members with an interest in advocacy to write conference proposals so that policymakers and news media representatives can appear on state and national programs of conferences and conventions. Work with others to prepare position papers that explain your organization's ideas with clarity. Embrace other organizations and individuals who share your concerns. A full-court press requires the dedication and total involvement of a variety of individuals. Working together, you will more frequently accomplish your group's desired goals.

Obviously, education advocates have many options at their disposal, and so far this book has presented you with many choices and strategies for action. We hope these will help you speak out and get involved in a myriad of advocacy activities. In the next chapter, you will learn how to look for subtle clues to assess your success as an education advocate.

In chapter 7 you'll see how these choices and strategies come together in a specific state and for a specific advocacy purpose. You'll be introduced to the advocates who worked the issue from start to finish, and gain insights into their thinking. You'll learn why they did what they did and how they mobilized others to help. The tale has a happy ending. Hard work, coordinated efforts, and well-developed advocacy skills led to a positive outcome and the children of the state did not have to participate in what these advocates believed were repressive educational practices.

CHAPTER 7

An Advocacy Tale of Success

The hair on the back of my neck stood up as I (Jill Lewis) read the e-mail message from the Associate Director of Government Relations for the New Jersey Education Association (NJEA), Linda Kassekert. She had written this day, September 7, 2000, to let me know that state Assemblywoman Connie Myers was introducing a phonics test bill that called for assessing all second graders to determine by the end of grade 2 whether they could read and spell phonetically. There would be consequences for schools where many children failed the test. Linda further indicated that the Assembly Education Committee might hear the bill in less than three weeks.

My initial reaction was pleasure in the fact that I'd actually been contacted by NJEA. After all, even though the New Jersey Reading Association (NJRA) was one of their affiliates, when I had first approached NJEA's Government Relations Director six or seven years earlier, he had not even recognized our organization's name. However, through ongoing communication with them, however—mostly from us contacting and informing them about our advocacy activities—over the years we had developed a positive relationship. Linda's notification was clear evidence that NJRA's members were now considered legitimate education advocates with some clout to put behind our words.

I also realized that there was not a lot of time to decide a course of action. I needed to see the full text of the bill, A–2652, and then strategize with members of the NJRA Legislation/Professional Standards Committee, which I chaired, and our association's executive board.

Note: While not everyone may agree with the New Jersey Reading Association's views, the organization has long advocated for evidenced–based instructional strategies that meet the differing needs of children and for the use of multiple classroom assessments to determine instructional goals for individual children. NJRA has written position papers on these topics, and its annual conference programs always have reflected this philosophy. The story Jill Lewis tells in this chapter describes a successful advocacy effort, not an attempt to sway readers toward her organization's point of view on these issues.

When I read the bill, I was mortified. In A-2652 (see Figure 12), the assemblywoman cited what she believed to be the findings of the National Reading Panel (NICHD, 2000). But she had misinterpreted them. This meant that we needed to get someone on the Panel to write to her about her error, and we had to make sure that the Assembly Education Committee was similarly informed. But this would never be enough to halt the bill.

I started my to-do list, realizing that the advocacy of our reading association would be critical. All members of NJRA who voted in Assemblywoman Myers's district had to be contacted and supplied with copies of the bill as well as talking points arguing against it that they could use either in a letter to or during a personal meeting with the assemblywoman. I also believed that members of the Legislation/Professional Standards Committee should meet with Assemblywoman Myers and members of the Assembly Education Committee. Another action would be to utilize NJRA's positive relationship with our State Department of Education, especially its Language Arts Literacy Coordinator, who had been serving on the Advisory Board for the NJRA Legislation/Professional Standards Committee. Although I felt that she would be in a difficult position, I did think she could take a stand on this bill and work with us to oppose it.

As I looked at my list, a few things became evident: (1) Accomplishing everything on the list would take a great deal of my time, and (2) I was depending on other people to participate in this work and was not sure if that expectation was realistic. For example, some members of the Legislation/Professional Standards Committee and also of NJRA were untenured classroom teachers. Would they take a risk? Others were working on advanced degrees. Would they have the time? Experience also told me that most educators, including classroom teachers, were less passionate about advocacy than I. This had become my life's work, not theirs.

I wasn't sure how things would unfold; I just believed that the bill would spell disaster if it became law. Unfortunately, the time was right for bills just like this. The United States, it seemed, was focused on getting reading programs back to basics (and nothing else), and the National Reading Panel report had become the clarion call for such views—but only because the media had seized on selected segments of the report that spoke about the importance of phonics, giving this reading instruction component high visibility. The media had pretty much ignored everything else the Panel had said.

Figure 12. Text of Bill A-2652

ASSEMBLY, No. 2652
STATE OF NEW JERSEY
209th LEGISLATURE
INTRODUCED JUNE 26, 2000
Sponsored by:
Assemblywoman CONNIE MYERS
District 23 (Warren, Hunterdon and Mercer)

SYNOPSIS

Directs the State Board of Education to revise the Core Curriculum Content Standards for Language Arts Literacy.

CURRENT VERSION OF TEXT

As introduced.

An Act directing the State Board of Education to revise the Core Curriculum Content Standards for Language Arts Literacy and supplementing Chapter 35 of Title 18A of the New Jersey Statutes.

Be It Enacted by the Senate and General Assembly of the State of New Jersey:

1. a. The State Board of Education shall revise the Core Curriculum Content Standards for Language Arts Literacy to include cumulative progress indicators which ensure that students demonstrate the ability to read and spell phonetically by the end of grade 2.

    b. By the end of the second school year following the revision of the Core Curriculum Content Standards for Language Arts Literacy pursuant to subsection a. of this section, each board of education that operates an educational program for students in grades 1 and 2 shall implement an assessment program to be administered to all students at the end of grade 2 that measures the student's ability to read and spell phonetically. Any student who does not successfully complete the assessment shall be provided with additional phonics instruction until the student is able to meet the cumulative progress indicators adopted by the State board pursuant to subsection a. of this section.

2. This act shall take effect on the 180th day following enactment.

STATEMENT

This bill requires that the State Board of Education revise the Core Curriculum Content Standards for Language Arts Literacy to include cumulative progress indicators which ensure that students demonstrate the ability to read and spell phonetically by the completion of grade 2. Presently, there are cumulative progress indicators establishing State required student abilities only at the end of grades 4, 8 and 12. Under the bill's provisions, each board of education would be required to establish an assessment program to be administered to all students at the end of grade 2 that measures the student's ability to read and spell phonetically. Students who do not successfully complete the assessment would be provided additional phonics instruction so that they are able to meet the cumulative progress indicators adopted pursuant to this bill.

(continued)

Figure 12. (continued)

Phonics instruction is a way of teaching reading that stresses the acquisition of letter–sound correspondences and their use in reading and spelling. The primary focus of phonics instruction is to help beginning readers understand how letters are linked to sounds to form letter–sound correspondences and spelling patterns and to help them learn how to apply this knowledge in their reading.

A recent study by the National Reading Panel, a panel convened by Congressional request, concluded that systematic phonics instruction beginning before grade 2 is significantly more effective in enhancing children's success in learning to read than instruction that teaches little or no phonics. Systematic phonics instruction was also found to positively and significantly improve the reading skills of students with learning disabilities and low-achieving students who are not disabled. Moreover, the National Reading Panel concluded that systematic phonics instruction was significantly effective in improving low socioeconomic status children's alphabetic knowledge and word reading skills.

Nevertheless, I started to work energetically on each task and found supporters along the way. To begin with, the president of NJRA that year, Natalie Smith, had been a member of the NJRA Legislation/Professional Standards Committee for several years and had become familiar with the importance of advocacy and some of the deliberate groundwork that had to be laid if anything were to be accomplished. She enthusiastically contacted the NJRA officers, committee chairs, and local council presidents, asking them to provide their district numbers or the names of their assembly representatives. This information allowed us to contact individuals whose representatives served on the Assembly Education Committee or, looking ahead, Senate Education committees.

I also contacted the Government Relations Division of the International Reading Association and spoke with Director Richard Long. He assured me that Timothy Shanahan—a member of the IRA Board of Directors who had also served on the National Reading Panel—would write Myers a letter. This would be terrific! (See Figure 13 for Shanahan's letter.)

A few days later, another e-mail message arrived from Linda. Apparently, NJRA was not the only organization with questions about the bill. Assemblywoman Myers was scheduling a meeting with representatives from NJRA and these different associations to hear our concerns. This was a real opportunity for us to present our evidence that this bill was too narrowly focused and misrepresented the National Reading Panel's conclusions.

Figure 13. Timothy Shanahan's Letter to Assemblywoman Myers

UNIVERSITY OF ILLINOIS
AT CHICAGO

Center for Literacy (MC 147)
1040 West Harrison Street
Chicago, Illinois 60607-7133

September 23, 2000

Assemblywoman Connie Myers
District 23

Dear Assemblywoman Myers:

I have read with interest your bill on literacy that has recently been introduced in the New Jersey legislature. As a member of the National Reading Panel (NRP), whose report you have cited in this proposed legislation, I was puzzled by the narrow focus of this bill. As you know, the NRP report addressed many issues in reading education.

I was curious as to why you singled out phonics—as this was only one aspect of instruction that our analysis found to be important. Your summary of our phonics is accurate. But we also found that phonemic awareness instruction, guided oral reading instruction, and explicit vocabulary and comprehension strategy instruction all helped children to read better (and each made about as much a contribution to achievement as did phonics). None of these were studied in isolation either, suggesting that focusing on phonics alone is likely to be a big mistake. We did not identify any missing ingredient or "silver bullet" in reading instruction, but found that children benefited from well-planned, explicit instruction in all of these areas simultaneously.

Your use of the NRP report seems misleading to me, but more important, I fear that a bill cast as narrowly as this one might result in lower quality instruction for children. I fully appreciate your commitment to education, and respectfully encourage you to broaden the scope of this bill to better meet the reading needs of all children in New Jersey.

Thank you.

Sincerely yours,

Timothy Shanahan
Director

UIC

Meeting With Assemblywoman Myers

Several of those who had been invited to the meeting lingered in the hall just prior to our scheduled meeting time—1:00 p.m. on September 27, 2000. Linda introduced me to two individuals, Robert (Bob) W. Sweet, Jr., and Anne Sweet, and commented, "I guess we're all here for the same reason." I knew something about both of these individuals and so could only reply, "I don't think so." Bob Sweet was cofounder of the conservative National Right to Read Foundation and had authored the Reading Excellence Act (REA) for Representative Bill Goodling, former Chairman of the U.S. House Education and Workforce Committee. The REA was the U.S. Department of Education's most recent attempt to apply pressure for back-to-basics reading programs and accountability. Although I had no problem with the accountability part, I certainly thought that there was more to learning to read than knowing phonics. I also recognized Anne Sweet's name; she was a pro-phonics reading researcher who now works for the U.S. Department of Education. The Sweets's presence signaled the importance of Assemblywoman Myers's bill and their hope to see it passed. They certainly had more resources than NJRA to put behind this effort, and I felt a little queasy as I reflected on this fact.

To say the meeting was contentious would be to minimize the severity of remarks that we made at the long table at which representatives from at least seven organizations sat, each ready to state their case for or against the bill. There were chairs down the sides of the table as well as a chair at each end. I wanted to slink into a chair somewhere in the middle of a long side and remain somewhat unnoticed. Unfortunately, Linda positioned herself at the head of one end and pulled up a chair for me to sit next to her. It was clear that I would be facing Myers head-on.

Assemblywoman Myers strode into the room and abruptly announced, "I'm hear to listen, but there WILL be a bill." This was not a great way to start what I had hoped could be a productive meeting. During introductions, I learned that to my right was a woman named Cathy Fox, a constituent of Myers who had been teaching her son to read because, in her view, his school had failed, largely because they did not teach him phonics. Myers gave Fox credit for drafting the bill. Further, Fox was the National Right to Read Foundation's State Director for New Jersey. Also present were members of the New Jersey School Boards Association (NJSBA), and the New Jersey Principals and Supervisors

Association (NJPSA). These two groups seemed primarily concerned about the cost of the bill to school districts because the bill made no provision to cover the assessment costs.

At one point during the meeting, I mentioned that the text in Bill A–2652 that cited the Panel's findings was simply incorrect. Then and there I offered Assemblywoman Myers a copy of the Panel's full report. I also offered her a copy of the letter from Tim Shanahan that I had in hand. She refused both, although she requested that the report be mailed to her. She also announced that she was aware that reading required more than phonics and would amend her bill accordingly. I offered to share a document I had prepared that illustrated how the percentage of New Jersey's students scoring at the "proficient" level in reading dropped dramatically between the fourth and eighth grades. Myers didn't want this document distributed, and Fox stunned me when she retorted, "That's because the kids don't know their blends!" I knew our work was cut out for those of us who didn't want to see reading instruction sink into a sea of phonics. I mentioned that New Jersey's Administrative Code for Licensure does not require that those pursuing a teaching license take any coursework in how to teach reading and that this was a critical dimension of the problem.

Few words were said on parting, and I had little doubt that I had violated a few of my own rules about appropriate behavior during meetings with legislators, especially the rules about being pleasant no matter what. I gauged the sentiment in the room. Only the representative from NJPSA, David Nash—the organization's lobbyist—seemed sensitive to some of the issues I had raised. Peter Fedorchak, a high school supervisor with whom I'd worked on the state's Language Arts Literacy Standards, also had been present as an NJPSA council representative. I decided that I'd contact both Fedorchak and Nash soon after the meeting to learn their thoughts and see if we might work collaboratively on next steps. I also earnestly believed I had to send a gentle note to Assemblywoman Myers, reiterating the points I'd made during the meeting (see Figure 14). At least that way they would be on record.

Follow–Up to the Meeting

Soon after the meeting, a letter came from Assemblywoman Myers's office to all who had attended the September 27 meeting (see Figure 15). It did mention some of the concerns that attendees had raised, although no promises were made

Figure 14. Jill Lewis's Letter to Assemblywoman Myers

| NEW JERSEY READING ASSOCIATION |
| STATE COUNCIL OF THE IRA & |
| AFFILIATE OF THE NJEA |

September 30, 2000
The Honorable Connie Myers
New Jersey Assembly
124 W. Washington Ave.
Washington, NJ 07882

Dear Assemblywoman Myers,

I enjoyed our lively conversation this past Thursday, September 28, 2000. Thank you for meeting with us.

Enclosed are the materials you requested, namely the report of the National Reading Panel with relevant portions highlighted. I have also included a letter from a panel member, Dr. Timothy Shanahan, which further elucidates the panel's findings vis à vis A-2652.

Also enclosed are materials developed by the New Jersey Reading Association that express our opinions on a number of issues related to reading achievement of New Jersey's children. The most recent one, "Literacy Teaching and Learning in Early Care and Education Programs," was developed in collaboration with several state professional associations and speaks to some of the questions you raised at our meeting. The paper on "Language Arts Literacy Assessment" offers many suggestions and you might find some of the language in it useful for your revised bill.

I do hope you will consider modifying your bill so as to include some of the recommendations made, namely:

 a. That districts be asked to develop benchmarks for each grade level (at least through grade 3) that would enable teachers to assess whether a child was making progress towards reaching the CPIs identified as necessary for children to reach by the end of 4th grade.
 b. That teachers be required to use a variety of informal assessments to determine whether children are making this progress.
 c. That teachers be required to use a specified portion of their professional development hours to increase their knowledge and skills about informal assessment.

I also hope you will consider writing a second bill, one that requires all teachers, regardless of grade level or content being taught, to take coursework in the teaching of language arts literacy. NJRA's position on this is elaborated in an enclosed paper. We know that unless teachers are trained in how to help children achieve literacy at all grade levels and for all types of text, no assessment instrument will result in the gains we desire.

I look forward to continued conversation. Please feel free to contact me at any time. My office number is XXX-XXX-XXXX. My address is on the enclosed materials.

Sincerely yours,

Jill Lewis, Ed. D.
Chair
NJRA Legislation/Professional Standards Committee

c. Natalie Smith, President, NJRA

Figure 15. Letter From Assemblywoman Myers to Attendees of Meeting on A–2652

NEW JERSEY GENERAL ASSEMBLY

CONNIE MYERS
ASSEMBLYWOMAN, 23RD DISTRICT
VARREN-HUNTERDON-MERCER COUNTIES
124 W. WASHINGTON AVENUE
WASHINGTON, NJ 07882
(908) 835-1202—WARREN
(908) 713-1608—HUNTERDON
(609) 466-7454—MERCER
FAX (908) 835-1205
asw.cmyers@worldnet.att.net

COMMITTEES
VICE CHAIR
AGRICULTURE & NATURAL RESOURCES
MEMBER
SOLID AND HAZARDOUS WASTE

October 16, 2000

TO: Attendees of meeting on A-2652

Thank you for attending the meeting on September 28, 2000. This is the summary from our notes.

First the issue was raised concerning which grade the students would be tested in for reading and spelling comprehension. I suggested that the students be tested at the end of grade 1, since research shows that if students do not read by the end of grade two, they are more difficult to remediate. Secondly, I suggested that those students judged not to be at grade level by the end of grade 1 should then receive additional phonics instruction in grade 2. The bill would be amended to reflect this.

The second issue was support for the provision in the bill that the type of assessment given to the students be left up to the individual school districts to formulate and implement.

During the meeting I was also promised material from some of you. I have received and read the NJ Reading Association material from Dr. Lewis. As I stated at the meeting, Dr. Lewis and I are unlikely to agree that an emphasis on phonics should be mandated. As I also stated, I will work with all interested parties to ensure that any mandate recognizes that not all children need an emphasis on phonics and that the mandate fits, insofar as practicable, the existing principles and practices in our schools. In addition, I am waiting for material from Bob Sweet, who is supposed to send me the VA standards for reading assessment, the teacher assessment for reading at the university level, and the definition of reading in the Reading Excellence Act. Finally, I am also waiting for material from David Nash, who is supposed to send me information on alternatives to phonics as effective strategies for remediating reading performance. As I stated at the meeting, I represent those who feel that an emphasis on phonics is necessary for certain children. I believe the report of the National Reading Panel supports this view. I am also currently exploring Dr. Lewis' request that I introduce separate legislation that would address licensing concerns for teachers.

The School Boards raised the issue of whether an appropriation is necessary. Since I feel that phonics should be incorporated as part of the Core Curriculum Standards, I have not envisioned the need for separate funding. However, it is my understanding that federal grant monies may be available to fund initiatives such as this. Another alternative we discussed was a pilot program. I will explore these options with Department of Education representatives.

Once again, thank you for attending the meeting and contributing your valued input on Bill A-2652. I will send you proposed amendments when they are ready. If you have any further comments or questions regarding this bill, please feel free to contact my office.

Sincerely,

Connie Myers
CM/tn/cm
D:\WINDOWS\SHARED\REVIEW\SUM.LTR

about changes to A-2652, except to indicate that the bill would now be revised so that the assessment would occur at grade 1 instead of 2.

I had first heard from Linda on September 7, 2000. It was now nearly a month later and NJRA was holding a Board of Directors meeting. I had hoped that many local council presidents would attend and that after the meeting they would communicate to their members the importance of both keeping abreast of developments with Bill A-2652 and being ready to act when called on. I had opportunity at the board meeting to summarize the bill and the nature of the meeting with Assemblywoman Myers. The talking points material was distributed, and the tenor of the room was such that I knew I could count on these association leaders to advocate as needed.

Fortunately, one member of the Legislation/Professional Standards Committee lived in Myers's district. She agreed to contact the Assemblywoman and arrange to meet with her. It was also the right time to send a letter to other NJRA members who lived in Assemblywoman Myers's district. There wasn't a lot of time to prepare the letter because even though we did not know when the bill would come before the Assembly Appropriations Committee, everyone believed it would be soon.

I sent an explanatory letter to the NJRA members Natalie Smith had identified, as well as to NJRA members living in Assemblywoman Myers's district, in which I outlined the major shortcomings of Bill A-2652 (see Figure 16).

Our organization also has a quarterly newsletter. Information about Bill A-2652 that had been distributed at the Board of Directors meeting appeared in the newsletter, with the hope that even more NJRA members would learn of the situation.

The Legislative Process

The NJRA officers, other Board members, and I expected A-2652 to be on the Assembly Education Committee agenda soon. It was time to get our legislative contacts identified and our advocacy plans moving forward.

One significant contact we had was with the Committee's chair, Assemblyman David Wolfe. NJRA's past president, Sue Hopson, lived in his district, and she, Natalie Smith, and I had met with him previously to discuss literacy needs for New Jersey's children. He seemed receptive to meeting with Hopson about Assemblywoman Myers's bill, but he was only able to

Figure 16. Jill Lewis's Letter to NJRA Members in Assemblywoman Myers's District

NEW JERSEY READING ASSOCIATION
STATE COUNCIL OF THE IRA &
AFFILIATE OF THE NJEA

October 3, 2000

Dear Language Arts Literacy Professional,

Your district Assemblywoman, Connie Myers, has submitted the enclosed bill (A-2652) to the NJ Assembly Education Committee. <u>It may be on the Committee's agenda for October 16th, 2000.</u> **The New Jersey Reading Association opposes this bill which calls for a phonics assessment of all New Jersey schoolchildren at the end of grade 2.**

We need you to **call Assemblywoman Myers at 908–835–1202, express your opposition, and let her know that you are a voter in her district.** Her address is: The Honorable Connie Myers, New Jersey Assembly, 124 W. Washington Ave., Washington, NJ 07882. <u>And share this information with others who may not be members of our association.</u>

NJRA opposes this bill because:

<u>It misrepresents the findings of the National Reading Panel.</u> The enclosed letter to Assemblywoman Myers from Tim Shanahan, who served on this Panel, confirms her misrepresentation. In the report, phonics is cited as only one of several areas that contribute to a child's reading achievement. Other factors cited by the National Reading Panel as making contribution include fluency; comprehension (vocabulary instruction and text comprehension); teacher education and reading instruction; computer technology. The National Reading Panel also noted throughout the document it was unable to review the research on all of the factors that contributed to a child's reading achievement including motivation and second language learning.

<u>The test called for imposes additional costs on districts for little purpose.</u> Districts already spend inordinate amounts of money implementing the state assessment system. A rough estimate is that the proposed test would cost Jersey City more than $67,000 to administer the test. This money could be better used; it would, for instance, pay the salaries of two teachers with some experience. In a tiny district such as Franklin Township, this test would be comparatively costly approximately $11,000 for the test, or the equivalent of one half-time classroom assistant.

<u>The test costs instructional time.</u> The state should review its current assessment instruments to determine whether there is already a way to obtain additional information about a child's language arts literacy development without imposing another test. For

(continued)

Figure 16. (continued)

instance, schools could be given a breakdown in terms of the types of questions students missed on the 4th grade test and instruction could be geared in those directions. This would be even more useful for the 8th grade test.

<u>The Core Content Curriculum Standards for Language Arts Literacy already include the need for phonics instruction</u>. The Cumulative Progress Indicators identify what every child should know by the end of 4th grade. **While it is not dictated HOW each child will reach these CPIs, certainly those for 4th grade cannot be achieved unless children have fundamental understanding of phonics and phonemic awareness.** The Frameworks provide sample lessons for developing these skills. Districts can, and many already have, develop benchmarks for each grade level that would lead to the CPIs for 4th grade; districts can, and many already have, use well-developed informal classroom assessments to determine how well children are reaching these benchmarks.

<u>The bill targets the wrong population</u>. It is in high school where a sharp drop in reading proficiency occurs, not in second grade. This is particularly true and is borne out on test scores in our poor, urban districts where there is a sharp drop in scores between 8th and 12th grade. This is a national trend.

Thank you for your commitment to quality language arts literacy programs for New Jersey's children. Let us know if you need any additional information from us, or receive any responses from Myers's office that we should hear.

Sincerely yours,
Jill Lewis, Chair
NJRA Legislation/Professional Standards Committee

c. Natalie Smith, NJRA President

Encs.

confer with her by phone. My understanding of the conversation was that basically Sue was told "not to worry." He seemed to suggest that the bill would not get through the Education Committee.

The hearing before the Committee was set for mid–October. Dorothy Strickland, past-president of the International Reading Association and Professor of Education at Rutgers University, and I planned to testify. Surprisingly, though, the bill was pulled from the Committee's agenda for that date. Linda let me know that the assemblywoman was revising her bill. Suddenly, I was optimistic. Had Myers heard what we were saying? Did Shanahan's letter make her reconsider? It was a bit of a mystery but one I didn't mind investigating.

An Amended Bill A-2652

I learned from my contact at the New Jersey Department of Education that Assemblywoman Myers had requested a meeting with their language arts people. During that meeting, she told them that she might request some funding for a pilot study on phonics. Although her agenda apparently hadn't changed, at least her new thinking bought some time for those of us opposing the bill.

I called the assemblywoman's office and, again, offered to provide assistance with the language of the bill. Her aide told me that Myers was modifying the bill and would include some of the points I'd made, especially the inclusion of comprehension as a dimension of the assessment.

In mid-January, I received a call from Myers's office, informing me that she was sending me an amended version of her bill and that she looked forward to my comments. What a turnaround! Of course, until I received the revisions, I offered no comment.

When the amended version of the bill arrived, it was a disappointment to say the least. A dollar allocation had now been included, thus addressing NJPSA's concerns. The Panel's findings—all of them—were summarized early in the bill's text, but then they were not mentioned again. Phonics remained the centerpiece of the assessment: The term *comprehension* appeared only once in the bill; however, in the summary of the Panel's findings, the word *phonics* appeared 23 times. The amended bill did not appear to address the questions I had raised nor the concerns of other groups opposed to the bill.

I decided to set aside all apprehension about contacting the Assemblywoman at this point and move quickly. I phoned Assemblywoman Myers's office and explained to her legislative aide my dissatisfaction with the revised bill. Much of the content did, in fact, contradict research. I followed up with a fax to the aide that included a copy of the revised bill and my detailed comments on different sections (see Figure 17). My notations made references to specific chapters in the Panel's report that refuted sections of the bill or that supported additions I made.

The cover sheet of my fax to the aide indicated that the recommendations I was sending were intended to "clarify some of the language so that test developers will have a clearer idea of what needs to be assessed." I also added provisions for special needs and English-language learners. Further, my cover sheet noted that, "A remaining question is what happens to children who do not pass this test? We hope grade retention will not be the consequence. Rather, we would like to see increased professional development in schools where children are having the greatest trouble."

Figure 17. Jill Lewis's Comments on and Additions to the Revised Bill A–2652 (additions appear in boldface)

P R O P O S E

1/9/2001

ASSEMBLY COMMITTEE SUBSTITUTE FOR
ASSEMBLY, No. 2652

STATE OF NEW JERSEY

Sponsored by Assemblywoman MYERS

AN ACT requiring a Statewide grade 1 reading assessment, supplementing Chapter 35 of Title 18A of the New Jersey Statutes and making an appropriation.

BE IT ENACTED *by the Senate and General Assembly of the State of New Jersey:*

1. The Legislature finds and declares that:

a. Learning to read is a complex and difficult task but is the foundation for proficiency in all of the core curriculum content areas and essential for full participation in all aspects of life;

b. In 1997, the U.S. Congress called upon the Director of the National Institute of Child Health and Human Development (NICHD) of the National Institutes of Health, in consultation with the Secretary of Education, to create a National Reading Panel to identify research-based practical findings on how best to teach children to read.

(1) On April 13, 2000, after nearly two years of analysis and assessment, the National Reading Panel officially released its report on scientific research-based reading instruction.

(2) The panel determined that effective reading instruction includes teaching children to break apart and manipulate the sounds in **spoken** words (phonemic awareness), teaching them that these sounds are represented by letters of the alphabet which can then be blended together to form words (phonics), having them practice what they've learned by reading aloud with guidance and feedback (guided oral reading), and applying reading comprehension strategies to guide and improve reading comprehension.

(3) More specifically,

(a) **with regard to phonemic awareness**, the panel found that:

[1] the research conducted to date strongly supports the concept that explicitly and systematically teaching children to manipulate phonemes significantly improves **many** children's reading and spelling abilities:

[2] although all levels of readers acquired phoneme awareness successfully, the impact of acquiring this awareness in the lower grades,

(continued)

Figure 17. (continued)

preschool and kindergarten, on a child's ability to read and spell was much greater than when this awareness was acquired by children in first grade and above.

(b) and, **with regard to phonics , the panel found that**

[1] the research literature provides solid evidence that phonics instruction produces significant benefits for children from kindergarten through sixth grade and for children having difficulties learning to read and that the greatest improvements in reading were seen from **systematic phonics instruction rather than nonsystematic phonics instruction.**

~~→ (c) for children with learning disabilities and children who are low achievers, systematic phonics instruction, combined with synthetic phonics instruction, produced the greatest gains;~~

(c) and, **with regard to fluency the panel found that**

[1] guided oral reading is important for developing reading fluency–the ability to read with efficiency and ease;

(d) and, **with regard to comprehension**, the panel found that:

[1] **reading vocabulary is crucial to the comprehension processes of a skilled reader**

[2] **Comprehension instruction can effectively motivate and teach readers to learn and to use comprehension strategies that benefit the reader.**

[3] **The preparation of teachers to deliver comprehension strategy instruction is important to the success of teaching reading comprehension.**

c. In 1999, the New Jersey Department of Education contracted with Achieve, Inc., a national organization formed in 1996 by governors and business leaders to serve as a clearinghouse for state educational standards, assessments and accountability, to evaluate the language arts/literacy and mathematics core curriculum content standards and the Statewide assessments of student proficiency in language arts/literacy and mathematics conducted at the 4th, 8th and 11th grade levels.

d. In its report dated November 2000, *Measuring Up: A Standards and Assessment Benchmarking Report for New Jersey*, Achieve, Inc. noted that:

(1) New Jersey's earliest set of core curriculum content standards describe what students should know and be able to do by the end of grade 4;

(2) since the most intensive early reading instruction occurs in the grades leading up to grade 4, grade 4 expectations assume that students have already mastered the early reading essentials. ~~including phonics;~~

(continued)

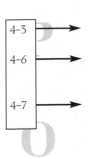

CUT THIS: It is not so. See pages 2-123, 2-93-94; no one systematic program more effective than another.

4-3

4-6

4-7

Figure 17. (continued)

P

> This is not true about the Standards. The Achieve report from which this was 'adapted' refers only to phonics study; this comment misrepresents that idea.

(3) however, ~~since virtually~~ no mention is made in the New Jersey core curriculum content standards of the early stages of literacy development, and no systematic phonics study is specified. ~~but the major strategy for mastering early reading essentials that appears to be advocated by the grade 4 expectations is the use of context clues, an important but not a sufficient strategy, according to....~~

(4) The National Research Council Report, *Preventing Reading Difficulties in Young Children* **(1998)** states that, "quality classroom instruction in kindergarten and the primary grades is the single best weapon against reading failure. Indeed, when done well, classroom instruction has been shown to overwhelm the effects of student background and supplementary tutoring." (343).

(5) Because early literacy is so important, New Jersey should consider launching an early reading initiative specifically addressing reading, writing, listening, and speaking expectations for pre-kindergarten through grade 3, including a balanced approach to reading that combines intensive instruction in phonics with significant exposure to rich literary experiences.

O

e. In its grant application for federal education assistance for a program for use only in the Abbott districts, the New Jersey Reading Excellence Act Program, the New Jersey Department of Education states, in part:

(1) that one of the most important foundations of reading success is phonemic awareness and that phonemic awareness skills assessed in kindergarten and first grade are good predictors of difficulties in learning to read; and

P

(2) if reading difficulties are not addressed through effective interventions in the early grades, the chances that children will catch up to their reading-proficient peers after third grade is unlikely.

O

f. New Jersey does not assess its pupils' proficiency in reading until the fourth grade in the language arts/literacy component of the elementary school proficiency assessment, an assessment which in 1998–99 found that Statewide 59% of the fourth grade pupils were not proficient in language arts/literacy.

S

g. It is urgent to implement a reading skills assessment, including an assessment of phonemic awareness **and reading comprehension** during the first grade in order to identify reading and spelling deficiencies, if any, at an early stage in a child's school life and remediate any deficiencies by third grade.

E

2. a. By the end of the 2001–2002 school year, the Commissioner of Education shall develop and administer an assessment to all pupils in grade 1 to assess the ability of pupils to read at grade level. This assessment shall be conducted annually thereafter. The assessment shall include

(continued)

Figure 17. (continued)

P

R

O

P

O

two components. The first component shall include items to assess the ability of pupils to read **with comprehension**. The second component shall include items to assess the ability of pupils to **segment, blend and** manipulate phonemes of spoken words, **particularly onsets, rhymes and syllables.**

b. The commissioner shall annually review the results of the assessment administered pursuant to subsection a. of this section with particular attention given to the relationship between a pupil's score on the reading **comprehension** and phonemes components of the assessment. The commissioner shall require any district with schools that do not meet State proficiency standards on the grade 1 assessment to develop and implement an improvement plan which includes measurable objectives to address the deficiencies identified through the grade 1 assessment.

c. The results of the grade 1 assessment required pursuant to subsection a. of this section shall be included on the School Report Card disseminated annually pursuant to the provisions of P.L.1995, c.235 (C.18A:7E-1 et seq.).

d. Alternative assessment formats will be available to ESL and special needs students.

e. Districts will provide professional development in the interpretation and use of test results.

3. There is appropriated from the General Fund $3,000,000 to the Department of Education to finance the administration of the grade 1 assessment.

4. This act shall take effect immediately.

Directs the Commissioner to develop and implement a grade 1 Statewide reading assessment.

A Hearing Before the Assembly Education Committee

Natalie Smith spoke about the bill at NJRA's annual meeting, hoping to garner more support and more advocates who would reach out to their representatives serving on the Assembly Education Committee. Linda informed me that the Committee was to hear the bill on March 22, 2001, at 2:00 p.m. at the State House Annex in Trenton, New Jersey. I confirmed this information by checking the online Legislative Calendar, provided by the Office of Legislative Services. Sure enough, the bill was listed for a committee hearing on that date. It was time to get the testimony together and be sure we had all the required supporting documentation for our case.

The hearing procedure was standard. Beforehand, Linda notified the Committee that representatives of NJRA would be testifying. Unfortunately, I was unable to attend the hearing after all, but Sue Hopson and Natalie Smith were prepared to testify. Linda also notified other NJEA affiliate organizations to attend and present their arguments for or against the bill. The day of the hearing, Sue and Natalie arrived on time, signed in as required, and waited for their turns to speak. At least four other professional organizations had come for a similar purpose—to express opposition to the bill. This bill had not changed in substance from the original language, except for the inclusion of monies for the assessments.

The hearing was a disaster. Chairman Wolfe did not allow testimony from anyone attending the hearing. No one prepared to testify, including Linda— who had attended hundreds of hearings—had ever experienced this treatment before. The bill was "moved out of committee" and on to the Appropriations Committee, without a single word of public testimony. This action by Chairman Wolfe made a mockery of the democratic process. It also raised a lot of questions by those opposed to the bill. Oddly, after the hearing Chairman Wolfe moved quickly toward Sue Hopson and Linda Kassekert to apologize to them about what had happened. He offered no explanation, and they did not seek one. We were confused by the uncommon practice of disallowing testimony but did not know the reasons behind it.

The actions of the Assembly Education Committee became a matter of public record. Linda sent me NJEA's Legislative Update on the meeting; it was circulated to NJEA members on March 29, 2001, and it read as follows (emphasis in boldface added by NJEA):

> ACS for A-2652 (Myers, Garrett): After taking no testimony, the Assembly Education Committee unanimously released this Assembly Committee Substitute for A-2652. The legislation **directs the Commissioner to develop and implement a grade 1 statewide diagnostic reading assessment.** The first component would measure items to access [sic] a pupil's ability to read. The second component would assess the ability of a pupil to manipulate phonics. As originally introduced, this legislation would advocate the teaching of phonics-only; the substitute subtly emphasizes the same goal. The results of the grade 1 test would be published in the State Report Card. The ACS would appropriate $3 million. **NJEA, as well as our affiliate, the NJRA (NJ Reading Association), and all other major education groups oppose the bill.** It now moves to the Assembly Appropriations Committee.

I think the word *tenacious* best describes my approach to advocacy, so I didn't feel defeated by the Committee's actions. Of course, I was surprised, but I didn't think it was over, and I certainly didn't feel the bill would ultimately pass. I was convinced that with the right plan, enough human resources, and enough time, we could defeat A-2652. There was a great deal of work ahead, and with a vengeance I orchestrated what we had to do. In fact, several things had to occur simultaneously.

We knew the bill would next come before the Appropriations Committee. We also knew that even if the Appropriations Committee approved the bill, it would still require approval of the Senate Education Committee before coming before the New Jersey State Assembly and then the New Jersey State Senate for a full vote. I believed that my colleagues and I needed to make contact with the chairs of both the Appropriations Committee and the Senate Education Committee to arrange meetings. Also, we needed to reach out to members of NJRA who lived in the districts of the committee members. I recalled that the legislative aide to the Speaker of the House had joined a meeting I had held recently with another assemblyman to express NJRA's support for his Spread the Word program (see chapter 3). I figured that it might be beneficial to contact that assemblyman and the Speaker's aide to let them know what was going on. Lastly (although there really is no *lastly* in advocacy work), I needed to be sure that the other organizations opposed to A-2652 were on board and were notifying their members about the latest developments.

Our Legislation/Professional Standards Committee's Advisory Board also includes an assemblyman, so I contacted his office as well and left a message explaining what had happened at the hearing before the Assembly Education Committee. The legislative aide there returned my call almost immediately. "That's incredible! I've never heard of such a thing," he said. "We're going to call the Speaker's office today and find out what happened." It was evident to me at that point how important building relationships for the long term is because you never know when you will need a friend and which friends will be able to help with which needs.

NJEA was very disturbed by the turn of events at the hearing. If the procedures that had been followed at that hearing became customary, NJEA would have great difficulty testifying on almost anything. The president of NJEA, Michael Johnson, decided to take action, and he sent a letter to the speaker of the House (see Figure 18).

Figure 18. NJEA President Michael Johnson's Letter to Speaker of the House Jack Collins

March 28, 2001
The Honorable Jack Collins
Speaker of the Assembly
63 East Avenue, Suite C
Woodstown, NJ 08098-1499

Re: ACS for A-2652

Dear Speaker Collins:

I am writing with respect to the above noted bill which was recently released from the Assembly Education Committee, without the taking of any testimony, and referred to the Assembly Appropriations Committee.

As released by the Assembly Education Committee, this substitute would direct the Commissioner of Education to develop and implement a Grade 1 Statewide reading assessment. Part of this assessment is to measure the ability of pupils to manipulate phonemes (phonics). As originally introduced, this bill would have mandated a phonics-only approach to the teaching of reading. Although this substitute is not as direct as the original version, the premise that phonics is the only way to teach reading is prominent in the bill. While phonics is an excellent method for teaching reading, NJEA believes that it should not be the only approach and whatever approach that is utilized should be based on the individual needs of the child.

NJEA opposes this legislation, not only because of the phonics aspect, but especially because of the mandated test. As you are aware, concerns have been raised by education groups and parents about the use of standardized tests and their impact on students and the instructional day. We believe that another mandated test, this time for first grade students, is not in the best interest of these children.

Additionally, you should be aware that the Appropriations Committee recently released A-2798 (Garrett), "The Standards and Assessment Accountability Act," which would require, among other provisions, that a thorough review of the Statewide assessments be conducted. Given this, we believe that great caution should be exercised prior to establishing any additional mandated assessments.

We would respectfully ask that ACS for A-2652 not be posted for a vote by the full Assembly.

Thank you for your consideration of this request.

Very truly yours,

Michael Johnson

Michael Johnson
President

MJ/LMK/ep

I also sent a letter to Speaker Collins, expressing NJRA's concerns and recalling the positive experience I had recently had with his legislative aide (see Figure 19). I requested a meeting. Soon after the letter reached its destination, I received a call from the speaker's aide to let me know that Speaker Collins would be contacting Assemblyman Bagger, chair of the Appropriations Committee, to express his opposition to the bill.

Figure 19. Jill Lewis's Letter to Speaker of the House Jack Collins

NEW JERSEY READING ASSOCIATION
STATE COUNCIL OF THE IRA &
AFFILIATE OF THE NJEA

March 27, 2001

The Honorable Jack Collins, Speaker
State of New Jersey–General Assembly
Majority Office–State House
PO Box 098
Trenton, NJ 08625-0098

Dear Speaker Collins,

I am writing you to request a meeting with you and your Education Legislative Aide as well as Mike Tolan to discuss A-2652 (Amended) (Myers). This bill made it through the Assembly Education Committee at that group's meeting last Thursday, March 22nd.

The New Jersey Reading Association had two representatives at the Committee meeting to oppose this bill, NJRA's President, Natalie Smith, and Past President, Sue Hopson. Also present to voice opposition were Linda Kassekert of NJEA and representatives from several other professional associations.

The Committee Chair, Assemblyman Wolfe, did not permit testimony on this bill. This was in spite of the fact that we had notified the appropriate office that we intended to speak and had completed the forms necessary to do so. Further, testimony was permitted on other bills on the agenda for that day. Interestingly, Assemblyman Wolfe later apologized to Ms. Kassekert and offered to assist us with the Legislature.

We have many, many concerns about this bill. Our organization had spent considerable time working with Assemblywoman Myers's office, making suggestions; we were assured that certain changes would be in the amended version—they were not.

We hope you will be willing to meet with us, and we would be happy to discuss possible days/times with your Scheduler.

Sincerely yours,

Jill Lewis, Ed.D., Chair
NJRA Legislation/Professional Standards Committee

In the meantime, NJPSA also objected to Assemblywoman Myers's bill, and in early April NJPSA sent an Action Alert to its members that outlined the bill, including the consequences and the dollar costs (see Figure 20). Members were urged to contact their legislators.

It was also important to bring more of the NJRA membership on board with our advocacy effort. The most efficient thing to do might have been to identify members living in particular legislative districts. For instance, we could have sent our note to just those members living in districts of Assembly Appropriation Committee members. But we didn't have our membership list set up for this kind of sorting. We also felt that it might be wiser to let all the membership know the status of the bill that Natalie had discussed at the Spring NJRA conference the previous month. Thus, the mailing went to everyone. As the letter in Figure 21 indicates, several pieces of information were included, along with suggestions of what the members could do.

Informing the Public

It had become almost impossible to pick up a newspaper during this period in public education without reading a piece on the state of U.S. education and children's poor performance on state, national, or international test scores. There was an angry mood toward public education; just a short time ago, outsiders from other states had publicly criticized our Language Arts Literacy Standards. I felt the criticism was unfair, and having worked on the Standards and as cochair of the Standards Curriculum Framework Committee, I was particularly offended. Bill A2652 simply increased my desire to get accurate information to the public. I felt that a letter to the editor of a major newspaper, including information about A-2652, might be worthwhile. From my perspective, the key was to find something in the press to which I could respond, preferably in a paper that reached both Assemblywoman Myers's and Assemblyman Bagger's constituents. These two Assembly members represented neighboring districts, so one paper with a wide circulation would suffice.

An incredible opportunity presented itself when a major paper in New Jersey published an article bemoaning the National Assessment of Educational Progress (NAEP) reading scores and using the poor results as evidence of children's poor phonics skills. I immediately sent a letter in response to the article. I kept my fingers crossed that my letter would be published. When it was

Figure 20. NJPSA Action Alert

New Jersey Principals and Supervisors Association
12 Centre Drive • Monroe Township, NJ 08831-1564
Tel: 609-860-1200 • Fax: 609-860-2999 • E-Mail: NJPSA@njpsa.org • Web: www.njpsa.org

-ACTION ALERT-

ACTION NEEDED TO HALT NEW GRADE 1 TESTING BILL

Legislation requiring the Commissioner of Education to develop a new state test to be administered in first grade, **A2652 (Myers)**, has been approved by the Assembly Education Committee and is awaiting action in the Assembly Appropriations Committee. The legislation mandates the new test be administered beginning in the 2001-02 school year, with the results included on the New Jersey School Report Card. The test will assess the ability of students to read and "manipulate phonemes." Where any schools in a district fail to meet state proficiency standards on the first grade test, the district is required to develop an improvement plan. Three million dollars in state funding is appropriated to develop and administer the new test.

-TALKING POINTS-

NJPSA members are urged to contact legislative leaders to express your opposition to A2652. Listed below are suggested talking points:

1) Any assessment tool designed by the NJDOE to address early literacy should be a purely voluntary, diagnostic tool to help educators identify students' educational needs and inform instructional practices. The NJDOE should conduct a pilot study of volunteer districts to determine the effectiveness of any diagnostic tool that is developed.

2) The Legislature should not consider any expansion of New Jersey's testing program until a comprehensive, independent review of the assessments that have already been developed is completed. Such a review is required under **A2798 (Garrett)**, now pending in the Assembly. Serious questions regarding the validity, reliability and length of current tests must be addressed. The NJDOE has had difficulty developing and scoring current state assessments and recently had to rescore the Language Arts Literacy portion of the ESPA exam. The NJDOE is also at the beginning of a review of the Core Curriculum Content Standards, which will impact future state assessment.

3) Because of the wide variation in the development of reading skills, it is inappropriate to report first grade test results on the New Jersey School Report Card.

4) In order to achieve the primary goal of A2652 - to ensure that all students are able to read at grade level by the end of grade 1 - some of the $3 million allocation in A2652 should be targeted to support professional

(continued)

Figure 20. (continued)

development in the most effective strategies for classroom teachers to use in diagnosing and remediating reading deficiencies.

KEY LEGISLATORS TO CONTACT

Acting Governor/Senate President Donald DiFrancesco (R-22)
Governor's Office: (609) 292-6000
Governor's Fax: (609) 292-3454
District Office: (908) 322-5500
District Fax: (908) 322-9347

Senate Education Committee Chairman Robert Martin (R-26)
District Office: (973) 984-0922
District Fax: (973) 984-8094

Senate Budget & Appropriations Committee Chairman Robert Littell (R-24)
District Office: (973) 827-2900
District Fax: (973) 827-0348

Assembly Speaker Jack Collins (R-3)
District Office: (856) 769-3633
District Fax: (856) 769-0049

Assembly Appropriations Committee Chairman Richard Bagger (R-22)
District Office: (908) 232-3673
District Fax: (908) 232-3345

NOTE: See NJPSA's Legislative Agenda Book and/or the Legislative Representation page on NJPSA's website at www.njpsa.org for information on how to contact your local legislators.

Figure 21. Jill Lewis's Letter to the NJRA Membership

NEW JERSEY READING ASSOCIATION
STATE COUNCIL OF THE IRA &
AFFILIATE OF THE NJEA

April 4, 2001

Dear NJRA Member,

We need you to get involved! **The advocacy work you do in the next few months will be a decisive factor in whether or not all first graders in New Jersey will be required to take a test on phonics and phonemic awareness, a test will be used to further erode the authority of local districts to develop child-appropriate curriculum for their schools.** If you attended the recent NJRA Spring Conference, then you know that there is a bill that has now passed the Assembly Education Committee, A-2652 (amended), which will lead to these results unless it meets with ultimate defeat.

What can you do? You can:

➤ **Learn** the enclosed materials, including A2652 (amended) and our reasons for opposing it.

➤ **Contact** your representatives on the enclosed list and ask them to oppose this bill. You can express your opposition to this bill by phone, in person, or by mail.

➤ **Talk** to teachers, parents, and administrators in your school; encourage them to do the same.

➤ **Write** letters to the editor of your local newspaper to express your opposition, and encourage others to do the same.

➤ **Contact** me for additional suggestions if you need them.

Enclosed you will find

(1) A copy of the amended bill. Note that some of our earlier suggestions to Myers were included in this amended version, especially funding for this test. The bill's intent and focus, however, remain the same.

(2) A copy of "bullet points" revised from what was distributed earlier and at the Conference, so as to reflect the amended bill's content.

(3) A copy of the "Making a Difference..." list of children's rights from IRA.

(4) A list of NJ Committees that will be making decisions on this bill in the near future.

(We aren't asking that you contact ALL legislators, only those that we expect to hear the bill between now and, perhaps, September.)

Please don't wait until it is too late to get involved. If the bill passes without anyone hearing from us, we will have only ourselves to blame.

Let me know how I can help you.

Jill Lewis, Ed.D., Chair
NJRA Legislation/Professional Standards Committee

Encs.

published (see Figure 22), I felt confident there would be more opposition to Bill A-2652. I should mention that I didn't give my letter the title "Shallow Literacy"; the newspaper editor created the title, but, thankfully, my point was understood.

My remaining and immediate advocacy task was to contact Assemblyman Bagger's office. It was the end of April and if things moved along as Myers expected, the bill would be posted for the May committee meeting, which was typically the final meeting of that committee for the year. I was a little nervous

---

Figure 22. Jill Lewis's Published Letter in Response to NAEP Reading Scores Article

THE STAR-LEDGER   THURSDAY, APRIL 19, 2001

p. 18

READERFORUM

Shallow literacy

Your April 7 report on the National Assessment of Educational Progress reading scores gives the impression that schools have failed to teach phonics. The findings do not support this notion. NAEP results show that while 37 percent read proficiently, another 63 percent could read simple words and sentences but were unable to draw conclusions from the material. That is, most could decode (use phonics) but could not think critically about text.

Unfortunately, some lawmakers support testing for only the most basic reading skills. A case in point is Assembly Bill 2652. If this measure becomes law, all first-graders' abilities to "manipulate phonemes" would be assessed, without regard for students' comprehension. This test would tell us whether children can sound out words but not whether kids understand what those words mean or how to use them. Test results would be used to penalize schools.

A-2652, based on a limited view of the requisites for successful reading, would lead to a narrowed curriculum and stunted literacy growth for New Jersey's children. As the recent findings of the national reading panel underscore, good readers have many tools at their disposal, including, but not limited to, phonics.

— *Jill Lewis, Highland Park*
The writer is a professor at New Jersey City University.

about making the call; NJRA had no history with his office—we had supported Democrats—and we had been told that Assemblyman Bagger was a friend of Assemblywoman Myers. Yet I felt I would be remiss if I didn't at least try to initiate a conversation and schedule a meeting with him.

When I phoned, I was put through to a woman who did not identify herself as a legislative aide, and I did not ask if she was. I was thankful I had a human voice on the other end of the phone line. I explained that I wanted a meeting with Assemblyman Bagger and I hoped she could help. She asked me to call back the next day, indicating that she'd have information for me then.

I was not optimistic; nevertheless, I did as requested and called back midmorning of the next day. Fortunately, the same assistant answered the phone. She said she had a message for me from the assemblyman. (I was really nervous now.) He wanted to know why NJRA was opposed to A2652. Referring to the points I had previously sent to NJRA's membership (see Figure 16 on pages 195–196), I was able to recite the numerous problems we had found with the bill. When I finished, the assistant gave a very brief but significant response: "Assemblyman Bagger doesn't like the bill either. He's not going to post it." I couldn't believe it! We had won! The bill would not be posted for the Appropriations Committee to hear in May. Because May was the Committee's last hearing for the year, legislators would have to resubmit bills again in the fall for the new legislative session, if they were to be heard. Any bills not heard by the current year's legislature would die with the end of the legislative session.

I was ecstatic. I also realized that many others who had worked on defeating this bill would be equally pleased and should take pride in the advocacy work they had done. Countless individuals had contributed, including many whose names I don't know and who are not part of the public record for A-2652. Some, such as Michael Johnson and David Nash, had encouraged their organizations to oppose the bill. There were others unfamiliar to me, including members of NJRA, who had no doubt written or phoned their legislators, sent letters to newspaper editors, spread the word to others about the dangers of the bill, and encouraged opposition. It had been a team effort, and I was thrilled to have been a part of it.

With delight, I contacted the office of Senator Martin, chair of the State Senate Education Committee. I had phoned him earlier in the week to try to schedule an appointment, figuring that once the bill made it through the

Assembly Education Committee, it would make its way easily through the State Senate. I was now able to tell his office that I would call again if I needed the appointment but that it was not currently necessary. In the back of my mind there was the memory of Assemblyman Wolfe's discourteous treatment of NJRA and others at the Assembly Education Committee hearing. I didn't want to completely discount the possibility that someone, Assemblywoman Myers perhaps, could get Assemblyman Bagger to change his mind about not posting the bill. I also had misgivings about whether Assemblyman Bagger had told me he wouldn't post the bill just to keep me from writing more letters to editors. As these thoughts crossed my mind, I realized I'd been doing advocacy work a very long time! I had become quite cynical and mistrustful.

A Reward for Work Well Done

As it turned out, Assemblyman Bagger was true to his word. He didn't post the bill in May, and it died with the legislative session. Soon after this information was known, one of the members of NJRA's Legislation/Professional Standards Committee's Advisory Board called me to let me know that Cathy Fox had a long editorial in a major newspaper, complaining about Assemblyman Bagger's decision not to post the bill. The editorial contained some of the same misrepresentations of the National Reading Panel report as those of the original bill. Fox concluded her lengthy piece by stating that constituents "have a right to know why this bill was not allowed out of committee."

I now had a chance to publicly thank Assemblyman Bagger for the work he did. I sent a letter to the editor of the same newspaper, offering a number of reasons why the bill had not been posted (see Figure 23).

Later that year, when NJRA was seeking someone to award as Legislator of the Year, as our organization had done each year for the past seven or eight years, the decision was very easy. We were thrilled to present the award to Assemblyman Bagger. This award is presented at our annual banquet to the legislator who has done the most for children's literacy that year, and some years it has been very difficult to find an appropriate recipient. In fact, some years no one is nominated, and this isn't surprising given how little some legislators have done for promoting reading and writing programs or addressing certification and professional development needs. We were fortunate that Assemblyman Bagger came through for NJRA and for the children and teachers of New Jersey.

Figure 23. Jill Lewis's Published Letter Thanking Assemblyman Bagger

Letters
to the
Editor

HERALD NEWS

Bagger Makes Right Decision on Education

Thursday, June 28, 2001

Cathy Fox raises a reasonable question in her June 19 letter to the editor when she asks why Assemblyman Richard Bagger, R-Westfield, did not permit A2652 to come before the appropriations committee. This is a bill that would legislate testing of first-graders to see whether they could "read and spell phonetically" and would penalize districts where children did not succeed. At the risk of being accused of trying to read Bagger's mind, I will attempt to provide some answers.

To begin with, Bagger may have understood how severely A2652, like Fox's letter, misrepresents the findings of the National Reading Panel. That panel found that there were several important contributors to reading development: comprehension strategies, including vocabulary development strategies, as well as guided oral reading, phonemic awareness and phonics.

A2652 only speaks to the last two and, in fact, a member of the National Reading Panel, Tim Shanahan, was so disturbed by the narrowness of A2652, that he expressed his concerns to Assemblywoman Myers when she was first drafting the bill.

To his credit, Bagger may have also done some checking around on what happened at the Assembly Education Committee meeting. As Fox says, "The bill passed the Assembly Education Committee...without discussion." That's because the opposition groups attending the meeting were not permitted to discuss it!

At last three groups there were prepared to offer testimony against the bill: New Jersey Reading Association, New Jersey Education Association, and New Jersey Principals and Supervisors Association. The committee chair, Assemblyman David Wolfe, R-Brick, did not allow comment. Later, he sent a letter of apology to each group, but he did not offer much in the way of explanation for his actions.

Probably Bagger also realized that testing whether children could "spell phonetically" was not the same as seeing whether children could spell correctly. After all, isn't Nu Jerzee the phonetic spelling of our state?

And testing whether students could "read," in the context of A2652, might just mean seeing whether they could "decode," or sound out words. In fact, I personally contacted Myers and asked her to change this language in A2652 to "read with comprehension." She did not make this change.

Obviously, comprehension didn't matter to her; only sounding out words was important. Is this what we want? Kids who can sound out words, but have no idea what the words mean?

Bagger may have also correctly realized that piling on assessments does not ensure good teaching. New Jersey is unique in that our state administrative code that dictates requirements for teaching certification does not stipulate coursework in teaching reading for any teacher. While most colleges and universities in our state see the folly in this and do require some coursework in their elementary education and early childhood teacher preparation programs, these schools are under no obligation to keep these requirements and, further, anyone seeking alternate route certification can avoid such courses altogether. We not only need to test kids' skills, we need to prepare beginning teachers how to teach these skills. A2652 ignores this reality.

The Department of Education is currently revising its standards for language arts literacy, in accord with the 1996 stipulation when the standards were first adopted that they would be reviewed/revised every five years. The original set of standards indicated what children should be able to do by the end of grade four. This time, there will be benchmarks for grade clusters, including K-2, that elaborate on the cumulative progress indicators. Phonics and phonemic awareness will be included, as will all other early literacy skills necessary for reading achievement.

If a test is to be legislated for these early years, then it must be designed to measure all of the skills that we know contribute to reading development in the early years.

While Fox's question was reasonable, so was Bagger's decision not to post this bill. Bagger is to be commended for his wisdom and his ability to see literacy in its broadest sense and to do what is right for the children of our state.

Jill Lewis
Professor of Literary Education, New Jersey City University and Chair, Legislation/Professional Standards Committee, New Jersey Reading Association

– 213 –

Conclusion

When the 2001–2002 legislative session began, NJEA notified me that another assemblywoman was introducing another reading test bill. I was notified as soon as the bill was introduced. Several legislators told me not to worry—the bill wasn't going anywhere. They were right. It didn't.

New Jersey is faced with the same assessment issues as most U.S. states now are, largely the result of the No Child Left Behind mandates and the lack of federal funding to implement the requirements. The battles over this issue are being fought primarily in Washington, DC. We can all be part of that process, if we choose. The important thing is to know that what you do can affect outcomes, large and small, and that if you don't do anything, you really shouldn't complain about the results if you don't like them, nor should you take credit for them if they reflect your thinking. Just ask yourself, Did I make this happen? Would I have wanted something different? What could I have done to contribute to implementation of the best policies for our schools, our teachers, our communities and our children?

CHAPTER 8

Evaluating Your Work
as an Education Advocate

As you no doubt realize after reading chapter 7, advocacy work is demanding and challenging. Jill told a strong story of her work with the New Jersey Reading Association (NJRA) to stop a bill that she and the organization felt was detrimental to students. Think of the dedication of these individuals to their advocacy issue and how much time, energy, and expense was involved in fighting this proposal so vigorously.

Jill's advocacy example shows that successful advocates are passionate and determined. To be successful, you need to believe that what you are doing is necessary and important; otherwise you are likely to abandon the effort. Advocacy is always labor intensive. Usually the pace is hectic and you operate on tight turnaround times and deadlines. There is often little lead-time. You have to be ready to jump into action and begin dealing with many different issues and audiences at the same time. After quickly establishing an advocacy plan and prioritizing your strategies, you begin your work, organizing yourself, others, or both for the many advocacy tasks that need immediate implementation. You might consider and implement simultaneously many of the strategies described in detail in previous chapters of this book: The e-mails, letters to the editor, and op-eds must be written and sent. Phone calls and letters to policymakers must begin. Information such as research summaries, position statements, and proposed alternatives or actions must be prepared and disseminated to the appropriate audiences.

In the rapid-fire action of your multiple and simultaneous advocacy initiatives, there appears to be little time for your reflection and evaluation. Yet the truly successful education advocate, the one who engages repeatedly in advocacy, is constantly reflecting on and evaluating the effectiveness of each advocacy strategy he or she has used. The successful advocate realizes the need to adjust the advocacy plan when implementation is not going smoothly and advocacy initiatives are not succeeding. The remainder of this chapter will focus on procedures you can use to evaluate the success of your advocacy efforts.

Looking Objectively at Your Advocacy Accomplishments

It often is difficult to step back and look objectively at how well things are working when you are very involved in putting your advocacy plan into action. As suggested in chapter 4, you are more likely to be reflective and evaluative if you build in specific times for evaluation when you are developing your overall advocacy timeline. Then, at those evaluation points, you should pause and consider what is working, what needs to be changed, and what your next steps are.

Be mindful of the many levels of your advocacy work. Consider that you may be successful in some activities but not in others. What audiences were reached? How were the messages received? What worked well? What didn't? How do you know? Brainstorm alternatives for strategies that seem to be going nowhere or leading the group away from the desired goals.

You also should learn from your mistakes. Sometimes your enthusiasm for your cause might get in the way. One of this book's authors, Kathy Jongsma, remembers a particularly difficult visit in the Washington office of one of her Senators. As she met with the Senator's aide, it quickly became apparent that the issues of concern to her were not the issues of concern to the aide. In fact, the aide was argumentative. The office visit was going nowhere. In hindsight, the best strategy for Kathy would have been for her to thank the aide for the time and to exit, but unfortunately, that wasn't the path the advocate chose. The ensuing argument brought neither clarity to Kathy's ideas nor goodwill between her and the aide. An apology in a follow-up letter helped to clear Kathy's conscience but may not have either smoothed over the breach in etiquette or helped her cause. What did Kathy learn that would apply to subsequent advocacy activities? She discovered the importance of remaining pleasant and polite even when baited and challenged. Indeed, keeping cool under pressure is an important advocacy trait.

After the debriefing session, determine and prioritize the next steps in your advocacy plan. Consider if additional resources are needed or if other people should be added to your advocacy team.

What Counts as Success?

The vignettes presented throughout this book have highlighted a variety of advocacy efforts. Not all of the described initiatives resulted in the changes or actions each advocate wanted. Yet for each advocate, there were successful elements to be celebrated.

It is easy to be discouraged when your hard work does not resolve a situation in the way you had hoped and planned. debbie smith's vignette suggests that advocacy stories include both positive moments and moments when events are not going so smoothly. If an advocate can monitor his or her efforts and adjust them, as debbie did, successful outcomes may be more likely.

Kenny, a New Student

debbie smith

Assistant Professor, Northeastern State University, Tahlequah, Oklahoma, USA

I had been advocating on behalf of students for over a year when I met Kenny, a Mexican American boy in the seventh grade. I noticed Kenny had given up on school. His teachers never complained about his behavior. He just didn't do the work.

Kenny failed seventh grade. His mother, Gina, was informed that if he took summer school he could be promoted to eighth grade, so he enrolled and passed. Subsequently, his mother learned that Kenny would repeat seventh grade. She called me. I called the vice principal who explained the school policy for appealing the retention decision: A letter needed to be in the school board office within two days. I composed a letter and hand-delivered it.

The next step was the hearing. I had never attended a school board hearing, so I called several school district employees for information. On the night before the hearing, an assistant superintendent returned my calls. He guaranteed me that the hearing would be friendly and designed to help Kenny. I had nothing to worry about, he said.

But I had learned from attendance/suspension hearings I had attended in the past that this might not be true and that procedures and policies are very important. So that night I prepared a two-page brief in Kenny's defense. In my brief I said that Kenny had shut down at school but nowhere else.

Kenny's mother and I arrived early and saw none of Kenny's teachers or his principal. We relaxed, thinking there wouldn't be any reason to present a defense. Finally, the assistant superintendent approached. I asked him what would happen if the teachers and principal didn't show up. He replied that they were currently meeting in his office. I was upset and said, "You told me this wasn't an adversarial meeting; yet you are having a pre-meeting in your office. I want you to know this sets off red flashing lights in my head."

Finally, the hearing began. The boardroom was full of people we didn't know. During the introductions, we heard the words *district lawyer*. I leaned over to Gina and said, "Maybe we should have gotten a lawyer." It was the school system against us. As a former teacher and part of this system, I was intimidated.

The school personnel presented their side. When it was our turn, I shared a different picture of Kenny. I was asked several questions. I quickly changed my strategy and referred to policies and not to Kenny. I pointed out that Kenny's mom had not been informed about the final decision to fail him until it was too late. She had asked for help but none was granted.

Kenny was ultimately promoted because the school district didn't follow due process; it would have been nicer if the reason for his promotion had been because it was best for Kenny.

When rules and regulations become more important than students, it is a shallow victory. Thinking about my past advocating experiences, I have lost when the policies demanded it to be so, and I have won when due process was not followed, but I have never won because the decision was the right thing and in the best interests of the students.

FOR YOUR CONSIDERATION

• What obstacles did this advocate face?

• How prepared was she for meeting these obstacles?

• If you win in an advocacy situation, how important is it that the win be for the right reasons? Explain your ideas.

As you proceed with your advocacy work, celebrate the small successes along the way. Take pleasure in the strategies that worked well. Praise your colleagues and yourself for what was accomplished. Consider where you and they might make strategy changes in the future; sometimes small advocacy successes at one moment can lead to bigger successes later.

The following vignette celebrates a successful program intervention for a few specific students. Consider how the ideas from this advocacy story could be spread to other settings so that other students could be as successful.

Meeting the Needs of Individual Students

Carol Karpinski
Programmer, New York City Public Schools, New York, New York, USA

In large urban schools, overcrowding, limited resources, and administrative policies and procedures often derail the correct placement of students. By the second week of school, Lisa, a foreign language teacher in a large New York City middle school, knew that Christine, one of her students, was having difficulty maintaining pace with others in the class. A docile child with mild learning disabilities, Christine received special services. Although she had trouble expressing herself verbally and was reading well below grade level, she had been scheduled for a foreign language class.

Although Christine was respectful, attentive, and never missed a homework assignment, she rarely came close to passing any kind of assessment in foreign language. Schoolwork was important to Christine, and her disappointment was intense. Lisa encountered many administrative hurdles as she tried to have Christine placed in a less frustrating class.

After several weeks of futility, Lisa decided to "correct" the situation herself. She arranged for Christine and several other students to have lunch in the classroom during one of her teacher preparation periods. In this small-group session, Lisa reiterated the day's lesson for Christine's benefit. The other invited students also interacted with Christine. Although Christine never became an honor student in a foreign language, she achieved passing marks, began to express herself more easily in English, and exhibited considerable pride in her ability to engage in simple conversations in a foreign language.

FOR YOUR CONSIDERATION

• What could you suggest as next steps for this advocate if she wanted to build on her advocacy success?

- What alternatives might you try if existing school policies seemed to interfere with your meeting the needs of the students you teach?

- Are there organizations in your community to whom you could turn for help for your students who are experiencing learning difficulties?

Do you remember Martha T. Dever's vignette in chapter 2? She worked on her advocacy issue for five years before her concern was resolved successfully. In chapter 7, Jill Lewis shared her extended advocacy story. Both of these advocates worked for long periods of time, but ultimately their advocacy made a difference for the children in their states. Few of us have the opportunity to have an impact on specific legislation in the way these two advocates did, but we can celebrate other advocacy successes. The two very different vignettes that follow illustrate that advocacy success takes many forms. Both advocates, working in very different ways, were successful in accomplishing their goals.

Meeting Student Needs for Self-Control Alternatively

Daniel P. Smith
Principal, North Middle School, Grants Pass School District #7,
Grants Pass, Oregon, USA

I have had the good fortune of being a middle school vice principal. As with most vice principals, my main area of responsibility was discipline. In the beginning, my teacher friends bid me farewell and cautioned me about the stress and discomfort I was about to endure as the "Don of Discipline." Four years later, on the eve of being named principal of a very prestigious elementary school in our school district, I gained some valuable insight about my experiences.

It happened while I was sitting at a table, after hours, with colleagues; one began to compliment my "record" on discipline. I began to feel uneasy with the terms he used to describe my no-nonsense approach to keeping the school safe: "Hard-nosed, big-stick wielding, setting them up and moving them out" and finally, "getting rid of the culls." I felt he had a rudimentary understanding of effectively managing student behavior, and I felt obligated to set him straight!

So I explained. In my first year as vice principal, the overall number of discipline referrals dropped by over 30%. This was due in large part to my predecessor's institution of Randy Sprick's nationally popular safe and civil schools discipline program. The following year, referrals were reduced by over 20%. For the remaining two years, we maintained improved student behavior and a positive school climate. Our expulsion rates averaged between 8 and 10 students for each year.

But the most important element in the equation was having *two* alternative placement sites, and, in special circumstances, a third option—homebound tutoring. Although it appeared that "problem" kids were being shipped out, a process of assessment, referral, and intervention was actually being implemented.

The guiding principle that I tried to follow was simply to meet the needs of all students. It is my belief that if a student has 30 behaviorals by midyear—and we did have such students—it was no longer the student that was not learning, rather it was the adults. The axiom, "One cannot expect different results by continuing the same behavior that created them," helped us identify which type of program might provide the best opportunity for success.

Behavioral interventions that involve changing student placement are complex and should be given thoughtful consideration. To engage in a process of "thinning out the culls" will never suffice. After all, there was a time when my name might have appeared on that list!

FOR YOUR CONSIDERATION

• What tools did this administrator use while advocating for good interventions for his students? Would any of his strategies be useful to you as you consider your goals and plans?

• What measures did the principal use to judge his success? Could any of these same measures be used to judge the success of advocacy work you might do?

Sometimes the success of our advocacy stares us right in the face and we acknowledge that we have done something worthwhile and deserve a pat on the back. You may agree that the author of the next vignette had such an experience. Thomas Lovitt shares the success of a group that created a support program for students experiencing serious learning difficulties. Without the work of many individuals and the support of several funding agencies, the Juanita Apartment School would not be functioning.

The Juanita Apartment School

Thomas C. Lovitt

Professor Emeritus, University of Washington, Seattle, Washington, USA

In 1993, an elementary school principal and I advocated for an after-school tutoring program at an apartment complex. The idea began when I was in the library at Hazel Valley Elementary School in south Seattle meeting with the principal, Leslie Perry, and a group of her teachers. They pointed out that about 100 students who attended Hazel Valley came from one apartment complex—the Juanita Apartments—and that many of these students had serious learning problems.

It occurred to us that we should set up classes after school at the apartments. We began with the idea of one apartment and one teacher. One of our first steps was to communicate the idea of the school to the owner of the apartment complex. Initially, he was skeptical about our plan because he was concerned about convening so many children in one place. There had been several previous acts of vandalism at his apartments. When we explained that the children would be in classrooms and supervised by a teacher and that we also planned to work closely with the children's parents, he agreed to support our project and gave us a modest break on the rent.

The Highline School District funded the teacher and paid for other expenses. It was a bare bones budget. We ran classes from 3:30 p.m. to 6:15 p.m. Monday through Thursday, and on Fridays took the children on field trips. Our program was based on academics, especially reading, but we sprinkled in time for listening to stories and music and having snacks.

Although initial responses to the program from the children, their parents, and their teachers at Hazel Valley were positive, establishing the school was far from simple. It took us more than two years of advocating to obtain grants from the Kellogg Foundation and other sources to sustain the program.

Eventually, we set up classes in two, two-bedroom apartments. As the program developed, several of the apartment mothers became tutors, as did youths from the neighborhood high school. Any student who lived in the complex was welcome, but children who were identified by their teachers at Hazel Valley as needing an extra boost received special encouragement to attend.

We also advocated for and received the services of a parent specialist, funded from a separate grant, who now assists at the apartment school site five hours a day. Her responsibilities include calling on parents of absentees, driving parents to school conferences and volunteer work, arranging appointments for parents and children with various social service agencies, and offering suggestions on childrearing and meal planning. Most of her time, however, is spent on adult education classes, which are scheduled throughout the day and evenings. In those classes, she assists parents with basic skills. She has also established a GED training program for adults, many of whom are parents of the children attending the Juanita School.

The program that began in one apartment building has now expanded to four such complexes in the same part of town. Although the acquisition of funds remains an issue, and we continually have to advocate for monies, the model has established itself so that now a number of agencies are willing to support it. And another sign of success? Although the apartment owner was initially skeptical, he now mentions the apartment school in all newspaper advertising for the apartments.

FOR YOUR CONSIDERATION

- How did a chance discussion turn into an educational accomplishment?
- What example can you give of a conversation you had that brought positive results in your school?
- How did Lovitt overcome obstacles to turn the idea into reality?
- What additional evidence might Lovitt be able to obtain to confirm that he was a successful education advocate?

So when should you celebrate? *Anytime you have accomplished something that gets you closer to your advocacy goals!* Be grateful for the small successes along the way as well as the big outcomes that may have long-lasting and wide-ranging effects. We believe you should celebrate on the following occasions.

Your name and face are readily recognized by your local school building administrator and by your school staff. You have now asked enough questions and engaged in enough conversations to be well known. You are no longer just one of many faculty members working at a specific grade level or in a specific content area. Your colleagues now know that you are an interested and concerned education advocate. They know that they can expect to hear from you on many issues, particularly if you do not agree with specific positions.

Your building administrator asks your opinion on a school-based issue or consults with you before either presenting an idea to the faculty or writing a comment for the parent newsletter. As your administrator knows, you may be vocal in your support or your opposition. Consider yourself successful when he or she enlists your support or listens to your arguments before presenting ideas to others.

The instructional and administrative staffs of your school district's central office know you and expect to hear from you about school district policies. Because of your past advocacy efforts, they may contact you to hear your questions and concerns about any policies or practices they are proposing for implementation. They may place you on important school district committees.

Members of your school board recognize you and know your name and your possible concerns when you call or come to their offices for an appointment. Your testimony at school board meetings or your past phone calls and visits to their offices have put you on a first-name basis with the school board members. They know that you are a citizen to be reckoned with and that listening to what you have to say is to their advantage. Some of them may call you in advance to hear your opinion about an issue or a school district concern.

Your input or testimony at a meeting triggers interest, curiosity, or discomfort among those attending. You were noticed! People listened to your ideas and were challenged by them, whether they agreed or disagreed.

People ask you questions after they hear you speak or send you e-mails or offers of assistance after you pleaded for your cause. Your message has resonated with them and they want to explore further opportunities for communication or collaboration with you. They see you as a credible source of information, as a potential colleague, or both. Based on what they heard you say, they feel you can be informative or helpful. They also feel that you are approachable.

You receive phone calls or e-mails from people who are strongly opposed to your ideas. You have touched a nerve. People have heard what you said or read what you wrote and they are concerned enough to get in touch with you. Their interest, even though you might be on opposite sides of an issue, is better than their apathy. Perhaps you can work together to find a compromise that will be appropriate for all interested parties.

People attending a meeting at which you presented your ideas ask you to send them additional information on your issue. Over time, your delivery of sound information may be a real asset. Someday people may ask you to present information at the formative stages of an issue.

You are asked to disseminate your information to people who were not present at a meeting. Those who attended the meeting and received your information found it useful. They want their colleagues who did not attend to have equal access to the same materials.

Your e-mail to policymakers at the local, state, or national level gets answered with something other than a stock message thanking you for your input. If your message generated a personal response rather than the usual, automatic form message, it means the recipient read what you wrote, reacted to it, and took the time to write a specific response. Possibly, he or she even addressed you by name.

Your legislator's aide knows your name when you call or walk into the legislator's office. The staff recognizes that you are a vocal constituent. They know they have heard from you in the past and they will hear from you again. You are no longer anonymous.

The same legislative aide calls you to ask you for information or your opinion. The aide now sees you as a helpful resource that can be tapped from time to time.

A policymaker cites you, your work, your organization, or your materials in committees, hearings, newsletters, or legislation. You, your organization, or both are now well fixed in the policymaker's mind. Your organization is no longer a confusing acronym to him or her. Your policymaker understands what you are about and how your organization and its concerns may affect his or her agenda.

A policymaker appoints you to serve on a specific committee or advisory board. Your policymaker now knows you well enough to think that your input on committees or advisory boards may be very helpful.

A policymaker recommends you and your organization to other individuals or organizations. Be thankful for this networking opportunity. Perhaps you will find new colleagues for future advocacy efforts.

Your op-ed or letter to the editor gets published in the newspaper. Not every piece submitted to a newspaper gets published. Be proud that the editors find your ideas well written and worthy of public exposure. Also, be glad when your published piece stimulates written responses from other individuals. When you see their comments published, know that they were inspired by your ideas. You motivated them to write a response, either to support or refute your ideas.

An article you write gets published in a newsletter, newspaper, or education journal. Your ideas are now published for others to read and your advocacy statements are reaching a wider audience.

Your local radio stations play a public service announcement (PSA) you wrote. Every time you hear your PSA played, think of how many people are hearing the message and processing your ideas.

A T-shirt or bumper sticker you designed is seen in many places. If you are reading these messages, others are too. Recall Richard Meyer's vignettes about using fliers and T-shirts for advocacy messages. If even one person is influenced by your message, consider your advocacy effort successful.

A reporter calls you for information before writing a story. You know your past advocacy efforts are recognized when you are called at the formative stage of an article or a feature. It is likely that the reporter wants to interview you because he or she thinks your responses have credibility.

People from other organizations call you when they have advocacy concerns. The time you have spent in laying the foundation for possible collaboration may be coming to fruition. Perhaps you will be invited to meet with representatives from those organizations. Honor the invitation and welcome the opportunity. Perhaps this meeting can lead to further collaboration and mutual benefit.

You are finally able to work with members of other organizations on joint goals. Past advocacy activities probably brought you to this point. Working with others may enable you to accomplish more than you could by working alone.

You are invited to make a presentation of your ideas at a meeting or a conference. Others recognize the importance of your advocacy work and honor your advocacy efforts. Use your presentation as a time to share your ideas and resources.

A legislator talks about you or your school when discussing education issues. Obviously those school invitations and visits and the information you sent made a difference. Because of your work, your legislator now has good information and good experiences to share when talking about education with others.

You are invited to be interviewed for the radio or television news. Others feel that you have important ideas to share. Remember that by participating in the interview you may be reaching a different audience for your ideas and that you may be sharing information that is unknown by them.

You are invited to appear on a radio talk show or a call-in program. Delight in the opportunity to respond to the concerns and calls of others. Your information may help them solve problems or give them alternative resources to consider. Celebrate when people call to thank you or to challenge you after you appear on any radio or television program. Be glad that people were listening and heard what you had to say. Whether they disagree or agree with you, your ideas challenged them and they took the time to call.

You receive calls and thank-you messages for your advocacy work. When others let you know that they appreciate your efforts on behalf of education, pause and be thankful that your ideas and your actions are helpful. Although you may not accomplish all that you wish, all your advocacy efforts are valued.

Celebrate any and all of these advocacy successes. Each one suggests that your advocacy work is making a difference. Over time, if you have done your homework and presented yourself clearly and fairly, you will be seen as a credible resource. Others will want to work with you and will seek you out when their areas of concern coalesce with yours. Still others will want to consult you to determine your opinion on ideas and solutions before they voice them to others. You may become a sounding board for emerging ideas of policymakers in your school district, your community, or your state.

What to Do if Your Advocacy Strategies Are Not Working

Unfortunately, advocacy work does not always go well or as originally planned. Often, we as advocates need to sit back, evaluate our efforts, and consider new strategies. Sometimes the best decision may be to concede the issue, determine what we have learned from the experience, and move on to other concerns.

We cannot always win. Often, the opposition is so well financed and organized that we can have little influence. We need to look at our time, talents, energies, and finances before determining if we should find other ways of approaching an issue or if we should abandon the fight and save ourselves for future challenges. There are times when our best plan may be to retreat and regroup.

Many times, however, we need to stick with our issue but find alternate ways of approaching it. At those times, what can we do?

We can reformulate our position in light of what we know of the opposition and their arguments. We can decide how we will rework our position so that our ideas will have more appeal to others. We can decide what ideas we will concede and where we can compromise. We also can consider if there are ideas from the opposition that we can accept and expand for our own use.

Are there additional coalitions that we can form? Are there groups that we can approach that we may not have considered at first? Will their addition to our efforts enhance our credibility with diverse audiences?

Are there resources, such as those described in previous chapters, that we have not yet considered but that we might want to try now?

Are there additional ideas we can consider? Is there new information or research emerging that would further support or amplify our position?

Are there additional individuals who might want to testify, write letters, or make phone calls on behalf of the issue we care about?

Revisiting our positions, revising our plans, and trying new strategies may put us back on the desired track so that we can accomplish much of what we originally set out to do.

Building an Advocacy Track Record

We believe that advocacy is an ongoing commitment. We think of it as a passion that keeps bringing us back for many diverse campaigns and causes. We would like to think that you see advocacy work as part of your professional responsibilities. There are many education issues that continue to deserve advocates' attention, energies, and resources.

Over time, your advocacy work will introduce you to many people. Your phone calls, e-mails, and office visits will help you build relationships with important policymakers. If you present credible information in an efficient and orderly manner, you will create favorable impressions. People will know you and come to trust your judgment. Although they may not always agree with your positions, they will respect your arguments and listen to what you have to say.

Relationships with policymakers can develop over time. A series of small steps and encounters may lead to more involvement. Do not be discouraged if your first advocacy initiatives are not as successful as you would wish. Plan for the long haul. Establish yourself so that you and the organization you represent are seen as having something worthwhile to offer.

If you deliver information when it is requested, you will provide resources that may contribute to policymakers' thinking. You may be consulted when issues related to your concerns arise. You will be even more effective if you can anticipate information that your policymakers will need and supply it before crises occur. Keeping your policymakers informed on significant education developments and research is an important contribution to their work. You and your organization will become recognized as an asset to policymaking activity.

As you recall several of the vignettes from previous chapters and Jill Lewis's tale of advocacy in chapter 7, note that many of the advocates' actions build on earlier steps. Coalitions formed on a current issue may have antecedents in other activities. Invitations for current meetings may result from past networking and contacts. Build a record of accomplishment over time. Keep information about your concerns in front of organizations and policymakers so that they may remember you and call on you when they have questions, need assistance, or want your input. Keep your list of possible resources and contact information for individuals current so that you can locate them easily. Developing relationships with like-minded people is an ongoing process that will reap rewards for your advocacy initiatives in ways and at times that you may least expect.

Revisiting Your Advocacy Self-Assessment

We hope you have enjoyed taking this journey with us. In chapter 1, we invited you along to learn how education advocates and education advocacy work. Throughout the chapters, we have shared our passions for advocacy and why the three of us feel that this work is an important professional responsibility. We have suggested that participation in advocacy can counter the feelings expressed in the preface by Barbara LaSaracina, 2001 New Jersey Teacher of the Year, that power in the education arena comes only through leaving the classroom and moving into administration. We hope you now agree with our view that engaging in education advocacy empowers educators.

In chapter 1, we invited you to take a self-assessment on the advocacy initiatives you had already pursued. You also considered what additional advocacy activities you might be willing to try. Then you set some goals for yourself.

During your initial self-assessment, you might have felt uncomfortable or intimidated by some of the suggested activities. You may even have concluded that advocacy work was beyond your capabilities. We ask you now to revisit this self-assessment (see chapter 1, pages 10–14) and to score yourself again on your current and potential advocacy initiatives. When you have completed the self-assessment, compare your original observations and goals to your new ones and discover how your thoughts, confidence, and goals have changed.

Ask what you now can say about yourself as an education advocate. Did we help you see that many of your activities were related to advocacy, even if you didn't realize that they were? Do you now know that advocacy includes ministeps and opportunities as well as large legislative initiatives? Do the vignettes increase your confidence that you can successfully advocate at a variety of local, state, and national levels? Do you feel more comfortable? Are you now more eager to participate in advocacy? When you revisited the goals you wrote, did you find that you wanted to change them? Did you discover that there is information you still want and need in order to be a successful advocate?

How will you use the awareness from your postreading self-assessment? Will you become a more active advocate? Will you seek out others with whom you can work on specific issues? Will you play a more active role in your building or district? Will you contact organizations to which you belong and suggest that you'd like to become more involved in their advocacy efforts? We hope so.

We feel that we will have been successful if our ideas have helped you to become more involved in advocacy and more aware of what initiatives others are taking that you might join. We would be excited if you would use this book for your future advocacy work. We hope it will serve as an important reference tool for you. Consider the many resources we have suggested as you undertake the necessary advocacy research. Try many of the suggested activities to accomplish your goals. Remember the vignettes and incorporate ideas you gleaned from these personal accounts as you create your own advocacy stories.

Conclusion

We hope our book has convinced you that all educators can engage in education advocacy. The vignettes throughout the book share the struggles and the successes of educators just like you who fought for change. Teachers, librarians, administrators, supervisors, professors, and parents who share their stories in the previous chapters all felt compelled to work for what they believed was important for their students, their schools, and their profession. Their advocacy initiatives involved many of the strategies that should now be familiar to you and that, perhaps, you are already using.

We hope we have convinced you that you can make a positive difference through your commitment to education advocacy. We urge you to work for change when you see something that is not in the best interest of students. As Cathy Roller told us in chapter 1, when we are confronted with educational stances that we find uncomfortable, we can vent, we can circumvent, or we can invent. We hope our book has given you the information, the vision, and the courage to act when you encounter policies and practices that need to be changed.

We close with three quotes written in very different decades that we find especially meaningful and inspirational. We hope you will find them thoughtful as you consider your advocacy journey.

Hargreaves and Fullan (1998) remind us of the importance of meddling. They remind us that we cannot be content to sit back when policies and practices interfere with what we consider is necessary and in the best interests of our students. They believe in the power of teachers to effect change. And we have a responsibility to share their optimism and to act on our hope.

> As citizens who refuse to mind their own business, teachers must not act as if their business is only in the classroom, and must realize that what happens outside the classroom can profoundly affect their work for better or worse. Most obviously, refusing to mind your own business means taking political action against wrong-headed reforms that railroad teachers through change at unworkable speed, or that put forward changes which will damage public education...teachers with purpose and passion must protest damaging government action, not because they are in despair, but precisely because they are hopeful and actively determined to make things better for their students. (Hargreaves & Fullan, 1998, pp. 99–100)

In an earlier decade, Ayn Rand expressed these ideas in another, politically stronger way. She suggested the dangers of accepting what is rather than the importance of working for what could be. Her quote reminds us that we must speak out and respond when we are challenged with inappropriate policies and, as Goodman states in "A Declaration of Professional Conscience for Teachers" (see Appendix A, page 234), we need to "make the welfare of our students our most basic criterion for professional judgment."

> The greatest guilt today is that of people who accept collectivism by moral default; the people who seek protection from the necessity of taking a stand, by refusing to admit to themselves the nature of that which they are accepting; the people who support plans specifically designed to achieve serfdom, but hide behind the empty assertion that they are lovers of freedom, with no concrete meaning attached to the word; the people who believe that the content of ideas need not be examined, that principles need not be defined, and that facts can be eliminated by keeping one's eyes shut. They expect, when they find themselves in a world of bloody ruins and concentration camps, to escape moral responsibility by wailing: 'But I didn't mean *this*!'
>
> Those who want slavery should have the grace to name it by its proper name. They must face the full meaning of that which they are advocating or condoning; the full, exact specific meaning of collectivism, of its logical implications, of the principles upon which it is based, and of the ultimate consequences to which these principles will lead.
>
> They must face it, then decide whether this is what they want or not. (Rand, 1938, writing in the author's foreword to *Anthem*)

And finally, the words of Pastor Martin Niemoller (1992), who was interned in Nazi concentration camps from 1938 until 1945 and who ultimately gave his life for his beliefs:

> They came for the socialists, and I did not speak out because I was not a socialist. Then they came for the trade unionists, and I did not speak out because I was not a trade unionist. Then they came for the Jews, and I did not speak out because I was not a Jew. Then they came for me, and there was no one left to speak out for me. (p. 684)

Will you speak out on behalf of education policies and practices you find inappropriate? We end this book as we started it, reiterating our prefatory statement to you: Education advocacy is rewarding, frustrating, time-consuming, exhilarating, and challenging. Those who do it are part of a responsive, expanding community that does important work. Won't you join us?

APPENDIX A

Advocacy–Related Publications and Sample Testimony

A Declaration of Professional Conscience for Teachers

Kenneth S. Goodman

T here is a time in the historic development of every human institution when it reaches a critical crossroad. Institutions, like people, cannot stand still; they must always change but the changes aren't always for the better. Human institutions are composed of people. Sometimes the people within the institutions feel powerless to influence the directions of institutional change. They feel they are swept along by a force beyond anyone. Yet people within institutions can determine the directions of change if they examine their convictions and take a principled stand.

That's what the founders of American democracy understood when they began the Declaration of Independence with "When, in the course of human events,..." Education in the United States is at such a crossroad. At the same time that schools have rededicated themselves to equal educational opportunity for all, laws and policies are being imposed on schools that limit the ability of diligent teachers to use their professional judgment to further the personal development and welfare of their students.

There are strong pressures today to dehumanize, to depersonalize, to industrialize our schools. In the name of cost effectiveness, of efficiency, of system, of accountability, of minimal competency, of a return to the basics, schools are being turned into sterile, hostile institutions at war with the young people they are intended to serve.

As teachers we hereby declare ourselves to be in opposition to the industrialization of our schools. We pledge ourselves to become advocates on behalf of our students. We make the following declaration of professional conscience:

We will make the welfare of our students our most basic criterion for professional work with parents and policymakers to formulate programs that are

From Goodman, K.S., Bird, L., & Goodman, Y. (Eds.). (1992). *The whole language catalog*. Santa Rosa, CA: American School.

in the best interests of our pupils. We will work with the kids to personalize these programs. We will respect all learners. We will cherish their strengths, accept and strive to understand their language and culture, seek to further their personal values, tastes, and objectives. We will oppose methods, materials, and policies that have the intent or effect of rejecting the personal and social characteristics of our students. We will, in all matters, and in all interactions, deal with our pupils fairly, consistently, honestly, and compassionately.

We will do all we can to make school a warm, friendly, supportive place in which all pupils are welcome. Our classrooms will be theirs. We will provide guidance and leadership to support our students in the development of problem solving, decision-making, and self-discipline. We will help them build a sense of respect and support for each other. We will help them appreciate and respect those who differ from them in culture, language, race, color, heritage, religion, sex, weight, height, physical strength or attractiveness, intelligence, interests, values, personal goals, or any other characteristics.

We will not use corporal punishment on pupils of any age for any offense. We believe violence begets violence. We will not use marks or schoolwork as punishment. We will seek causes for problems and work with pupils to eliminate the causes of antisocial behavior rather than simply control the symptoms.

Neither will we use tangible, extrinsic rewards such as candy, prizes, money, tokens, or special privileges as a means of controlling behavior. We regard all institutionalized forms of behavior modification as immoral and unethical. We will work with pupils, building on intrinsic motivation in all areas of curriculum and development.

We will accept the responsibility of evaluating our pupils' growth. We will make no long- or short-range decisions that affect the future education of our pupils on the basis of a single examination no matter what the legal status of the examination. We will evaluate through ongoing monitoring of our pupils during our interactions with them. We will strive to know each pupil personally, using all available professional tools to increase our understanding of each and every one.

We are teachers. We are not actors following scripts. We are not technicians servicing an educational machine. We are not delivery systems. We are not police officers, babysitters, petty despots, card punchers, paper-shufflers, book monitors. We are not replaceable by machines.

We are professionals. We have prepared ourselves for teaching by building knowledge of human development, human learning, pedagogy, curriculum, language, and cognition. We know the history of education. We know the competing philosophies of education. We have carefully built personal philosophies that provide us with criteria for making teaching decisions in the best interests of our pupils. We have a broad liberal education and an in-depth knowledge of the content areas in which we teach.

We will use our knowledge base to support our students in their own quest for knowledge. The real curriculum is what happens to each learner. We, as teachers, are the curriculum planners and facilitators. We will not yield that responsibility to the publishers of texts or management systems. We will select and use the best educational resources we can find, but we will not permit ourselves or our pupils to be controlled by them.

We will continually update our knowledge of education, of our fields of instruction, of the real world, because of our dedication to use all means to improve our effectiveness as teachers. We expect school authorities to support us in our professionalism and self-improvement. And we will oppose all policies that restrict our professional authority to use new knowledge or new pedagogical practice on behalf of our students.

We believe that schools can serve pupils, parents, and communities well if the teachers in them function as responsible, dedicated, and compassionate professionals.

To that purpose we make this declaration of professional conscience.

New Jersey's Literacy Initiative Mission Statement

In order to achieve the goal of literacy for all New Jersey's school children, we
believe there must be the following initiatives:

1. Development of language arts literacy benchmarks for all grades from pre-K
   through 12, with particular attention to kindergarten through grade three.

2. A requirement of coursework in teaching of language arts literacy skills for all
   teacher certifications, including alternate route, in the state Administrative
   Code. These should include the NJEA Delegate Assembly's (November 1998)
   recommendation that there be required 12 credits in this core area for elementary certifications; 6 credits for secondary certification. Twelve credits
   should also be required for early childhood certifications. Further, it is the
   view of the undersigned that 6 credits in language arts literacy should be required for all other certifications, including special education. Alternate route
   teachers should have the equivalent in instructional time in learning how to
   teach language arts literacy.

3. Professional development training that is ongoing, sequential, comprehensive,
   coordinated, and required as inservice for all teachers and that is directed
   toward developing students' language arts literacy skills. It should include

but not be limited to: reading curriculum, language development as it relates to literacy, informal classroom assessment, teaching diverse learners, research based reading practices, critical thinking and comprehension across disciplines.

4. Use of multiple, varied, comprehensive, research based reading programs and assessments, tailored to meet the individual needs of students, including meaningful use of students' first language skills. *

5. Employment of a full-time reading specialist on the staff in each school building who will provide intensive direct services to students and consultation with teachers and school staff. *

6. Use of speech-language specialists in each school building to foster oral language development and language acquisition skills, and to identify students at risk for reading and/or writing problems due to speech/language disabilities.

7. Programs for parents and other caregivers to build awareness and skills so they can participate in the early literacy development of their children.

8. An Intervention and Referral Services system in each school building (NJAC Chapter 16, 6A:16-7.1-7.3) that includes the parent, classroom teacher, reading specialist, speech language specialist, school psychologist, learning consultant, and other educational support staff to develop reading intervention plans for students.

9. Access to technology used for the improvement of reading instruction and a Library Media Center in each school staffed by a certified education media specialist. *

10. Use of classroom assistants to supplement, not replace, certified teachers for reading instruction. *

11. Implementation of a process for identifying children with potential reading difficulties; such identification should take place in pre-K and be part of continuous K-12 evaluation. *

12. Creation of appropriate physical space in each school to focus on individual or small group reading instruction based on developmental needs of at risk children. *

13. Inclusion of students who are eligible for special education and related services in this literacy initiative.

* Supported by NJEA Delegate Assembly's November 1998 recommendation.

Rev. 04/02/02 **

NOTE: NJEA has since endorsed this statement with an exception (Delegates Assembly, January 11, 2003). They withdrew support for item 2 that the Delegates Assembly had endorsed previously.

Teachers of Special Education Classes Must Improve Student Reading Skills

Jill Lewis

While concerns about the large number of teachers with emergency certification in special education, bilingual and English-as-a-second language classrooms are legitimate and critically important ("Many special-ed teachers not fully certified," Oct. 28), it would be a mistake to think that holding teacher certification in these fields is *synonymous* with being prepared to help children with unique learning needs. Special education is a case in point.

Research confirms that large numbers of children are placed into special education because of their difficulties with learning to read. In the past decade alone, the number of students aged 6–21 identified as learning disabled (LD) under the Individuals with Disabilities Education Act has increased 38 percent. And it is estimated that approximately 80 percent of all LD students have difficulties learning to read.

Nevertheless, New Jersey's Administrative Code for Licensure, the code that specifies requirements for every teaching certification field, does not require that any certification program include a single course in how to teach children to read. This is particularly devastating for special education teachers, most of whom work with children who have the greatest need for expert teaching in reading.

These teachers may or many not have been in a teacher preparation program at a college that required a reading course or two for special education certification. Certification alone does not guarantee such preparation.

The consequences of this situation are apparent in data available from the state's school report card. The data for 2000–2001 on the fourth grade ESPA and eighth grade GEPA Language Arts Literacy tests provide results in three categories: advanced proficient, proficient, and partially proficient.

Reprinted from Asbury Park Press (November 1, 2002), p. A27.

If we look at the scores for students in special education, we see a reduction between fourth and eighth grade in numbers of children scoring in the proficient category. On the ESPA 44.5 percent of the children achieved proficient rating, but on the GEPA only 24.9 percent of the special education children were determined to be proficient. This means 20 percent fewer special education children read proficiently by the end of eighth grade.

The cause for this decline in scores among the special education population is easy to identify. Reading needs become greater and more complex as children advance through the grades. The reading is harder; the homework is more demanding.

Revisions should be made to New Jersey's Administrative Code. Those entering the teaching profession must be better prepared to assist all children, especially struggling readers at all grade levels, with those literacy tasks they need to reach the high standards we are expecting all children to achieve.

Writing About Reading for the Public

Allen Berger

> One of the things that strikes me as wrong with educators is that we talk to ourselves too much. Now there's a lot right with that: it's what in part makes a profession.
>
> But what's wrong is that while we're communicating with each other in educational publications others are talking about us in other publications. (Berger, 1995, p. 11A)

This is the way I began an article that received the Distinguished Achievement Award for editorial writing from the Educational Press Association of America. I mention this fact not for self-aggrandizement but to alert the literacy community that we are contributing to a crisis of unprecedented proportions if we do not write more than we do for the general public.

Our critics write in influential periodicals such as *The Public Interest*, *Commentary*, and *Daedalus*. I would venture to guess that very few teachers and teacher educators have ever read a copy of any of these publications. Yet the articles that appear in these publications find their way into the popular media.

For example, Pulitzer Prize-winning syndicated columnist George Will launched a vicious attack on the teaching of writing. He began his column: "Summertime, and the living is easy. Schools are empty, so the damage has stopped." He continued:

> During this seasonal respite from the educational system's subtraction from national literacy, consider why America may be graduating from its high schools its first generation worse educated than the generation that came before. Particularly, why is it common for high school graduates to be functionally illiterate, uncertain when reading, and incapable of writing even a moderately complicated paragraph? (Will, 1995, p. 17A)

Reprinted from *The Reading Teacher* (September 1997), *51*, pp. 6–10.

Will says that he knows this is so because he read an article, "Why Johnny Can't Write" (Mac Donald, 1995), in *The Public Interest*.

Multiply this particular example a hundred times, and it is no wonder that the public thinks we're doing a lousy job improving literacy—and that politicians, who are part of the public, write laws affecting the teaching of reading and writing in classrooms throughout the United States.

Robert Barro, an economist, wrote an attack on education in *The Wall Street Journal* (Barro, 1996). His attack was based on a study that appeared in a specialized periodical, *Quarterly Journal of Economics*. I responded to the attack with a letter that was published in abbreviated form:

Don't Judge Teachers By the Dropout Rate

The September 27 editorial-page piece "Teachers' Unions Don't Deliver Quality" by Robert J. Barro doesn't make sense. Mr. Barro defines quality solely by the "high school dropout rate." Is that the way corporations define quality—solely by dropouts? And dropout isn't even defined in the piece.

What about all the other ways to assess quality in education? Process? Product? ACT and SAT scores? Reading, writing, math and science improvement? Library usage? Growth in the arts and music and physical education? Honors and scholarships? Citizenship? Preparation for the marketplace? To mention just a few.... (Berger, 1996b, p. A23)

These two examples show that we're making a major mistake if we don't respond to the baloney in the popular media. We can respond with an opinion/editorial (op/ed) piece or with a letter to the editor.

What we must not do is become paranoid: Just because something we write isn't accepted doesn't necessarily mean that editors don't like our views.

There may be many reasons why something we write isn't accepted for publication. For example, I had a wonderful neighbor when I lived in Pittsburgh. His name was Fred Bonach and he was a retired steelworker. His wife ran the three bookstores at the University of Pittsburgh.

One day Fred died, and I was moved to write the following:

I would like to pay a small tribute to Fred Bonach. You can read about him in his obituary (July 1). But an obituary contains only bare facts—occupation, memberships, church affiliation, survivors. What is missing is the life of the person who died.

Fred was the mayor of the street he lived on. People trusted him, and when they had problems, they called Fred. He helped people and brought them together. They asked him to watch over their homes when they went away.

During bad snowstorms, Fred organized neighbors to get the street plowed. In the summer he worked in his front yard and watched over the street.

For eight years I lived across from Fred. During that time he had heart trouble so he had to be careful. He had an attack while stopping to pick up a newspaper on his way to meet his wife after work on Wednesday.

If you have a friend and neighbor like Fred, you are fortunate. They add to the community, and they make a better world. People like Fred are rare. They add to our lives. When they die, we are all diminished. (Berger, 1983a, p. 6. Copyright, *Pittsburgh Post-Gazette*, all rights reserved. Reprinted with permission.)

When I wrote that little piece I drove to the offices of the major evening newspaper in Pittsburgh. I shared it with an editor who read it and said he liked it but wasn't going to publish it. I asked why. He said that if he did, he might be deluged with similar pieces. I asked about publishing it in the morning newspaper. He said its offices were upstairs (in the same building). So I went upstairs. Everyone was at a meeting, so I just left the piece on an editor's desk. It was accepted for publication and given the title "Our 'Mayor.'"

Another reason why some of what we write may not be accepted by newspapers and magazines is because we don't know how to write for them. Rarely does anyone in any of my college classes know the answer to a simple question: How many sentences are there in a newspaper paragraph? They are dumbfounded when I tell and show them that newspaper paragraphs are usually one sentence long. I explain that the climax is in the first sentence and information of less and less importance is in following sentences—almost the opposite of a short story. (They also don't know that the major article is on the righthand side of the front page because, as Miles Tinker [1965] observed in his research, our eyes hit a little left of center and then move to the right in reading English.)

I once sent an op/ed piece to *The Cincinnati Enquirer* and, after a couple of months without seeing it in print, I phoned the newspaper. I was told that it was too long to be published. So I revised the article to the appropriate length and had it published with the title "Attacks Distort Literacy Gains" (Berger, 1996a).

A third reason for lack of acceptance is that we educators tend to use big, empty words, long sentences, and jargon unnecessarily. It is small comfort that this same problem exists in other professions. When I did consulting work with one of the leading credit-rating firms in the world, I asked the evaluator/writers (many of whom had gone to high-class, private schools) to define a *financial parameter*, a term they used often in their writing. They couldn't agree. I said that if they couldn't agree, how were others supposed to understand? In nearly every field, editors of leading journals encourage a great deal of rewriting to make clear what is being said.

But in education there is a movement called critical pedagogy that praises obtuse writing. Literacy educators/researchers belonging to the National Reading Conference recently participated via computer in a discussion of *Breaking Free: The Transformative Power of Critical Pedagogy* (Leistyna, Woodrum, & Sherblom, 1996). I personally thought the book was boring and ran a readability formula on a number of random parts of the book. The readability ranged from the 20th- to the 26th-grade levels!

In addition, some of the writers of chapters in this book flatly state that "writing clarity represents a pernicious mechanism used by academic liberals who suffocate discourses different from their own" (Freire & Macedo, 1996, p. 216). If we have this kind of attitude, how are we going to communicate with the general public? This view of critical pedagogists and many of their believers reminds me of another letter I wrote for *The Wall Street Journal*:

Write Thinking

There is not a shred of evidence for the Carnegie Foundation's assertion (news story, Sept. 16) that "clear writing leads to clear thinking." It is far more likely that clear thinking leads to clear writing. Brandeis once noted that "to think hard and persistently is painful." (Berger, 1983b, p. 33)

The Wall Street Journal, incidentally, is extremely interested in education. Just recently it published a major front page article on "How Whole Language Became a Hot Potato In and Out of Academia" (Duff, 1996) with the following headings: "Reading Method Ditched Phonics," "Won Adherents But Test Scores Tanked" and "A Boomer-Christian Coalition." I was curious to see how many among the approximate 400 members on the National Reading Conference listserv would comment on this major article (all the way down the righthand column and inside) in this extremely influential publication. Only two people responded: Ken Goodman, who is quoted in the article and alerted members to read it, and a person who asked to know the date of publication.

Through thinking and writing we reveal ourselves, and how many of us want to expose ourselves through our exposition? Perhaps, like politicians, we like to hide behind words and passivity. For not only does our writing reveal our soul, it also tests our thinking, and how many of us want to be so exposed in public? In Chaim Potok's (1967) wonderful novel *The Chosen*, a father tells his son's friend who is being brought up in silence by a father who is a brilliant scholar: "In your father's writings I look at his soul, not his mind" (p. 280).

How to write for the public

One of the paradoxes affecting those of us who teach teachers and future teachers is that we are evaluated on something that is often ignored in our training. That is, we need to write articles for promotion, tenure, and salary increases, and yet many potential professors go through graduate school without learning how to write an article for publication. Eventually we do learn how to write articles in professional journals. But if we want to write for the public, we have to write differently—almost backwards! Why? Because research articles tend to begin with what happened in the past, followed by what is occurring in the present and suggestions for the future. But to write for the public, you need to first tell what you found out and then how it connects with previous research. This can be learned—sometimes through trial and error, occasionally more directly.

When I taught at the University of Pittsburgh, a doctoral student took an independent study course: She wrote 15 articles—one a week—about reading and writing and studying for readers of her hometown newspaper. She first wrote a draft, I made constructive suggestions, and she rewrote the draft and submitted it to her local newspaper. My recollection is that about 10 of her articles were published. Her name is Bonita Wilcox, and her articles now appear in *The Reading Teacher* and the *Journal of Adolescent & Adult Literacy*.

This experience with Bonita leads me to another dimension in writing for the public. Instead of choosing to respond to misleading information in the public media, we should take it upon ourselves to write first and let our critics respond. There are many ways to do this. For example, my article, "Misuse of Language Hampers Reading and Writing" (Berger, 1989), in *The Plain Dealer* (Cleveland, Ohio) began as an invitation from the news bureau at Miami University. I've had op/eds in Cincinnati newspapers as a result of simply sending them. One was reprinted in newspapers in other major cities in Ohio.

Another, on the intriguing question of when exactly is a publication a publication, appeared under the title, "Perish the Thought" (1985), in *The Baltimore Sun*. "Disguising the Issues in Education" (1986) appeared in the *Pittsburgh Post-Gazette*.

If you are on vacation and are in the mood, you can write a relaxing article about literacy. That's what I did when I had time on my hands while vacationing in Fort Myers Beach, Florida. I spoke with an editor and then wrote "In Defense of Teachers" (ca. 1980) for the *Fort Myers News-Press*.

With nearly everything I write I first ask my students (undergraduates and graduates) and colleagues to read and comment on drafts. When they are finished writing their comments in the margins, we discuss what they think are the strong and unclear parts. Then I collect the drafts, and the next day I examine their comments and make changes as appropriate. I do this because it's useful and also because I want to encourage my students to act similarly when they teach writing in their own classrooms.

Sometimes my students get so angry at what appears in newspapers that one or two decide to write their own retorts. Last year syndicated columnist Walter E. Williams, a distinguished professor of economics at George Mason University in Virginia, attacked future teachers and the education profession. To bolster his argument he quoted an unnamed "knowledgeable academic" and the president of Harvard University who "retired in 1933"—more than a half century ago!

Laura Bunker, then working toward a Master of Arts in Teaching degree at Miami University, became so concerned that she wrote to Williams. To his credit, he sent her a gracious letter in which he enclosed "two tables that tell a large part of the story." To our astonishment, one table dealt with "Test Performance by Undergraduate Major" for 1977–1982, over 15 years ago! The other table with the same title was also published over a decade ago.

This year Williams continued his attacks on education in another syndicated column in which he stated that students 100 years ago knew more than students today because of

> the deliberate dumbing down of educational standards, half-baked, failed education theories, school time wasted on fads like AIDS awareness, homelessness, environmentalism, sex indoctrination and endangered species, learning how to feel good about yourself, even if you're an academic idiot, and finally, teachers and administrators who, for the most part, represent the very bottom of the intellectual/academic barrel. (Williams, 1996, p. D3)

An older student, Arthur Ftacnik, working on his master's degree, became so incensed that he wrote directly to Williams, beginning his response as follows:

> Since you are part of the educational system in the U.S., are you not including yourself in the group identified...as the "very bottom of the intellectual/academic barrel"? Or does being a professor of a "hard" subject, economics, absolve you from the alleged stupidity you conveyed on March 24th? (Ftacnik, personal communication, 1996)

Ftacnik went on to politely defend teachers and explained why they shouldn't be blamed for society's shortfalls.

I'm not sure how effective these letters are in changing the minds of our critics, many (but not all) of whom are touched more by anecdote than by reason. Nonetheless, examining such letters and articles can be a useful classroom exercise that increases our students' political awareness and professional responsibility.

Writing for the general public (as well as for one another) is easier said than done. Educators tend to be social—to write well is hard and lonely. And writing well takes time to learn. We easily accept the idea that it takes years to become, say, an accomplished pianist. Why should it take less time to become an accomplished writer?

Years ago, when I taught at the University of Alberta, I began a periodical unlike any at that time (and perhaps even now) in the world. It was a six-page newsletter called *Elements: Translating Theory into Practice.* It appeared once a month—nine times during the school year. Each month's issue focused on one area of the curriculum: art, language, math, music, physical education, reading, science, social studies, and a bonus issue on a special topic. Each article started where most articles ended—with the conclusions and implications for education. The publication lasted for 20 years—longer than even Wayne Gretzky lasted as a hockey player in Edmonton, Alberta. (Its success resulted in its demise: It was changed into a magazine and, within several years, died.)

I mention this because translating research is not considered as important as doing research, which, in many places, is not considered as important as directing research. But my simple belief is that we must follow our conscience: We must do what we think is in the best interest of students and teachers whether it is directing, doing, or translating research for students, teachers, or the general public.

What now?

Nowadays we can not only write for print media but we can also communicate electronically. Where can we start? Most universities have their own radio and television stations: Phone or drop in to see the director and offer to share ideas about literacy. Let your students and colleagues critique your early drafts before talking over the air. If you have the time, take a workshop in writing for publication. (I teach a 3-day workshop each summer; it's a joy to exchange tips with teachers who are current and future writers—and an "overjoy" a few months later to receive a phone call or note saying that an article worked on in the workshop was accepted for publication.) And don't forget about the possibility of sharing ideas through a website on the Internet. If you don't know how to begin, ask a teenager! (That's what I did with my son, and, with his help and that of a graduate student, we now have a website called Teens for Literacy at www.muohio.edu/~bergera/teensforliteracy.)

In short, as literacy educators we need to publish outside as well as inside the profession. How else will the public know, for example, that whole word has nothing to do with whole language? How will the ordinary citizen know that phonics and whole language can live together cheerfully and productively? If we and other educators don't share honest ideas in newspapers and other influential publications, how are we supposed to make sensible and sound educational laws? If we don't, we'll end up reading people like George Will writing abominable lyrics to George and Ira Gershwin melodies.

Author note

I thank Liz Shafran and Mark Krabbe, graduate student and professor at Miami University, respectively, for their suggestions on earlier drafts of this article.

References

Barro, R.J. (1996, September 27). Teachers' unions don't deliver quality. *The Wall Street Journal*, p. A18.

Berger, A. (ca. 1980). In defense of teachers. *Fort Myers News-Press*, editorial page.

Berger, A. (1983a, July 5). Our "mayor." *Pittsburgh Post-Gazette*, p.6.

Berger, A. (1983b, October 4). Write thinking. *The Wall Street Journal*, p. 33.

Berger, A. (1985, April 3). Perish the thought. *The Baltimore Sun*, p. 11A.

Berger, A. (1986, Feb. 1). Disguising the issues in education. *Pittsburgh Post-Gazette*, p. 7.

Berger, A. (1989, April 11). Misuse of language hampers reading and writing. *The Plain Dealer*, p. 5B.

Berger, A. (1995, July 18). Ivory towers are often tempting targets. *The Cincinnati Post*, p. 11A.

Berger, A. (1996a, May 13). Attacks distort literacy gains. *The Cincinnati Enquirer*, p. A13.

Berger, A. (1996b, October 8). Don't judge teachers by the dropout rate. *The Wall Street Journal*, p. A23.

Berger, A. (1997, April/May). Let's mend fences with our newspapers. *Reading Today*, p. 37.

Duff, C. (1996, October 30). How whole language became a hot potato in and out of academia. *The Wall Street Journal*, pp. 1+.

Freire, P., & Macedo, D.P. (1996). A dialogue: Culture, language, and race. In P. Leistyna, A. Woodrum, & S. Sherblom (Eds.), *Breaking free: The transformative power of critical pedagogy* (pp. 199–228). Cambridge, MA: Harvard University Press.

Leistyna, P., Woodrum, A., & Sherblom, S.A. (Eds.). (1996). *Breaking free: The transformative power of critical pedagogy*. Cambridge, MA: Harvard University Press.

Mac Donald, H. (1995, Summer). Why Johnny can't write. *The Public Interest*, pp. 3–13.

Potok, C. (1967). *The chosen*. New York: Simon & Schuster.

Tinker, M. (1965). *Bases for effective reading*. Minneapolis: University of Minnesota Press.

Will, G. (1995, July 3). Why can't Johnny write? Because nobody taught him. *The Cincinnati Post*, p. 17A.

Williams, W. (1996, March 24). Dumbed-down U.S. values curtail wealth. *The Cincinnati Enquirer*, p. D3.

On Continued Government Intrusion Into Professional Decision Making

Resolved, that the National Council of Teachers of English assert that any legislation that focuses on reading and writing needs to reflect best practice and sound research;

that NCTE declare that neither Congress nor any federal or state agency should establish a single definition of reading and writing or restrict the type of research used in funding criteria for preservice or inservice teacher education and professional development programs;

that NCTE affirm that neither Congress nor any federal or state agency should bypass professional standards and procedures for peer review of research; nor should they centralize authority for decision making and review by putting these vital functions in the hands of a single individual or extraordinary authorities;

that NCTE proclaim that no federal or state law or program be framed in such a way to provide substantial advantage to any commercial reading or writing program. No person who could personally profit from any legislation or regulation should hold a staff position or be a paid consultant with the government agency that develops or monitors the legislation or regulation;

that NCTE immediately distribute this resolution to members of the education committees and the full bodies of the U.S. Senate and House of Representatives, as well as to state legislatures; and

that NCTE distribute this resolution to federal and state education agencies, professional education associations, teacher unions, the media, parent groups, and appropriate organizations, and urge them to voice their support of this resolution.

This resolution was approved by the Board of Directors of the National Council of Teachers of English.

Literacy Teaching and Learning in Early Care and Education Programs

A joint position statement of:

New Jersey Reading Association (NJRA)
New Jersey Association for the Education of Young Children (NJAEYC)
New Jersey Association of Kindergarten Educators (NJAKE)

Adopted Spring 2000

Even before they begin school, children learn a great deal about reading, writing, and communication. It is, therefore, essential that parents and other caregivers provide even the very youngest children with quality experiences that encourage and extend this learning. Everyone has an important role to play in developing young children's emerging literacy. For this reason, three state education associations have joined together to formulate a position statement on early literacy that provides a set of principles and recommendations to guide those who are in a position to influence a young child's learning and development.

Clearly, we have considerable research-based knowledge about developing literacies in the early years. We firmly believe that this knowledge should serve as the basis for decision-making about literacy programs for young children.

What do we know about young children's developing literacies?

Parents and other who speak often to infants are establishing the building blocks of early literacy.

Reading and writing experiences create a bond between children and the important people in their lives.

Starting at birth, all children benefit from hearing stories and songs.

Very young children who have lots of opportunities to talk are more likely to develop literacy strengths than children who don't.

Play is an important component for developing literacy.

Children become aware of print in their environment (newspapers, magazines, logos, store signs) before preschool.

Very young children learn to create some of their first stories from viewing pictures and illustrations.

Children benefit from hearing books read aloud and being exposed to many different kinds of books.

Reading to young children on a consistent basis has a profound effect on children's later literacy development.

Children's literacy develops when they have many opportunities to handle the books on their own.

Children learn about reading and writing by watching and imitating readers and writers.

Vocabulary is best learned in conversation and through hearing and reading stories.

Finger play, scribbling, and "pretend reading" are children's early attempts at literacy.

Once children master their home languages, developing literacy in the English language is easier.

Who should teach preschool and kindergarten children?

Those who teach should be certified in early childhood education from accredited higher education programs with appropriate coursework in early childhood literacy.

Non-certified classroom staff and volunteers, under direct supervision of certified teachers, provide much needed additional support in the learning environment.

What should very young children learn about literacy?

Communication occurs in many different forms.

Print in the environment has meaning.

Pictures and stories can tell us about ourselves and others.

Speaking, listening, reading, and writing bring pleasure.

Speaking, listening, reading, and writing are interrelated.

Speaking, listening, reading, and writing are done for meaningful purposes.

Language follows grammatical patterns.

Letters and sounds are related.

Letters are combined to form words.

What should teachers do to inspire children's literacy?

Early care and education agencies and schools should promote developmentally appropriate models of literacy.

Early childhood teachers must continue to provide the same kind of learning experiences children receive at home as well as appropriate additional experiences as children become ready for them.

Create environments where children have many opportunities to use literacy in meaningful ways.

Be supportive of children's early attempts at literacy.

Respect individual and cultural differences.

Model reading and writing in everyday activities.

Model reflective thinking about literacy experiences.

Provide developmentally appropriate literacy experiences.

Discuss and demonstrate strategies for making meaning from books.

Demonstrate effective writing strategies.

Provide student-led sharing opportunities.

Encourage creative and critical thinking in the expression of ideas.

Encourage students to ask questions.

Encourage students to take risks with speaking, reading, and writing.

Ask questions that help children to think about how they read and write.

Who else is responsible for the literacy development of young children?

Parents, family members, and other caregivers are children's first teachers, starting at birth.

Our society must demonstrate, through actions and programs, that it values literacy.

Public leaders must model literacy behaviors and sponsor educational initiatives for developing literacy.

We are all responsible!

Testimony of Susanne B. Hopson on Behalf of the New Jersey Reading Association Before the New Jersey Assembly Education Committee

May 21, 2001

Mr. Chairman and members of the committee, I am Susanne B. Hopson. I appear before you today on behalf of the New Jersey Reading Association, an organization of nearly 2,000 members who represent nearly one half million schoolchildren in our state. Currently I am a member of NJRA's Executive Committee and am the 1999–2000 Past President.

I want to thank you, Mr. Chairman, for offering NJRA an opportunity to participate in this hearing. Since its inception, NJRA has been outspoken about the need to strengthen our literacy programs in New Jersey. The focus of most of NJRA's policies and advocacy activity is on teacher preparation and quality programs in our schools. Naturally, we are strong supporters of The Spread the Word Program, A3151.

1. The goals of A3151 are valuable. A3151 calls for a state literacy initiative to provide books to elementary school-aged children who have few books at home. It has the potential for placing thousands of books in the hands of children who need them most and that they will be able to share with parents and siblings. We believe the design of Assemblyman Azzolina's Spread the Word bill for New Jersey, including its amendment, will promote in our young children the spirit of giving to those who are less fortunate. It will also help young readers understand the meaning books have for others. When you open a book, you open your mind. You learn new words, new places and you develop new ideas that are all your own.

2. Research supports the intent of A3151. Getting books into the hands of young children is essential to the development of their literacy skills. Research suggests that reading proficiency increases with the amount of time spent reading voluntarily. The U.S. Department of Education's Assistant Secretary designee, Susan B. Neuman, found a significant difference in the print materials available in poor communities as compared to wealthier ones, and attributed the poorer children's lower literacy levels to this absence.[1] According to the American

Association of School Libraries, "to become life-long readers, students must have access to current, quality, high interest, and extensive collections of books and other print materials."[2] Our parent organization, the International Reading Association, has issued a children's Bill of Rights to Excellent Reading Instruction. One of those rights is that "Children have the right of access to a wide variety of books and other reading material in the classroom, school, and community libraries."[3] A3151 contributes to the realization of this right.

3. This program has a history of success. A *Spread the Word* program was initiated in 1995 by Governor Cellucci of Massachusetts and his wife Jan, who is a librarian. Since its inception, the Massachusetts program has given half a million books to more than 100,000 children across the Commonwealth. Each year, that state gives 12,000 students in kindergarten through third grade a total of 60,000 books; that is an average of 5 books per child. We should be able to do no less than this.

"All students are readers. All teachers are reading teachers"

4. The program has a well-conceived plan. Like the Massachusetts program, Assemblyman Azzolina's bill will provide a mechanism for collecting books from children and families who have extra books at home and distribute them to children who have few books at home. According to the amendment, there will be an individual assigned half-time to the New Jersey Department of Education specifically to ensure effective coordination of effort. We also know that Assemblyman Azzolina will reach out to professional organizations, like New Jersey Reading Association, as well as to parents and businesses for support and assistance for this program. This should assure its success.

5. A3151 is a positive step for literacy. Unlike other literacy bills that have recently come before this committee that are punitive and seek to narrow the scope of literacy education for our children, A3151 opens opportunity and promotes civic mindedness in even our youngest schoolchildren.

Assemblyman Azzolina was the recent recipient of the New Jersey Reading Association's Legislator of the Year Award because we believe his bill, as amended, will make a significant contribution to literacy and social awareness of the young children in our state.

We urge you to support this bill. We should recall the words of Mark Twain who said, "The man who does not read good books has no advantage over the man who cannot read them."

If our children do not have them, they cannot read them.

[1] Susan B. Neuman, presentation at International Reading Association Annual Convention, New Orleans, LA, April 30, 2001.

[2] American Association of School Librarians, American Library Association position statement on Independent Reading (adopted June 1994; revised July 1999).

[3] International Reading Association (March 2000). *Making a Different Means Making It Different: Honoring Children's Rights to Excellent Reading Instruction.* Newark, DE.

Testimony prepared by Jill Lewis, Chair, NJRA Legislation/Professional Standards Committee

Taking Stock: Knowing What's Worthwhile and Advocating for It

Jill Lewis

D o you feel like the teaching profession has unfairly taken a lot of heat the last few years? It's not surprising. Sharp criticism has been leveled at our schools, teacher, and students. News reports unabashedly say we are not teaching very well, we are not doing enough, and that our students will not be ready to enter the workforce capable and productive. What is causing such animosity towards us? Most of it results from test scores—national, international, and even state tests.

But wait a minute. It's pretty clear to experienced teachers what our critics are looking at the wrong things. While tests—on the surface—are fine, they do not tell the whole story and they should not be used to condemn an entire system or an entire profession. Just as we do not judge an individual's well-being by his or her weight or height, but by many different measures, we need a fuller, richer picture of our classrooms and our teaching in order to make any judgments about our successes or failures.

What we literacy advocates must do is to provide policymakers with a lens that offers an analytical journey into our classrooms to see what makes them worthwhile spheres of influence and learning. This view must show features that may not be measurable on a test but that are immeasurable insofar as developing and maintaining civility, democracy and a productive citizenry.

Beginning Our Analytical Journey: Looking Through a Cross-Cultural Lens

We can begin this analytical journey with a cross-cultural comparison, on that highlights dimensions of classroom activity that are critically necessary in order for us to achieve the goals of the U.S. education agenda, but that may not be evident in classrooms elsewhere. We could for instance, visit a classroom in Macedonia

Adapted from *The Reading Instruction Journal* (Spring/Summer 2001), pp. 25–28.

where I have been working for the past four years as a volunteer for the Reading and Writing for Critical Thinking project, cosponsored by the International Reading Association and the Soros Foundation's Open Society Institute. To contrast this classroom with one in the U.S., imagine that outside, not far from the Macedonian classroom window, is the scene described in this press release:

> Peaceful Atmosphere in Tetovo After the Action of the Security Forces
>
> The spokesman of the Ministry of Defense, Gjorgji Trendafilov, stated that the Old Tetevo Fortress is under complete control of the Macedonian security forces from yesterday, and that armored vehicles of the Macedonian army are positioned on the site. Yesterday the special forces of the Macedonian army and the police continued to clear the villages of Gajre, Selce, Lavce, Lisec and the Old Tetovo Fortress from the presence of the terrorists. There was no organized resistance from the side of the terrorists. The security forces clearing the terrain found artillery mines, snipers, uniforms, automatic infantry weapon and an improvised kitchen for making bread, all left behind by the extremists while they fled under the attack by our forces two days ago. About 900 Albanian terrorists, in the last 24 hours, fled in panic from the terrain in the vicinity of Kobilica and, passing Karanimolichka Shija and Karani-kolichko Ezer, returned to Kosovo, inform police sources. Trails of blood were found on the Old Tetovo Fortress, also three rocket launchers-type "zolja," hand grenades and explosives. The Albanian terrorists defiled the holy ground of the church "Sv. Atanasij" as well, that is located on the Old Tetovo Fortress, using it as food storage for bread and such. Yesterday morning, occasional fire came from the terrorists' positions in the vicinity of the villages Germo and Veshala. Distant battles are taking place in the depth of the Shara Mountain. According to information, the terrorist groups had a great number of casualties, but there is no official confirmation on that. Remains of terrorist groups, yesterday morning, tried to make their way through to Kosovo using the region of the massive Plocha, but their number was drastically diminished and, in panic, they retreated in the direction towards their bases above the village Bozovce. ("Dnevnik")
>
> —Daily briefing from Macedonian press about Macedonian crisis (3-27-01)

If we put our analytical lens into many of the social studies classrooms of Tetovo, Gajre, Selce, Lavce, Lisec, what might we see? No doubt we would witness frontal teaching—the teacher giving facts about Macedonian heroes from 500 years ago, students responding by reciting facts upon request, and teachers making no connection between classroom activity and the events occurring outside of it.

In fact-driven classrooms such as these, standardized paper-and-pencil tests might be useful. But in classrooms where a premium is put on critical thinking and cooperation, such tests are woefully inadequate and certainly don't provide a complete picture of student achievement.

Continuing the Journey: A Subtle Lens Into Our Own Classrooms

Classrooms in New Jersey look quite different from most of those in Macedonia; our two countries' goals for education are not the same. Interestingly, there is no word for "reflection" (meaning "inward thinking") in the Macedonian language. However, in the United States, reflection by both teachers and students is an important part of educational activity.

Be cautious though! Words alone will not convince policymakers of the richness of our teaching. Our language will not convince legislators of the loss we would face by narrowing our definition of successful teaching and student progress in order to focus on helping students attain high scores on state and national standardized tests.

Instead, policymakers, who for the most part are neither teachers nor reading experts, should be invited into our classrooms to <u>observe</u> what we do. During their visit, we might ask them to consider several questions, the answers to which could offer an analysis of some of the subtle dimensions of our classrooms that shape how we instruct our students. These answers might explain why we respond as we do to policymakers' criticisms of our teaching and test results. Some suggested questions follow.

1. WHAT DO OUR STUDENTS THINK IT MEANS TO BE LITERATE IN THIS CULTURE?
Literacy is a social and historical construction. Its definition in Western culture has changed considerably over time as we have become more aware of how people learn about their worlds and, as we have seen, different kinds of literacies become valued. In the past, literacy was defined as the ability to read and write. But being literate in Western culture today also includes creative thinking and problem-solving, being able to use visual information such as artifacts, web pages, facial expressions, and body posture, to obtain meaning from them and to provide a response to them.

For instance, consider the artifact described in the next paragraph and what we can learn about ourselves by noting how it has changed over time.

The very first Barbie doll captured the imagination of young girls everywhere. Her voluptuous pencil-thin figure, blonde hair, and blue-eyed countenance conveyed the contemporary notion of "perfection," something to aspire to. This was in 1959. A decade later, Barbie looked pretty different. She was now dressed in a somewhat shapeless astronaut's garb, but that's not all. A number of years before man even landed on the moon, Barbie was headed into outer space. Little girls now were being told they could have careers—even scientific and dangerous ones. In the 1990s, "Share a Smile Becky," a young girl in a wheelchair, joined the Barbie entourage, illustrating our culture's new social awareness and shift towards inclusion. It would take reams of explanatory detail to relate the same information that we are able to glean from analyzing just these three dolls.

In addition to a changing definition over time, the meaning of literacy changes in different contexts. In some cultures, listening, speaking and viewing are valued more than reading and writing. Imagine, for instance, the importance for the Yannomamii of the Amazon to recognize the variety of meanings conveyed by feather ornaments of their clansmen, or the need for native Americans to understand the symbolism of the patterns in their weavings.

One of the goals for the students in our schools should be to know what it means to be literate in this culture. The tools we use to develop students' concepts of literacy will influence how they define it. There are countless resources we use for achieving this goal: newspapers, the world wide web, fine textbooks, wonderful literature, artifacts that are important to our lives—art, clothing, advertising, music, furniture, hairstyles, dance—that convey the richness of our ideas and who we are.

Unfortunately, for some policymakers being literate simply means the ability to sound out words, without regard for meaning, critical reflection, or personal response. We, as educators, know better than that. A standardized test may yield valuable information for particular audiences, e.g. parents, and for particular purposes, e.g. determining whether traditional basic or functional literacy has been achieved. But these are minimal, socially constructed values, certainly not all that a formal education can accomplish.

One thing is certain—we must convey to policymakers that being literate is not synonymous with passing a test. By visiting our classrooms, witnessing and analyzing literacy-in-action, policymakers may come to appreciate that a single paper-and-pencil test cannot tell us much about the multiple ways in which students successfully use their literacies in their lives.

2. HOW WOULD OUR STUDENTS DEFINE THE TEACHER'S ROLE IN THIS CULTURE?
We know that in Macedonia, a teacher could easily be defined as a dispenser of information. What about in our classes? How would our students define us? Possibly as

Friend	Leader
Facilitator	Convener
Disciplinarian	Problem Solver
Collaborator	Task Master
Facts Dispenser	Energizer
Tester	Manager
Thought Provoker	Model
Guide	Prober
Bridge Builder	Authority
Challenger	Empowerer
Gatekeeper	

In which roles would your policymaker/visitor find you? Probably several of these would characterize your activity. But your visitor might be even more surprised at the extent to which you were working to improve each student's skills in reading and writing. Regardless of grade level or subject area, we know that these skills provide the foundation for all other learning and that all teachers have a responsibility for their development.

Because of the importance each of the teacher's roles makes to developing the students' literacy, we cannot afford to let the role of test-giver predominate. In spite of a "Leave No Child Behind" rhetoric, even children who are performing at a high level on the ESPA <u>will</u> be left behind unless each of us places a premium on continuing the literacy development of our students...no matter what we teach, and even at the expense of preparing students for tests. We need time away from tests so we can do some <u>real</u> teaching and to use the many tools include those that go beyond test-taking and fact transferring, to helping students realize their own strengths as learners.

Teachers know how to be successful at their craft and how to prevent students and schools from literacy failure. Our policymakers must visit our classrooms and enter into discussions with teachers that redefine what the most worthwhile teaching behaviors are, and which student behaviors are best assessed with measures outside standardized instruments. This kind of opportunity for critical analysis of our instruction and of our students' performance will point our policymakers in responsible and valuable directions when they are drafting legislation.

3. HOW WOULD OUR STUDENTS DEFINE THEIR ROLE(S) IN OUR CLASSES?

Your visitor will no doubt observe a variety of roles reflecting students' perceptions of what it is that they should do in classrooms. Some possibilities include:

Audience	Mentor
Partner	Leader
Debater	Follower
Creator	Team Player
Community Member	Mediator
Critical Thinker	Apprentice
Antagonist	Friend
Test Taker	Critic
Information Source	Comedian
Disinterested Observer	

For certain, a student's role as *Test Taker* least resembles classroom life, or for that matter, life outside the classroom. New Jersey's teachers know the power of student discussion and active engagement. They know from research that the quality of student thinking about content is affected by the quality of the questions we ask them and that students create for themselves.

Policymakers have put such an overemphasis on testing for basic skills that we are becoming fearful that if we go beyond the test, beyond basic skills, we are "wasting time" because our students won't do as well on these high-stakes assessments. In such an environment, there is no time for student inquiry.

<u>With all the emphasis on testing for basic skills, we may never get to the learning that really matters.</u> Students' roles in our classrooms will become increasingly narrow and our graduates will be unschooled in how to participate in a democratic society, with all of the responsibilities this entails.

We know how important it is to engage students, not just drill them. We have to stay true to our course. To paraphrase Pamela Adams, editor of *Radical Teacher* magazine,

> Successful teachers have a relatively coherent set of commitments and assumptions from which they teach, and they are aware of it; this awareness distinguishes them from rocks, mollusks, and unsuccessful teachers. They possess the capacity to listen well and the self-control not to always fill silence with the sound of their own voices. They believe that theory and practice are not separable and they are concerned with process as much as product. They assume that minds do not exist separate from bodies and that the bodies or material conditions, in which the potential and will to learn reside, are female as well as male and in a range of colors that thought grows out of lived experience and that people come from a variety of ethnic, cultural, and economic backgrounds; that people have made different life choices and teach and learn out of a corresponding number of perspectives. These teachers demand a lot from their students; they do not assume they know it all.

We must not be distracted from what we know will contribute the most to student learning; focusing solely on standardized tests that assess recitation of fact and low level skills will ultimately do our students a disservice. While they will do well on the political agenda of test-taking, they will likely suffer setbacks in competition with students who have had the advantage of a more informed and forward-looking educational system.

I suggest that we consider the outcome we prefer—high test scores or students who can succeed in the competitive world outside of school, and advocate constructively for those things that are most worthwhile.

Reference

Annas, Pamela. (undated). *Radical Teacher*. Available: http://www.wpunj.edu/radteach/default/htp, p. 1 [2001, May 5]

Additional Online Resources

American Education Association	http://amedu.com/polls/
Association for Supervision and Curriculum Development	www.ascd.org/advocacykit/gettingstarted.html
Center for Community Change	www.communitychange.org
Medical Health Association of Alaska	www.alaska.net/~mhaa/advocacy.html
National Consortium for Policy Research in Education (CPRE)	www.cpre.org
Ombudsman's Office, Washington State University	www.wsu.edu/~ombuds/history.html
Public Education Network/ Education Week polls	www.publiceducation.org
State Government Offices	www.statelocalgov.net/index.cfm
State Legislature Home Pages	Go to www.lsb.state.XX.us, where "XX" is the state abbreviation, or using a search engine, type in "[Name of State] State Legislature" to get to the homepage for the state.
The Laboratory at Brown University	www.lab.brown.edu
Video Camera Use	www.videomaker.com

Website Hosting & Site Building	http://geocities.yahoo1.com www.tripod.lycos.com
Wright's Law	www.wrightslaw.com/advoc/articles/advocacy_ intro.htm

APPENDIX C

Resources for Grant Writing and Funding Information

Allison, M., & Kaye, J. (1997). *Strategic planning for nonprofit organizations: A practical guide and workbook.* New York: Wiley.

Annual Register of Grant Support (35th ed.). (2002). Medford, NJ: Information Today.

Barbato, J., & Furlich, D.S. (2000). *Writing for a good cause: The complete guide to crafting proposals and other persuasive pieces for nonprofits.* New York: Simon & Schuster.

Barber, D.M. (2002). *Finding funding: The comprehensive guide to grant writing.* Long Beach, CA: Author.

Bauer, D.G. (2001). *How to evaluate and improve your grants effort* (2nd ed.). Westport, CT: Greenwood.

Belcher, J.C.C., & Jacobsen, J.M. (1992). *From idea to funded project: Grant proposals that work* (4th ed.). Westport, CT: Oryx Press.

Blum, L. (1996). *Complete guide to getting a grant: How to turn your ideas into dollars.* New York: Wiley.

Brown, L.G. (2001). *So you'd like to...win grants for your nonprofit program.* San Francisco: Jossey-Bass.

Brown, L.G., & Brown, M.J. (2001). *Demystifying grant seeking: What you really need to do to get the grants.* New York: Wiley.

Browning, B.A. (2001). *Grant writing for dummies.* New York: Wiley.

Burke, J., & Prater, C.A. (2000). *I'll grant you that: A step-by-step guide to finding funds, designing winning projects, and writing powerful grant proposals.* Portsmouth, NH. Heinemann.

Carlson, M. (2002). *Winning grants step by step: Support centers of America's complete workbook for planning, developing and writing successful proposals* (2nd ed.). San Francisco: Jossey-Bass.

Clarke, C.A. (2001). *Storytelling for grantseekers: The guide to creative nonprofit fundraising.* San Francisco: Jossey-Bass.

Corporation for Public Broadcasting. (n.d.). *Basic elements of grant writing.* Retrieved December 6, 2002, from http://www.cpb.org/grants/grantwriting.html

DeVaul, D. (1989). *Federal grant programs: A shrinking resource.* Washington, DC: Northeast–Midwest Institute.

Drucker, P.F. (1992). *Managing the non-profit organization: Principles and practices.* New York: HarperCollins.

Ferguson, J. (1994). *The effective grant office: Streamlining grants development and management.* Alexandria, VA: Capitol.

Ferguson, J., & Gershowitz, M.V. (1995). *The grantseeker's answer book: Grants experts respond to the most commonly asked questions.* Alexandria, VA: Capitol.

The Foundation Center. (n.d.). *Foundation finder.* Retrieved December 18, 2002, from http://lnp.fdncenter.org/finder.html

The Foundation Center. (n.d.). *Proposal writing short course.* Retrieved December 18, 2002, from http://fdncenter.org/learn/shortcourse/prop1.html

Frost, G.J. (Ed.). (1993). *Winning grant proposals: Eleven successful appeals by American nonprofits to corporations, foundations, individuals, and government agencies.* Rockville, MD: Taft Group.

Geever, J.C. (1997). *The foundation center's guide to proposal writing.* New York: The Foundation Center.

Geller, R.E. (1986). *Plain talk about grants: A basic handbook.* Sacramento: California State Library Foundation.

Golden, S.L. (1997). *Secrets of successful grantsmanship: A guerrilla guide to raising money.* San Francisco: Jossey–Bass.

Grant writing tools for nonprofit organizations. (n.d). Retrieved January 9, 2003, from http://www.npguides.org

Hall, M.S., & Howlett, S. (2003). *Getting funded: The complete guide to writing grant proposals.* Portland, OR: Continuing Education Press, Portland State University.

Henson, K.T. (1996). The art of writing grant proposals, part I. *Contemporary Education, 68*(1), 61–63.

Henson, K.T. (1997). The art of writing grant proposals, part II. *Contemporary Education, 68*(2), 136–138.

Henson, K.T. (1997). The art of writing grant proposals, part III. *Contemporary Education, 68*(3), 197–201.

Hoffman, D., Lamoreaux, D., & Hayes, L. (Eds.). (1999). *Winning strategies for developing grant proposals.* Washington, DC: Thompson.

Internet Nonprofit Center. Homepage. Retrieved December 18, 2002, from http://www.nonprofits.org

Kiritz, N.J. (1980). *Program planning and proposal writing*. Los Angeles: Grantsmanship Center News.

Lauffer, A. (1997). *Grants, etc.* (2nd ed.). Thousand Oaks, CA: Sage.

Locke, L.F., Spirduso, W.W., & Silverman, S.J. (1999). *Proposals that work: A guide for planning dissertations and grant proposals* (4th ed.). Thousand Oaks, CA: Sage.

McIlnay, D.P. (1998). *How foundations work: What grantseekers need to know about the many faces of foundations*. San Francisco: Jossey-Bass.

Michigan State University Libraries. (1996, June 1). *Nonprofit resource guide: A directory of organizations of interest to or serving nonprofits*. Retrieved January 4, 2003, from http://www.lib.msu.edu/harris23/grants/znprofrg.htm

Miner, L.E., & Miner, J.T. (2003). *Proposal planning and writing* (3rd ed.). Westport, CT: Greenwood.

Minnesota Council on Foundations. (n.d.). *Writing a successful grant proposal*. Retrieved November 28, 2002, from http://www.mcf.org/mcf/grant/writing.htm

Nauffts, M.F. (Ed.). (1994). *Foundation fundamentals: A guide for grantseekers* (5th ed.). New York: The Foundation Center.

New, C.C., & Quick, J.A. (1998). *Grantseeker's toolkit: A comprehensive guide to finding funding*. New York: Wiley.

Northern California Community Foundation. *Foundations on-line*. Retrieved January 9, 2003, from http://www.foundations.org/page2.html

Reeds, K. (2002). *Zen of proposal writing: An expert's stress-free path to winning proposals*. New York: Crown.

Riddle, J. (2002). *Streetwise managing a nonprofit: How to write winning grant proposals, work with a board, and build a fundraising program*. Avon, MA: Adams Media.

Ries, J.B., & Leukefeld, C.G. (1995). *Applying for research funding: Getting started and getting funded*. Thousand Oaks, CA: Sage.

Robinson, A. (2003). *Grassroots grants: An activist's guide to grantseeking* (2nd ed.). San Francisco: Jossey-Bass.

Schladweiler, K. (Ed.). (2003). *The Foundation Center's guide to grantseeking on the Web* (2nd ed.). New York: The Foundation Center.

U.S. Department of Education. (n.d). Information for new grants seekers. Retrieved June 22, 2004, from http://www.ed.gov/policy/elsec/leg/esea02/index.html

U.S. Federal Register. (2004, January 5). Retrieved April 20, 2004, from http://www.gpoaccess.gov/fr/index.html

Warwick, M. (1999). *Five strategies for fundraising success: A mission-based guide to achieving your goals.* San Francisco: Jossey-Bass.

Warwick, M. (Ed.). (2001). *Fundraising on the internet: The ePhilanthropyFoundation.org's guide to success online* (2nd ed.). San Francisco: Jossey-Bass.

Warwick, M. (2001). *How to write successful fundraising letters* (Rev. ed.). New York: Wiley.

Warwick, M., & Hitchcock, S. (2001). *Ten steps to fundraising success: Choosing the right strategy for your organization.* San Francisco: Jossey-Bass.

Annotated List of Online Publications

The Chronicle of Philanthropy: The Newspaper of the Nonprofit World

http://philanthropy.com/

> This publication features grant-related conferences, seminars, and workshops. It also includes current issues, funding announcements, and a "Guide to Grants."

Community of Science Funding News

http://fundingopps2.cos.com/news

> This free newsletter is published each week and includes a sampling of new and updated award information from the Community of Science Funding Opportunities, which is one of the most comprehensive sources of funding information available on the Web.

Philanthropy Journal Online

http://philanthropy-journal.org

> This nonprofit publication provides news on numerous topics such as fundraising, foundations, and corporate giving.

REFERENCES

The American Heritage College Dictionary (3rd ed.). (1993). Boston: Houghton Mifflin.

Association for Supervision and Curriculum Development. (2002). *ASCD advocacy kit*. Retrieved October 30, 2002, from http://www.ascd.org/advocacykit

Carlton, J. (2003, September 15). The best way to organize a protest. *The Wall Street Journal Reports*, p. R13.

Clearinghouse on Educational Policy Issues (n.d.). Homepage. Retrieved 1/15/2004, from http://www.nga.org/center/topics/1,1188,D_5444,00.html

Cummins, C. (1998, November 11) *Noise makes news, so school critics make noise*. Retrieved June 2, 2003, from http://www.educationreportcard.com/columns/1998-11-22

Dilley, B. (1995, November 22). Building a broad constituency for change. *Education Week, 15* (12), 33.

Hargreaves, A., & Fullan, M. (1998). What's worth fighting for out there. New York: Teachers College Press.

International Reading Association. (n.d.). *IRA advocacy manual*. Newark, DE: Author.

Kaplan, G.R. (2000). Friends, foes and noncombatants: Notes on public education's pressure groups. *Phi Delta Kappan, 82*(3), 213–225.

Keresty, B., O'Leary, S., & Wortley, D. (1998). *You can make a difference: A teacher's guide to political action*. Portsmouth, NH: Heinemann.

Lewis, J. (2003). *Academic literacy: Readings and strategies* (3rd ed.). Boston: Houghton Mifflin.

Manzo, K.K. (2003, February). Trends and changes in education. Speech given at the Government Relations Symposium of the International Reading Association, Washington, DC.

Mental Health Association in Alaska. (2002). *Advocacy*. Retrieved October 30, 2002, from http://www.alaska.net/~mhaa/advocacy.html

National Commission on Excellence in Education. (1983). *A nation at risk: The imperative for educational reform*. Washington, DC: U.S. Department of Education.

National Governor's Association Clearinghouse on Educational Policy Issues. (2003). *Closing the achievement gap*. Retrieved May 18, 2004, from http://www.subnet.nga.org/educlear/achievement/index.html

National Institute of Child Health and Human Development (NICHD). (2000). *Report of the National Reading Panel. Teaching children to read: An evidence-based assessment of the scientific research literature on reading and its implications for reading instruction* (NIH Publication No. 00-4769). Washington, DC: U.S. Government Printing Office.

Niemoller, M. (1992). In J. Bartlett & J. Kaplan (Eds.), *Familiar quotations: A collection of passages, phrases, and proverbs traced to their sources in ancient and modern literature* (16th ed.). Boston: Little, Brown.

No Excuses. (n.d.). *Think tanks and researchers*. Retrieved June 27, 2003, from http://www.noexcuses.org/resources/think_tanks.html

Nua. (2003). *How many online*. Retrieved September 18, 2003, from http://www.nua.ie/surveys/how_many_online

Pipkin, G., & Lent, R.C. (2002). *At the schoolhouse gate: Lessons in intellectual freedom*. Portsmouth, NH: Heinemann.

Public Agenda. (n.d.). *Where we are now: 12 things you need to know about public opinion and public schools*. Retrieved November 19, 2003, from http://www.publicagenda.org/specials/wherewearenow/wherewearenow.htm

Public Education Network. (2003). *A community action guide to teacher quality*. Retrieved September 28, 2003, from http://www.publiceducation.org/pdf/TQ/PEN_CommActionGuide.pdf

Rose, L.C., & Gallup, A.M. (2003). The 35th annual Phi Delta Kappa/Gallup poll of the public's attitudes toward the public schools. *Phi Delta Kappan, 85*, 41–53.

Routman, R. (1996). *Literacy at the crossroads: Crucial talk about reading, writing, and other teaching dilemmas*. Portsmouth, NH: Heinemann.

Snow, C.E., Burns, M.S., & Griffin, P. (Eds.). (1998). *Preventing reading difficulties in young children*. Washington, DC: National Academy Press.

U.S. Department of Education. (1998). *Turning around low-performing schools: A guide for state and local leaders*. Washington, DC: Author.

U.S. Conference of Mayors. (2003). *About the United States Conference of Mayors* . Retrieved October 23, 2003, from http://www.usmayors.org/uscm/about/what_is/what_is_uscm.html

Washington State University. (n.d.). *Office of the university ombudsman*. Retrieved October 23, 2003, from http://www.wsu.edu/~ombuds/history.html

Willinsky, J. (2001). Raising the standards for democratic education: Research and evaluation as public knowledge. In J. Kincheloe and D. Weil (Eds.), *Standards and schooling in the United States* (pp. 609–621). Santa Barbara, CA: ABC-CLIO.

Wrights Law. (2002). *Advocating for your child—Getting started*. Retrieved October 30, 2002, from www.wrightslaw.com/advoc/articles/advocacy_intro.htm

LITERATURE CITED

Rand, A. (1938). *Anthem*. New York: Cassell.

INDEX

Note: Page numbers followed by *f* indicate figures.

HERNANDEZ, A., 133, 135
HIGH-STAKES TESTING, 38–40; lobbying against, 185–214
HOPSON, S., 194, 196, 202, 256–258

I

INDIVIDUALS WITH DISABILITIES EDUCATION ACT (IDEA): public comment on, 15
INFORMATION SOURCES, 58–86; Chambers of Commerce, 69; National Governors Association, 69–70, 70f–72f; national research and development centers, 62, 63f; online, 59, 60f, 148–154, 266–267; for pending legislation, 81–84; public opinion polls, 77–79, 79f; regional educational laboratories, 62–64, 64f; special advisory groups, 61–62; think tanks, 64, 67, 65f–66f; U.S. Conference of Mayors, 73; U.S./state departments of education, 59–61
IN-PERSON STRATEGIES, 156–184; adopt-a-legislator programs, 174–176; campaigning for legislators, 178–179; hearings testimony, 156–161, 201–202, 256–258; legislative action teams, 161–163; policymaker breakfasts, 164–167; public hearings, 156–161, 169, 256–258; rallies and marches, 167–169; running for office, 179–182
INSTITUTE OF EDUCATION SCIENCES, 61
INTERNATIONAL READING ASSOCIATION, 20, 21, 123, 188, 196
INTERNET, 148–154, 266–267; chat rooms, 152–153; e-mail, 133, 136–137, 153–154; listservs, 152–153; websites, 59–60, 60f, 148–152, 266–267
INTERVIEWS: on public radio, 145–147

J–K

JOHNSON, M., 203, 204f, 211
JOURNALS, 73–74; themed, 132–133
KAPLAN, G.R., 49
KARPINSKI, C., 29, 219
KASSEKERT, L., 185, 190, 201, 202
KERESTY, B., 33–34
KRAMER, M.A., 48–49

L

LEGISLATION: lobbying for/against, 185–214; monitoring of, 81–86
LEGISLATIVE ACTION TEAMS, 161–163
LEGISLATIVE AIDES: meeting with, 172–174, 176–177
LEGISLATORS, 155–179; developing relationships with, 155–179; in-person contact with, 156–177; letters to, 133, 134f, 135–137, 193f; meeting with, 40–41, 189f, 205f, 170–179; newsletters of, 113f; phone calls to, 155–156; recognition for, 178–179, 212, 213f
LEISTYNA, P., 245
LENT, R., 32–33

Invest in your future—join the world's premier literacy organization.

The International Reading Association can help you reach the pinnacle of your career with a variety of resources and networking opportunities that are unparalleled in the education field. An IRA membership is a convenient, affordable way to be a part of the world's leading literacy organization and gain access to a rich array of resources.

If you subscribe to one or more of the following IRA peer-reviewed print journals, you'll become a member:

- *The Reading Teacher*: Packed with useful, classroom-tested information and practical insights for educators of children ages 5–12. (8 issues/year)
- *Journal of Adolescent & Adult Literacy*: For teachers of middle school, high school, and adult learners, *JAAL* encourages innovative ways of teaching and studying literacy. (8 issues/year)
- *Reading Research Quarterly*: Focusing on original and innovative research, *RRQ* promotes the exchange of information and opinion on theory, research, and practice among learners of all ages. (4 issues/year) *RRQ* is available online as an optional add-on service. Get more information about *RRQ Online* at www.reading.org/rrqonline.
- *Lectura y Vida*: This Spanish-language quarterly provides information about the most current reading instruction issues in Latin America. (4 issues/year)
- *Thinking Classroom* (English version)/*Peremena* (Russian version): Provides new and different perspectives and experiences from all over the world and challenges teachers at all levels to consider how changes in classroom practice have implications in larger cultural contexts. (4 issues/year)

The benefits don't stop...

Membership to the Association also includes the following benefits:

- A 20% member discount on all IRA books and videos
- Eligibility to join IRA's exclusive Book Club and annually receive nine new titles for one low fee
- A subscription to *Reading Today*, the Association's bimonthly newspaper
- A discounted subscription to *RRQ Online*
- Significant discounts on IRA conferences

Visit www.reading.org for comprehensive and up-to-date information about all activities, programs, products, services, and membership opportunities.

Join today! Together, we can make a difference.

Call toll free 800-628-8508, or join online at www.reading.org/membership. (Outside the United States and Canada, call 302-731-1600.)